For most Australians, the Pilbara region of the continent's north-west conjures up images of rugged and majestic country, huge mining projects and roughcast pioneers. Histories celebrate the triumph of European ingenuity over difficult conditions, naming the resilient white settlers who turned this arid land into an economic asset.

But there is another history of the Pilbara, one that both cuts across and is intermeshed with the white history. *Karijini Mirlimirli* reveals this history through stories told by the people who were there before the white man came, and are still very much there today. Struggling to retain their culture, the Aboriginal people were drawn inexorably into the new economy imposed by the invader. They played a crucial role in the development of the pastoral industry, and watched their lands being swallowed up by the cattle stations and then mines, but they never gave up the fight to retain their heritage.

The stories collected here — living narratives by and about the Karijini peoples — cover the period from the 1920s to the present day, revealing a seamless continuity between the life before the invaders and the pressing issues of the 1990s.

Cover design by John Douglass. Photographs by Noel Olive.

Royalties accruing from the sale of this book are to be paid to the Karijini Aboriginal Corporation, as directed by the editor.

Noel Olive was born in Sydney during the Depression years, into a Communist family with strong views on social equality. In his early years he worked as an apprentice electrician and then as a drover. In the pastoral industry he witnessed first-hand the destructive government policy of removing Aboriginal children from their families. Later he worked in heavy industry in Sydney, becoming a union delegate. He retrained as a lawyer, qualifying in 1982. He has represented Aboriginal families before the Royal Commission into Aboriginal Deaths in Custody, and worked in the early 1990s as coordinator for the Karijini Aboriginal Corporation. He now lives in New South Wales, still doing law work for those most in need and participating in the Central Coast Community for Reconciliation. He has three children and two grandchildren.

Karijini Mirlimirli

Karijini Mirlimirli

Aboriginal histories
from the Pilbara

EDITED BY
NOEL OLIVE

FREMANTLE ARTS CENTRE PRESS

First published 1997 by
FREMANTLE ARTS CENTRE PRESS
193 South Terrace (PO Box 320), South Fremantle
Western Australia 6162.

Consultant Editor Bryce Moore.
Designed by John Douglass.
Production Coordinator Cate Sutherland.

Typeset by Fremantle Arts Centre Press
and printed by Lamb Print, Perth, Western Australia.

National Library of Australia
Cataloguing-in-publication data.

Karijini Mirlimirli : Aboriginal histories from the Pilbara.

ISBN 1 86368 204 X.

1. Karijini (Australian people). 2. Karijini (Australian
people) - Social life and customs. 3. Karijini (Australian
people) - History. 4. Aborigines, Australian - Western
Australia - Pilbara - Social life and customs. 5.
Aborigines, Australian - Western Australia - Pilbara -
History. I. Olive, Noel. II. Fremantle Arts Centre Press.

994.1300415

artswa

The State of Western Australia has made an investment in this project
through the Department for the Arts.

Acknowledgements

The preparation of the manuscript of *Karijini Mirlimirli* proceeded throughout 1993 and early 1994. It required considerable field work in the Pilbara, transposing and editing the cassette material in Perth.

Though this was a cooperative effort, I wish to thank the Karijini storytellers: Dulcie, Mirru, Listen Listen, Chubby, Nellie, Judy, Daji, Henry, old girl (Jukari), Wobby, Mabel, Queenie, Joyce, Peter, Auntie Alice, Gregory, Lola, Bonny, Guy, Trevor, Maitland, Margaret, Marjorie, Slim, Doreen, Doris, Donald Ard, David, Lorraine, Julie, Suzanne, Darren, Donald Hicks, Sally, Ruben, Vivian, Adrian, Rodney Butler and Rodney Parker. They were patient and forebearing when so often the process of obtaining information, and of verifying its correctness, was an intrusion on their lives.

Further, the greatest debt is owed to Traudl Tan for her comradely gift of editorial skills, dedication and genuine care for the editor and the project. My heartfelt thanks goes to Leslie Knox for her unstinting research work and support, and to Anne Butorac and Janet Ristic for their unfailing support and assistance.

Tribute is paid to the linguistic and anthropological skills of Lorraine Injie for her contribution in identifying the correct Aboriginal words and, with Di McCullam, Alan Dench and Nick Green, for proofing the spelling of Aboriginal words. Nick Green with Elliot Johnston also gave practical support in a variety of other ways necessary for the project's survival.

Finally I thank the Institute for Aboriginal and Torres Strait Islander Studies for their initial support of my efforts in collecting and placing the materials in their archive, and to the Fremantle Arts Centre Press for publishing the manuscript.

May your labours not be in vain.

Except where otherwise indicated, the photographs in this volume were taken by Noel Olive. The line drawings used at various points throughout the text are all the work of Rodney Parker (see page 235).

CONTENTS

Introduction

The Karijini Mirlimirli presents a powerful Aboriginal voice from people whose traditional lands lie in the West Pilbara region of Western Australia. This voice is rich in experience and expresses such variety that the reader will be surprised that the contributors have come from similar backgrounds. The Mirlimirli, it is to be hoped, will help along the process of consolidating the position of Aboriginal people in their rightful place as equals in an evolving multicultural society.

The word Karijini is used in three different ways. It is a place, the Karijini National Park in the Hamersley Ranges, an Aboriginal organisation, the Karijini Aboriginal Corporation, and the members of that organisation, who are referred to as the Karijini. Thus the title *Karijini Mirlimirli* means 'writings of the Karijini people'.

The collection brings together many experiences perhaps unfamiliar to other Australians. The towns in which most of the Karijini Aboriginals now live — Onslow, Roebourne, Karratha, Wickham, Port Hedland, and Tom Price — are all north of the twenty-sixth parallel and at least fourteen hundred kilometres from Perth.

The roots of the Karijini peoples can be traced to the magnificent landscape of the Karijini National Park and its surroundings in the Hamersley Ranges. That is their homeland: a beautiful montage of yellow spinifex, red soil, white snappy gums, hauntingly beautiful low hills and mystic gorges. It is an arid country, ever changing from harsh reds and yellows to soft blues and greens, under the commanding influence of the sun, which at times can be merciless.

Landscape and nature have always been essential elements in the Aboriginal way of life, but more recent Aboriginal history speaks of other matters. The effect of displacement wrought by colonisation is apparent from the stories, and today there often remains little correlation between birthplace, workplace and ancestral home. Of particular note is the wide use made of Aboriginal labour on pastoral leases, until the 1968 Award requirement made it mandatory to pay Aboriginal stockmen at least equal wages with other station hands.

The subsequent rejection of Aboriginal labour by pastoralists caused a massive dislocation of family and community, as people were forced to live in the towns as fringe dwellers. Their belated recognition as citizens of Australia by the 1967 Referendum, though a vital political act, did little to halt the corrosive processes eating at the fabric of Aboriginal life.

The disruptive consequences of European settlement in Aboriginal lands on the lives of those indigenous Australians cannot be overemphasised, and the misery of the Aboriginal people since can be laid squarely at its door. The stories detail experiences of native welfare policy which tore children from their families, of lives spent working for the station owners, and of the present torment endured in a government village.

Throughout the contributions a central theme emerges, a deep longing and unwavering determination to return 'to country', a great desire to maintain intimate contact with their homelands in order to nurture their culture. This is at the core of the lives of Aboriginal people, the intimacy and interdependence of their relationship with land and culture.

In the 1980s members of three tribal groups, the Yinhawangkas, Punjimas and Kurramas decided to pursue their claims for traditional lands. They joined together in one united organisation, the Karijini Aboriginal Corporation, based in Onslow. They clashed with iron ore miners, who had State Government support, on the controversial Marandoo mine project. The media were not supportive of the Karijini case, while the Aboriginal people simply sought to protect their inheritance, the land and their culture. Their demand for recognition as major stakeholders in land issues in the Pilbara was a new direction for Aboriginal politics there.

Other voices, more strident, speak of the racism of a paternalistic society, or the failure to warn of or protect the people from the menace of asbestos at Wittenoom. Yet, others speak with pride of achievement and hope of a better future from the lessons learned from life.

Aboriginal people in the Pilbara have called for the respect for their culture and authority in cultural matters, rights in land and the protection of sacred sites, employment for Aboriginal workers in the resource and tourism industries, and training for such jobs. Aboriginal unemployment is said to be as high as ninety-eight per cent in some areas of the Pilbara. These measures are seen as necessary to replace the hand-out system, with its 'sit down money'. Aboriginal people want to control their own lives.

The idea of producing a collection of Aboriginal histories germinated in discussion with the Karijini people when I was an employee of the Karijini Aboriginal Corporation.

The gathering of these histories commenced in early 1993, after I had ceased working for the Corporation. I returned to the Pilbara and began to collect material, completing the field work in April 1994. I was known to all contributors, having worked with the people at Onslow for over fifteen months and stayed periodically at other Pilbara towns over a period of four years.

Contributors were randomly selected from among members of the Karijini Aboriginal Corporation and its supporters, interviewed at the towns of Onslow, Karratha, Roebourne, Wickham, Tom Price, Port Hedland and South Hedland. Often the basis of selection was the person who happened to be available to talk at that moment. The interview was conducted at a place indicated by the interviewee, either the home, in the work place or under a tree.

The process used was to record an interview on cassette, then reduce it to a statement by eliminating the interviewer's questions and comments, or minor matters which detracted from the story's flow. Finally the document was read by (or to) the contributor to verify its accuracy. In some cases there was more than one such reading. Where it was not possible to verify accuracy due to the inability to make further contact, the material was not used. In all cases the finalised story has been authorised for publication, in writing, by the contributor.

The histories reveal the cross-cultural nature of the people's lives. Ensuring comprehension in conventional English and maintaining accuracy in the Aboriginal language, required a system of checking relevant Aboriginal words with Pilbara and Perth linguists.

Aboriginal people had no written language at the time of the colonisation of Australia. Written Aboriginal language is a non-Aboriginal construct. Rules laid down by linguists for writing Aboriginal language lack consensus, with the result that the written word may vary according to the writer. This situation is unsatisfactory. The sooner the Aboriginal people take charge of their language and declare how it shall be written the better the chances of its

13

preservation. For the treatment of Aboriginal words in this work the reader is referred to the Glossary (Appendix 2).

Every effort has been made to preserve the cultural idiom of the contributors' language in the course of recording, in order to ensure the integrity of the message.

The lives of Aboriginal communities have characteristics unique to the West Pilbara region, which are reflected in their stories. Aboriginal people may speak of having had 'bad luck', which invariably means they have lost a family member. Outsiders will often have difficulty in finding out who has passed away because custom forbids the mention of the deceased's name. This is overcome in ordinary communication by providing a name to replace the given name of the person who has died. For the Karijini peoples that word is 'Jukari'. It is used in conjunction with the surname of the subject person.

Ordinarily the death of a person will mean that all direct reference to them will cease. In the case of this Mirlimirli the elders have given their consent to the document being published and distributed, should that unfortunate event take place.

Some storytellers refer to 'give away' brides. This is a reference to traditional marriage practices, in which parents arrange partners well in advance of the actual marriage. In other places the reader will encounter such references as 'cousin-brother' 'cousin-sister' 'uncle dad' or 'auntie mum'. Such terms are consistent with extended family construction, where people have multiple obligations to each other.

The skin groups of the contributors are indicated at the lead to each history. There are four such groups: Banaka, Burungu, Karimarra and Milangka. In traditional society skin grouping is a key means of regulating social relations, by determining the obligations of all tribal members to each other. These relations are still strong today, and people still recognise others as brother or sister according to their skin grouping. Skin group relationships are every bit as strong as those created by blood, giving a new meaning to 'relation', unknown in Australian–European cultures.

Two pastoral stations, Rocklea and Mulga Downs, (see Map 2, page 18) were central to the people's cultural and spiritual needs. Many contributors were born there. The Wakuthuni block referred to in the text is a piece of land on the Rocklea Station, near Tom Price. Wakuthuni is the name of a hill which has great significance for the group of Karijini members belonging to the Wakuthuni Incorporated

Aboriginal Association. In recent times they have successfully negotiated their claim for some living space in their traditional lands. Fifty members have moved onto the land and live there today, in sight of their hills.

There has been no attempt to title the contributions, though each is preceded by a fragment of the text to give the reader some guide to the story's content. It is hoped that in the future many of the contributors will write full accounts of their lives, bringing their wisdom to bear on current problems. It is sorely needed.

The histories in the Mirlimirli are randomly representative of the members of Karijini of varying ages. They are men's stories and women's stories. They are stories of dignity, love and compassion. Above all they show the unending courage and hope of a people who have endured, and continue to endure appalling deprivation. In the land of plenty they have had a meagre hand-out.

Survival for Aboriginal people of the West Pilbara has demanded an unrelenting struggle against domination by mainstream society and their marginalisation by the welfare state. They take pride in their successes, and are optimistic of their future and in their own strength of purpose to build that future.

We should all welcome and acknowledge the Karijini's struggle as a genuine contribution to a reconciliation process which is to be founded on the existence of genuine equality for all.

Abbreviations used in the text

AAPA   Aboriginal Affairs Planning Authority
AETB   Aboriginal Employment and Training Branch
ALO   Aboriginal Liaison Officer
ALS   Aboriginal Legal Service
ALT   Aboriginal Land Trust
APB   Agriculture Protection Board
ATSIC   Aboriginal and Torres Strait Islander Commission
CALM   Department of Conservation and Land Management
CBH   Co-operative Bulk Handling Ltd
CBI   Chicago Bridge Iron Company
CDEP   Community Development Employment Program
CES   Commonwealth Employment Service
DAA   Department of Aboriginal Affairs
DCD   Department of Community Development
DEET   Department of Employment, Education and Training
DSD   Department of Social Development
EPT   Electrical Power Transmission
HACC   Health and Community Care
KAC   Karijini Aboriginal Corporation
KNP   Karijini National Park
NAC   National Aboriginal Conference
NACC   National Aboriginal Consultative Committee
NPAWS   National Parks and Wildlife Service
REDSA   Roebourne Employment Development Scheme for
        Aboriginals
SAAP   Support Accommodation Assistance Program
STD   Sexually Transmitted Disease
TA   Trades Assistant
TAFE   Technical and Further Education
TSI   Torres Strait Islander
UAM   United Aboriginal Missions
WAIT   Western Australian Institute of Technology
YMCA   Young Men's Christian Association

16

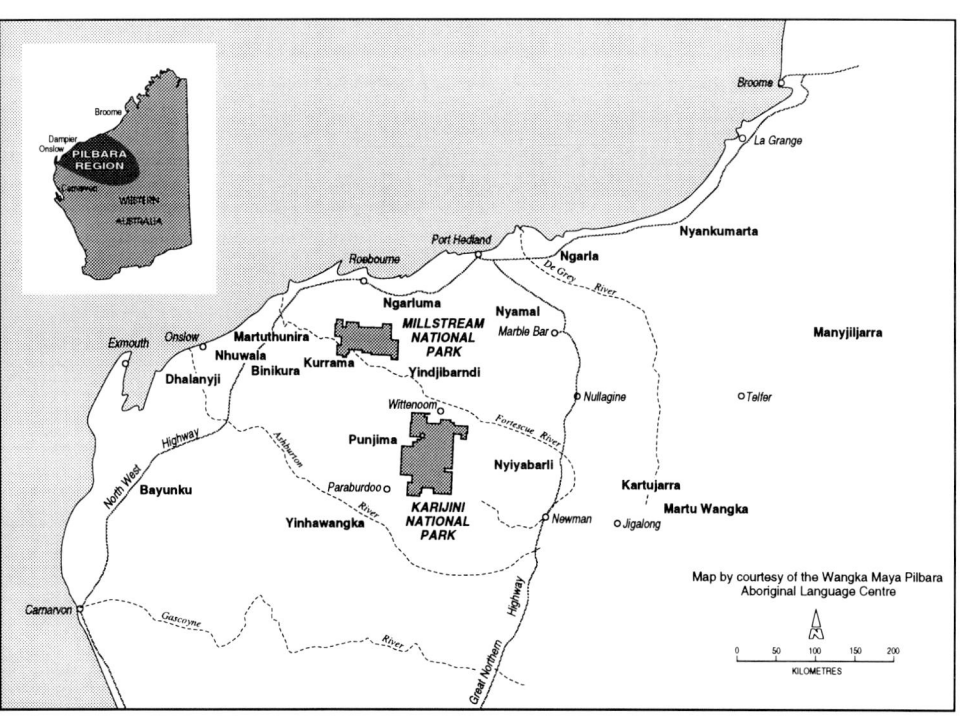

Map 1: *The West Pilbara region of Western Australia, showing major*
towns, national Parks and Aboriginal tribal lands.

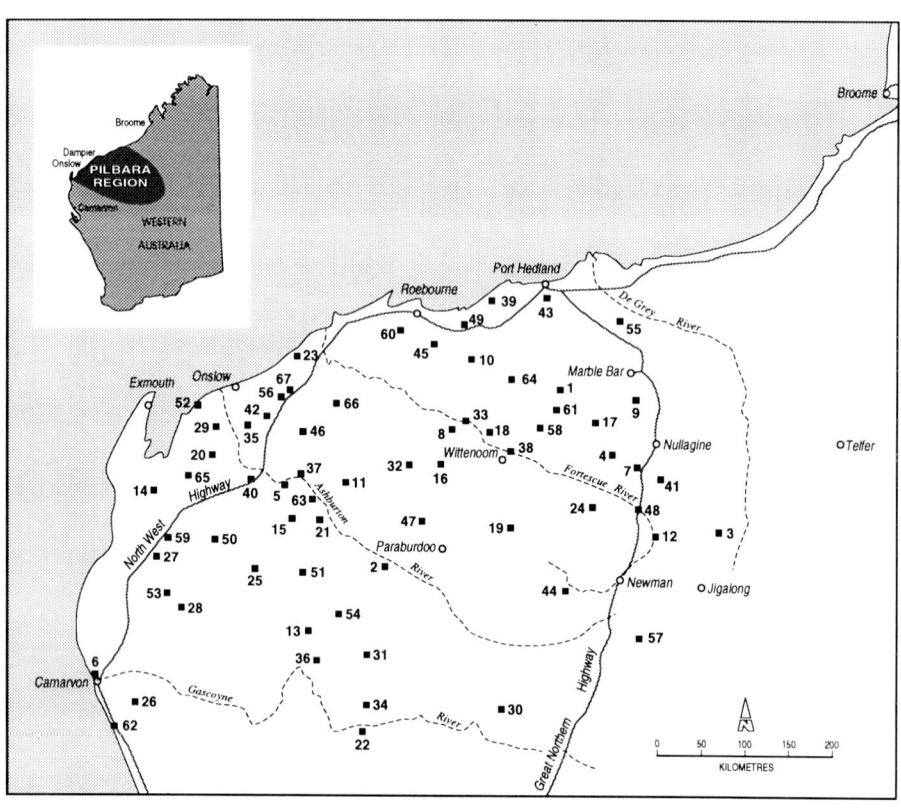

Map 2: Pastoral stations in the West Pilbara region, with which the storytellers are associated through work, history or culture. See key, opposite page.

18

1. Abydos (Alma out-station)
2. Ashburton Downs
3. Balfour Downs
4. Bamboo Springs (formerly Bellary)
5. Boolaloo
6. Boolathena
7. Bonney Downs (Cobbore out-station, formerly Cherratta)
8. Coolawanyah
9. Corunna Downs (Cowra out-station)
10. Croydon (formerly Dignam's)
11. Duck Creek
12. Ethel Creek
13. Gifford Creek
14. Giralia
15. Glenflorrie (formerly Glenroy)
16. Hamersley
17. Hillside
18. Hooley
19. Juna Downs
20. Koordarrie
21. Kooline
22. Landor
23. Mardie
24. Marillana (formerly Murimamba)
25. Maroonah (formerly Medawandy)
26. Meeragoolia
27. Mia Mia
28. Middalya
29. Minderoo (formerly Mintina)
30. Mulgul (Munjina)
31. Mount Augustus
32. Mount Brockman
33. Mount Florence
34. Mount James
35. Mount Minnie
36. Mount Phillip
37. Mount Stuart
38. Mulga Downs
39. Munda
40. Nanutarra
41. Noreena Downs
42. Peedamulla
43. Petermulla
44. Prairie Downs
45. Pyramid
46. Red Hill
47. Rocklea
48. Roy Hill
49. Sherlock (formerly Tambrey)
50. Towera (formerly Turee Creek)
51. Ullawarra
52. Urala
53. Wandagee
54. Wanna
55. Warralong
56. Warramboo (formerly Warrie)
57. Weelarrana
58. White Springs
59. Winning Pool
60. Woodbrook
61. Woodstock
62. Wooramel (formerly Wolli)
63. Wyloo
64. Yandeyarra
65. Yanrey
66. Yalleen
67. Yarraloola (formerly Yangkalinha)

DULCIE CONDON

Birth Date: Not Recorded
Birth Place: Hamersley Station
Tribal Group: Yinhawangka
Skin Group: Karimarra

*When I was working at Hamersley I would go by mail truck
to Roebourne or Onslow. There was no Karratha, Tom Price,
Paraburdoo, or railway.*

I was born between Hamersley and Rocklea Stations. My mother
gave birth on her own except for help from Mabel Tommy's old
mother. This was not unusual for our people. My mother and father
were living on Hamersley and Rocklea stations at the time. He was a
dogger catching dingoes and we used to go with him. We were up
and down the hills with him all of the time.

When she had children, mother stayed behind on the stations
looking after them. She had ten kids but lost three. Her kids are:
Jukari Cox, Thomas Cox, and Gilbert Cox who live at Bindi Bindi
village, Onslow, and Hilda Cox who is in Onslow hospital. Leary
Delaporte and me live in our own houses at Onslow. Arthur Cox
lives in Roebourne. David Cox lives at South Hedland, and brother
Mitchell and sister Trixie passed away. Mitchell was the eldest and
David the youngest. My mother's name was Daisy Dick before
marriage. She was a Yinhawangka. My father was a Kurrama, Frank
Cox. My father's mother was a Kurrama, and her father and her
mother were Kurramas. My mother was Yinhawangka and her
mother's mother was Yinhawangka.

I have nine children. Three were born in the bush. Sally, the oldest,
and Barry were born at Mount Stuart Station. Another one, Noel, was
born here in Onslow under two gum trees, just this side of the
Gilliamia Hostel, before it was there. My husband had to come in a
motor car and pick me up and take me to the hospital with the baby in

arms. I had no problem having my kids. I had Cathy, Thomas, Pamela, Adrian, Lisa, and Melanie, in hospital.

I have lived in Onslow since I had four kids. We were out on Wyloo Station cattle mustering then, on Cheela Plains out-camp.

Mick, my husband, and I met at Hamersley Station. We were both working on the station. I was a house worker and he was mustering. We liked each other and got together. Then I came up to Nanutarra Station. Mick was still working at Hamersley. My mother had gone to Nanutarra because my father was there. He had gone away from my mother when we were little fellas and we never saw him till we had all grown up.

Now he went to work at Nanutarra and wanted to see us kids. He told my mother to bring us to Nanutarra. He had another wife. My mother didn't get another husband. I would have been about fifteen or something like that.

Mick and I met up later at Onslow. He was bringing horses from Rocklea Station to the Onslow races. I went back with him to Nanutarra. That's where I had the first baby, Sally. We stayed at those three stations in a row there, Nanutarra, Boolaloo and Mount Stuart. I had Barry there at Mount Stuart and then we shifted to Wyloo, and had Noel down here. I worked at those stations, and when they were mustering I was the musterers' cook. We were mustering at Cherrita Plains, back of Wyloo. Then we came back to Onslow and got a job at the pumping station out at Peedamulla. We had Thomas then. He was sick so I sent him to Perth. We've been here all of the time then, and I had the rest of the kids here. I worked in the shops helping them clean up. I also worked for the Pilbara Water Department and was paid money. At Wyloo they paid me money as a cook.

In the days when I was a little girl at Rocklea and Hamersley, there used to be big mobs of people and corroborees. They had corroborees at the place where I was born, and down at the old reserve at Bindi Bindi, when we come in from the station. There was a lot of people staying here in town then. They held initiation ceremonies here at the Cane River 'till this year. When I was little they had them at Rocklea. From the old days when I was a kid only old Amy Smith (from Roebourne) is left.

When I was working at Hamersley I would go to town by mail truck. We would go to all those stations between, Hooley, Mount

Florence and others. Town in those days was Roebourne or Onslow. There was no Karratha, Tom Price, Paraburdoo, these only come lately. There was no railway.

My country is the other side of Minthacoogina (a spring in the Karijini National Park), out near Paraburdoo. Bellary Creek is part of Yinhawangka country.

My mother, father and grandmother taught me about bush tucker, bush medicine and fruit trees. Some of the medicines I remember are jilarn, that's a green tree, a medicine bush in the water country. You boil it and use the water to wash the skin to heal sores. Nhiidi, that's another one for sores. Baddawa was another medicine tree.

Then there are fruit. Nyirrilyi, that's another tree like a cherry. Wild orange we call kajawari. Jilbukarri is wild passionfruit, and bathara that's like strawberry.

One of the bush vegies we would eat is like a bean and is called marna. Little white onions we dug up from the ground that were good to eat, was called ngarlku. We also had the jiddha, a yam. One like a long white carrot is called marla. They used to eat these raw or cooked by throwing in the ashes. These gum trees here have a little white things coming on the leaves (lerp), we call these marlbanunku and they are very sweet. Another one on the bark is like chewing gum, sweet too. I taught my kids about these things too.

The old people always told us what we shouldn't eat.

MIRRU GEORGE

Birth Date: Unknown
Birth Place: Rocklea Station
Tribal Group: Kurrama/Punjima
Skin Group: Banaka

You look at the photo of me, there near the tree where I was born, that is my country.

My name Mirru comes from our Aboriginal name for tip of the throwing stick.

My father's name was George Pinda. I'm a full uncle to Doris Cooke. Wakin was my uncle dad. He was the owner of that hill we call Wakuthuni, that's being mined. My mother was Dinah. They belonged to Rocklea Station.

I was born near the government well on Rocklea. That place we now call Mirwida. Two years ago we all camped there for the night and you (Noel Olive) lost a water bucket when lowering it down the well to get water. You took a photo of me there near the tree where I was born. That is my country. It's the other side of the hill we can see from this Wakuthuni block we're sitting on today. This Wakuthuni block is our traditional land and we want to live here.

I never went to school as a kid but worked at Rocklea and Kooline Stations. I was eighteen years at Kooline. I was treated all right and was paid in money. I was mainly a musterer.

I married Maybee, we've been together for years. She's at Meekatharra now because of her crook knees. I'm crook in one eye. I can't see out of it. The doctor operated on it at Carnarvon.

Elder Mirru George stands by the tree under which he was born, as another elder,
Jambu Giggles, looks on.

LISTEN LISTEN JAMES

Birth Date: Unknown
Birth Place: Rocklea Station
Tribal Group: Kurrama/Punjima
Skin Group: Banaka

I'm a stockman, sheep, cattle and ... I've never worked for an Aboriginal boss, always worked for the whitefellas.

People call me because I've always said, 'listen listen' when I've been talking with people. My real name is Herbert James. My mother's name was Dinah, Bumbah. My step-father was Johnny. My father was Wakin. I'm a full uncle to Doris, Lola, Colin Cooke, Kevin Gilba, Brian Gilba and Nicholas Cooke. My parents worked at Rocklea when they were young. Kathleen Johnny, Nellie Johnny, Eileen Parker are my three sisters and Mirru George my brother, the younger one is gone. This country was my father's country and the hill on the horizon was my father's. I was only a little fellow when my father passed away. My children are Eilane James, Terry James, Jamie James. One lives here on the Wakuthuni land, one is in the Regional (prison), and the other lives at Carnarvon.

I never went to school in my life. I've worked at Kooline Station for fifteen years. I've worked at Rocklea, Mount Minnie, Nanutarra, Mount James and Wyloo Stations. I'm a stockman, sheep, cattle and fencing, looking after windmills. I've never worked for an Aboriginal boss, always worked for the whitefellas.

The first job for money for me was Kooline but I was always given money. I stop at Kooline Station in my own bedroom. I eat at my own table and I sometimes would have some friends eat with me. The boss and his family eat by themselves. There are eleven people working at Kooline, this included the boss. When he wants me back there he will come and pick me up, for mustering or something like that.

When I was little I always spoke our language.

CHUBBY JONES

Birth Date: Unknown
Birth Place: Rocklea Station
Tribal Group: Yinhawangka
Skin Group: Karimarra

> *The hills you see from this Wakuthuni block are named*
> *Nyimirli and Wakuthuni. That one is my grandfather's hill,*
> *and now it's being mined.*

My father was Cutacross George. His Aboriginal name was Dhurlja. He was a Yinhawangka. My mother's name was Wankja, she was a Kurrama. They lived on Rocklea Station. My mother worked in the house and father was a stockman. I had one brother and one sister, they are finished. There are many cousin brothers.

There was a big mob of people living at Rocklea in the days when I was little. Peter Stevens, Jukari Cox, Injie, Limerick, Jambu Giggles, and Thomas Cox now elders or passed away, were some of the kids there then.

I went through the law at Jigalong. These fellows went through the law at other places. But I was working out at Mount Augustus Station and at Meekatharra, that's why I went through at Jigalong.

There is a big community of Aboriginal people at Mount James Station and many of them come from this Rocklea area. I've come to Wakuthuni to be with my people, Doris Cooke and Lola Young. Doris is my step-daughter by my brother.

This is my country, Bellary and Mud Springs and all around here from Rocklea to Turee Creek Stations. The hills you see from this Wakuthuni block are named Nyimirli and Wakuthuni. That one is my grandfather's hill, now it is being mined (Wakuthuni). I expect to live here where I can see that hill.

In the old days there used to be plenty of our culture at Rocklea. There was corroborees and plenty of dancing there. Every Christmas

The hills are called Wakuthuni. They belonged to Chubby Jones' father, Wakin, a respected elder, deceased.

there would be a meeting. Some people would come from Turee Creek, Mulga Downs, Wyloo, Hamersley Stations and the Communities.

Old Cookie Cutacross, Doris' father, taught me how to track and other bush craft. The old people taught us the names of fruit and other things, like honey. We would go camping out with them, walking round the river looking for kangaroo, bunkurra (goanna) and other food. I used to use the spear then. I would have been about ten to thirteen years old. Us young people would all go together with the older ones.

I left my traditional lands because my brother took me to work on other stations. He's gone now. There were still Aboriginal people working at Rocklea then.

I worked at Juna Downs Station, Turee Creek Station, then Jigalong Mission, Prairie Downs Station, droving at Meekatharra, and then went to Landor and Mount Augustus Stations. Then I came back home to Rocklea Station. I went to Mount James for a long time and returned to Rocklea. Now I'm back at the Wakuthuni block.

Life on the stations was good then. I was treated all right. When I started working there was only salt meat, spuds and damper. We ate together when we were out mustering. When I came back to the station I would then go and live out in the bush with my people.

There were more than fifty people living at Rocklea in those days and they received tucker. I was not paid in money in those days. The first time I got money was when I worked for George Parks at Juna Downs Station. I was about sixteen at the time. We were cattle mustering. It wasn't much. I was paid always after that.

I'm married. My wife is Nellie. I had three boys but have lost two in motor accidents. One daughter died as a baby from pneumonia. Another boy was born with bad ears and was deaf and dumb. He died when he was about ten.

I never went to school, but the kids did. Churchill my only son now, went to Gilliamia Hostel in Onslow and primary school there, then went to high school in Port Hedland, staying at Moorgunyah Hostel.

I think it's a bit rough the mining companies mining that hill without talking to us.

NELLIE JONES

Birth Date: Unknown
Birth Place: Rocklea Station
Tribal Group: Kurrama
Skin Group: Banaka

The bad luck I had with my son was caused by alcohol.

My father was Wakin. But Johnny Dick was the one that reared me up. My mother took his name when she lived with him. My brothers are Mirru George and Listen Listen James. They are living in a camp on this Wakuthuni block of land.

I come from the Rocklea Station where there was a big mob of kids. That's where I learned our culture. Us kids went around everywhere. My old step-father, Johnny Dick, he would teach me. My grandmother had died when I was little. We used to go out in the bush at Christmas time and stop down by the creek at Ashburton Downs for a holiday. There we'd have a corroboree.

Chubby Jones and I are married Aboriginal style. I met him at Ashburton Station when my family moved there. I was a full grown girl and had been working at Kooline and then Nanutarra Station. I came from there to be with Chubby. We weren't promised in marriage. We had four kids.

I spoke language with my parents when I was little. I spoke all of the time and I still talk language with Listen Listen, Chubby and others. But my kids don't have a language, they have lost it since they have to go to whitefella school.

I never was chased by Native Welfare but do remember two kids who were caught. They were on Kooline.

I worked at the stations setting tables and doing housework. The jobs were washing up, polishing floors, washing and looking after kids, bathing them. There were three of them at Ashburton Downs. At Mount James Station where I've lived for the last few years, we'd do the gardening. There's a big mob there and Charlie Snowball is the boss. We're finished there now and have come back to our own country. I decided this after my son died there last year with that accident. Young people at Mount James do fencing and things like that. Children have a school to go to. They are taught by teachers in our Aboriginal culture. No alcohol is allowed there.

The bad luck I had with my son was caused by alcohol. I used to tell him not to drink but some people used to carry the drink in the motor car. They have the money but my son didn't. The old fellow in the car with the pension money was getting the grog. There was a slide on a bend of the road. The old fellow who was the driver was my brother-in-law and he died too.

About this Wakuthuni block, I think the Shire should come and bulldoze the spinifex, and put up a couple of houses and water tank on the hill. We've got a bore and small tank that Karijini has helped us with, but it's not big enough for the mob.

I get the old age pension. It started last year.

JUDY JULY

Birth Date: Not Recorded
Birth Place: July Springs
Tribal Group: Kurrama
Skin Group: Karimarra

*They are drinking. The kids are playing around
for half of the night, the parents don't control them, they
don't respect us old people.*

My mother was a full Kurrama. Her name was Amberly James. I am a Kurrama. My father was Jerry James, a Yinhawangka. I was born at July Springs on Duck Creek Station and called Judy July, whitefella name. I now live at Bindi Bindi village, Onslow.

My father used to go all over the place working for stations, cattle mustering or with the sheep, dingo trapping, or as a station hand. He worked at stations near Duck Creek, Red Hill, and Wyloo. One place he worked only had a bough shed for sleeping. We were there with some other workers, Jack Butler, and Maudie Dowton of Onslow. My father had a buggy at some time. And we travelled in the buggy, me, my mother, father and our swags. There had been three children in our family, but a brother and a sister died. I was the oldest. Once father worked at the Melrose gold mine on the Onslow side of Wyloo Station. We stayed there with him in a bough shed and tent.

Father got crook and mother brought him in to Onslow where he passed away. Maudie Dowton's mother looked after us. We lived on the old reserve in a tent. There was only one building there at the time, the toilet block.

My grandparents worked at Red Hill and went from there to Kooline Station. Their names were Dick and Diana. They were on my mother's side. Grandfather on the father's side was a full blood Kurrama. I don't remember his or my grandmother's names.

I never went to school. In those days there wasn't any schools. The first time I went to work was after I lost my father. I worked at Wyloo Station as housemaid and cook, and was there for a long time with Maudie Dowton's mother, Topsy Ashburton. She taught me how to cook. Bob Bell was the manager of Wyloo in those days.

There were no iron ore mines when I was a little girl. Tom Price and Paraburdoo only came lately. There was a Welfare Officer in those days taking the kids away to Perth. They went from Rocklea. No one went from Duck Creek, he only took half castes. I wasn't frightened but he took Peter Steven's brother and sister.

After I worked at Wyloo I got married to Jambu Giggles (Mabel Tommy's brother). It was a long time ago. I was promised to him and stayed with him for two or three years. I went to Rocklea and lived there with Jambu. Later we worked at Wyloo and Ashburton Downs Stations.

Me and him finished then, and I came to Kooline Station to work. We used to fight. He would fight me with a boomerang. He was too hard for me. We split up and have not been friends since. My daughter Angeline was born at Kooline. Her father was Jukari Cox. He was just a boyfriend, not my real husband. I never had a male friend for a long time after I left Jambu. Men are too much trouble. I did get another man for thirteen years, but he passed away. I stay by myself now. My daughter Angeline lives at Bindi Bindi village and works in their administration office. She has six kids. Three boys and three girls. The youngest goes to school.

There were plenty of corroborees in the old days. Some were held at Duck Creek, others at Wyloo, Kooline, Ashburton Downs, I can't remember all of the places. We used to go to law ceremonies in the Rocklea area when I was little. We also went to ceremonies in the Robe River area. My parents taught me about our culture. My skin group is Karimarra. We followed the law here in Onslow when old Parker was alive, and we'd put the young fellows through the law. In those days my father would catch the kangaroo and cook it. He wouldn't go shooting, he'd go with a spear. My brother Cliff James used to shoot them. I used to go back to my country in the days when I was at Rocklea. But I can't get back to July Springs these days.

Living at Bindi Bindi is very downheartening. The boys here don't bring kangaroo to the old people, they're too lazy. They get it for themselves. They don't care about us. I have to wait till the shooter comes around and buy some.

The village is a noisy place to live in at night, and on some days. They are alcoholics. The young people go everywhere when they are drinking. The kids are playing around for half of the night, the parents don't control them. The parents don't respect us old people. I don't worry too much about them. They've got the pensioner houses too close up to the family houses. Sometimes I have a good rest, sometimes not. They've gotta stop the drinking. They need a strong man.

I used to drink but I gave it away. My feet used to swell up all of the time. It was not worth it. I feel better now. I still go to the doctor. My problem now is sugar diabetes and blood pressure. I don't have sugar in my tea. I've had this problem for a long time, since I've been in Onslow. When I was out in the bush I didn't have it. There are a lot of other women here with this sort of problem, like me, and they get it when they come to live in town.

Some of the old people have gone back to their block of land at Bellary Creek, that's Rocklea country, Old Mabel and her man. And Lola and Doris Cooke have gone bush to their block at Rocklea. I think this is good for them, but we don't have a block in my country.

It can be very boring at Bindi Bindi, I do nothing all day. I get up before sunrise. Sometimes I have a cup of tea and sometimes I don't. If I don't feel like it I have cool water instead. I just wander around, or go to Lilly McKay's place and play cards, just a game. Sometimes I have a cup of tea for lunch and sometimes cool water. In the afternoons I'll watch TV. My niece has a TV set. Sometimes I get tired and go to sleep. My main feed is in the night time when I have meat and bread. Sometimes I have raw cabbage, carrots, apple, or orange if I don't want meat. Sometime diet coke, but mainly it's water, cool water. At night, if I watch TV I might go to bed at midnight. It depends on whether I watch TV and what is on. Sometimes I look after someone's child at night while they go to town. When it cries it can be hard to get a night's sleep. I go down town on pension day, once a fortnight, on Wednesdays. I spend my pension on tucker, all of it. Rent is taken out by the office, $85 a fortnight. Pension is $300 and something. There's $250 left when the rent's taken out. I don't smoke or drink. I get tobacco to make burlku and chew it. It gives me a good feeling.

DAJI LIMERICK

Birth Date: Unknown
Birth Place: Mount Vernon Station
Tribal Group: Yinhawangka
Skin Group: Karimarra

> *I had the seven kids out in the bush, one died. We stayed at*
> *Yanrey Station.*

I don't remember my mother's name, she died when I was a baby. I
was reared up by my uncle Jimmy. His wife was Diane. My father
was old father Jerry Ireland, same as my cousin sister, Maisie.

I have three brothers, Vernon Ireland, Clarrie Mass he's my white
father, and born not far from Rocklea homestead. I can't remember the
other brother's name he is down near Mount James. I am the only girl
and the youngest. I was born near Mount Vernon homestead, no
doctor. None of us had a doctor. I never knew my grandparents they
had passed away before my time. I only knew the one uncle and aunt.

I used to speak my language but I've lost it here at Onslow, where
they speak Punjima. My brother's still got it.

After leaving Mount Vernon we came to Ashburton Downs
station. Uncle Jimmy was a station hand. At this time I was still little,
about eight years. I grew up there. I worked there. I pushed the
wheelbarrow with sand. Doris Cooke's mother, Lorna, taught me
how to cook there. We didn't get paid, any of us. All we got was food
and dress. We lived in a little house at the station.

My promised one was the long and skinny one, Teddy Tumbler. I
had seen him, he worked at a station near Mount Vernon. I was only a
short little girl and didn't want to marry him. I didn't marry him and
so he married Kathleen Hubert. I married Joe Limerick, Mabel
Tommy's brother. There was no problem about me marrying Joe
Limerick.

I had the seven kids out in the bush, one died. We stayed at

Yanrey Station. Some of them have children. Diane married an old man they had three kids. Joseph married but she left him with one child. Peter lives at Roebourne doesn't want to marry. Donald married but she cut him with a knife and ran away in fear. He has two little girls. Matthew's not married and lives at Mount James with uncle Chubby Jones, my cousin brother. Rose my daughter has three kids and lives at Mount James.

We were at Giralia Station a long time. We saved money when we worked there. We owned a motor car, not long before Joe died.

I never went to school. We learned things in the bush. How to track goanna and get them, where to dig up yams, how to get wild honey and wild potato, they're nice. I used to take Mabel and we'd go bush.

We came to Onslow from Yanrey because we had no job. We stopped on the old reserve. My husband had a job cleaning the toilet.

Jambu was too rough for my friend Judy July, she left him. My old husband was rough when he got drunk. This was when he lived on the reserve where Bindi Bindi village now is. He didn't drink when we worked on the station. My husband would accuse me of going after other men, but I would stay in the one place. He got jealous for no reason, just the drink.

I live with my daughter Di Limerick in Onslow. Sometimes we fight. I have never lived at Bindi Bindi, and only visit my friend Judy.

They used to have corroborees on the stations, and sing. Mabel was a good singer. I'd go to the ceremonies at the Cane River.

I've been back to Mount Vernon a couple of years ago and I've been camping out in the Karijini Park with the people here at Onslow.

HENRY LONG

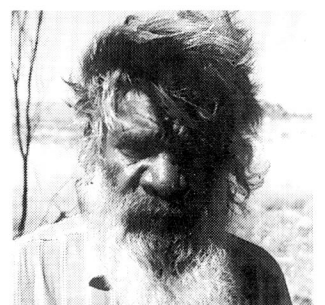

Birth Date: 1 July 1957
Birth Place: Top end of the Shaw
   River
Tribal Group: Nyiyaparli
Skin Group: Milangka

> *I got speared in the leg ... the spear came out*
> *of the calf of the leg. My old father did that. I was*
> *a cheeky bloke fighting.*

I was born on the top end of the Shaw River near Hillside Station, not far from Marble Bar.

My mother was Nyiyaparli and so was my father. My mother's name was Lucy, her Aboriginal name was Nhuthabah. My father's country was Nymbiliyundah. His name was Bahbinah. There were four of us kids in the family, three boys and one girl, but there are only two left now. Horace Parker's wife Olive, she's my sister. She was born after me. Patrick Long, he was my oldest brother, I'm second and she is third. We had a young brother who was killed in a car. The young boy walking around here, Junior Long, it was his father.

The mother, father and uncles taught me the culture. What to do and not to do, this and that, so that I could carry it on. There's very few young blokes now that I know of who are learning the culture, no culture meetings. The young fellows are always there though, a few of them may dance at a corroboree and so on, and things like that.

I learned about dance when I was a kid. I used to like it when I was a kid until I became a man. And I still go today with the singing and the dance. I don't make songs but I sing a lot of them and join in the corroboree. My great-grandmother on my mother's side was named Yunibah. My father's mother's face I remember, but not her name. These old people took us bush and taught us the bush tucker to eat, and how to get it. We had a good old time. That's how I came to know about the bush life.

We ate wild oranges and ones that look like a passionfruit, and ones like they put in the cake, you know. They call it a bathara, wild plum. Wild honey and all that. We ate the same as today, kangaroo, emu, porcupine (echidna) or munkinah in our language. And lizards, kughali in our language. The best tucker for me is kurrumanthu or goanna, and the big one bunkurra. There are two. The other one is the cheeky one with the black spots, but not him, he's yellowish colour. We call him yallakarah. We call the one we eat marundu. He's nearly the same colour as the cheeky one. The cheeky one is the bigger. We eat them both. We don't touch them skinny lizards, the racehorse lizard, jyntarndah in my language. We learnt about things to treat sores with plants but I don't see any around here. They treat itch with that passionfruit thing, boil it up. We had plenty of bush vegetable.

I never went to school. My school was with the old people and from them I learnt to hunt. I used the spear to get my tucker.

I got speared in the leg, too, for being cheeky. I got hit on the head, too, by all my old people. The spear came out of the calf of the leg. My old father did that. I was a cheeky bloke fighting the other fellas over some silly things I been doing in my young days. I was going with the wrong girls. My skin group is Milangka. I was with someone from a wrong skin group. Even Wobby Parker used to flog me too. Queenie was my old girl friend. I used to fight them over that old girl. Wobby was married to her Aboriginal way before I came along. Then she became my girl friend and he bashed me up. Queenie and me were kid mates. We used to stop around the Shaw River, all of us, that's our country. When Wobby was gone away I used to sneak around her place. That's how stupid I was. I got caught in the finish. I fought them back, too.

I got bashed up with the boomerang also. I used to make trouble where I shouldn't do. I never finished my culture law really and this led to trouble. I was a troublemaker in my time. I wanted to do the things I liked, but I couldn't because they bashed me up.

After you've taken your punishment then people don't worry about you. When I finished my law right through, they didn't care about me. Then, I wasn't a problem whether I was wrong or right. They didn't worry about me much, not like in the time before I had gone through the law. They didn't care as much if I went and got a wrong woman and all that, because I had finished my law. That's how hard they were. These days I see young fellas, as soon as they've been initiated in the law they think they can get a woman, and they never been bashed. You couldn't do this in the old days.

I went through the law up Bamboo Springs way, that was my country. I married Lena Long. I got into trouble over her too, until I married her and had a son, Leslie Long. She was never my 'give away' bride. The decision was made by our parents. Her younger sister was my 'give away' but she had an accident up in Mulgul Station, and burnt to death. We never lived together. She was a member of the Punjima tribe and cousin sister to Doris and Lola.

I worked on stations all of my life. When I was young I used to work around Bamboo Springs Station and Mulga Downs. Then I worked Coolawanyah, Roy Hill, Marillana, Bamboo Springs and all around there. When I first came to this country I got a job at Rocklea. Then I went back again, after I finished up working at Minderoo, Mount Stuart, Wyloo, Kooline, Ashburton Downs, Duck Creek, Glenflorrie, Nanutarra Stations in that area. I was a station hand. I did a bit of droving but it wasn't too far though. I was paid wages in money. But when I first started I was paid in tea, flour, tobacco and things. Then I was paid ten bob a week as a young jackeroo and yardman until I got older, this was at Mulga Downs Station.

I used to break in a lot of horses with my old father. He was a horse breaker and so I took up with him breaking in horses. I've seldom been thrown from a horse. I met a match one day at Nanutarra. There was a grey horse, Amos. He was the first horse ever to throw me off, right in Nanutarra. The locals knew the horse could buck and so they put me up on him. I got back on him and rode him then, right back to Mount Stuart. I later broke in his brother, the same family. He could buck, too. They could buck hard, twist and turn. They were good horses when they got some work. They were the Mount Stuart breed, old Teddy Leonard's station. His family had Nanutarra and Duck Creek Stations.

I was breaking in horses over at Marillana and Roy Hill. I like horses, riding them, I used to own some. The last riding I did was at Peedamulla. They are good company and good friends if you look after them. They take care of you too and they know you. When you sing out for them they'll come to you. They'll support you, when you teach them, you know. They are just like a dog. Whistle at them if you teach them. They'll come to you. They know the feed too, they won't leave you when you take them out.

One man's horse will go mad if somebody else rides it. But I didn't teach them like that. I would teach them so that anyone could ride them. I had a couple of yankee saddles, you know with the big horn, but they got burnt.

What really finished me off was when I was at Peedamulla they got me on the bike, mustering cattle. This put me right out of balance with the horses. I've been riding them now for about eleven years. This has changed me, and I couldn't ride a wild horse. I don't ride horses these days. And I still go back to Peedamulla, it's sort of my home these days.

I'm going back to Yangkalinha now. I've been in hospital at Roebourne with pneumonia. After that I got my tooth pulled out at Karratha. I'm taking pills and feeling better now. I'm here at the Wakuthuni block, on my way to Yangkalinha. I'll stay there for while and go to Peedamulla and do some work when they need me.

I still speak language. I can talk to these Punjimas, Yinhawangka, Yindjibarndi people. These groups of people are like cousins to each other. They are all family. I'm part of their people, too. I come here visiting. I used to be here when I worked at Rocklea, I used to muster around here.

I'm not on the aged pension yet. But I get Social Security because I've got no job. They pay about $200 a fortnight.

I don't live with a woman these days, that's finished. But I might catch someone somewhere.

JUKARI PARKER

Birth Date: Not Recorded
Birth Place: Sherlock Station
Tribal Group: Ngarluma
Skin Group: Banaka

> *On stations we were treated not like humans ... we would get
> a tray of tucker and have to go and sit on the wood heap to
> eat it.*

Ngarluma people's country is around Roebourne. Sherlock, Croydon, Munda and Pyramid Stations are some of the leases on their country, and then it goes out near Python Pool on the Mount Herbert Road from Roebourne.

My mother, Daisy Wedge, was a Ngarluma and so was my father. My brother Jack Wedge, sister Elsie, and me from the same father. Another sister passed away after she was burnt. Then Jimmy and Amy Fredrick were my brother and sister, but they belonged to another father. All live at Roebourne except me, I live at Onslow.

I never went to school. I lived with mother and father at Sherlock Station until we shifted to Croydon Station. We were big girls then, me and Elsie, and so we started to work, helping out with housework. My mother did the cooking and we helped, and washed clothes, cleaned house. As I remember we were treated not bad, but no money only clothes. Same for my mother, just a few bob for cooking. Father would get some money.

There would be great mobs of Aboriginal people on the stations. We would go to corroborees at Croydon, down near the creek, and people would come at holiday time to get together, and do a bit of dancing. Sometimes when we had taken a holiday we took the motor car, and we would go away for ceremonies, for initiation. We would visit all around the place. In the Pyramid country there was a big law ground.

From Croydon I went to Mount Florence Station to live. I went with a man. It happened like this. I had been given away in marriage by my parents to this man. From the time I was told I was to live with this fella it was about one year before we actually lived together.

In that period he would come and visit us with his mother and father. We were a bit shy at that time. I didn't think anything about us, I was just really frightened. One day the father came with his son, Richard Andrew. And my parents said to me 'you'll have to get your gear together because you are going with him to Mount Florence Station in the morning.'

They had brought horses with them. And we left early in the morning. I couldn't ride then, but they put me up on a horse and off we rode. I was about sixteen at this time. We travelled all day through the Yindjibarndi's country and camped overnight in the bush. We rode the following day until that afternoon we reached Mount Florence, in sight of the Hamersley Ranges.

We worked at Mount Florence. Richard was a station hand, and I would set the dinner tables. There were five at the table, the husband and wife, and three children. I wasn't paid money, women never got nothing. The man was, and so Richard was paid. I also worked mustering. I would go out all the time with the men. I'd learned to ride by then. My mother-in-law was the cook at the muster camps. Carrie Andrews was her name. I got on all right with her, and with my husband, though I had not really settled down to this marriage.

We had a son Trevor after a couple of years. Then when Trevor was a baby I left Richard. There was trouble to do this in Aboriginal law, but I got away with it. How it came about was that Richard and me went on holidays to Mulga Downs. We did this a lot. Many people used to go there and meet up. This would be for initiation ceremony, dancing, and such things. This was in the days before they had races at Wittenoom. Well, we were at Mulga Downs and I met Herbert. We found each other.

Richard spotted me with Herbert, and back at Mount Florence he said: 'That's what you're doing, eh? All right, if you feel that way and you don't want me, you can roll your swag and get.' I rolled my swag and camped at Herbert's place and stayed with him for the rest of his life. I had another five children. And I was pretty strict with them when they were growing up. We made them do their work, getting wood, and water, washing up, sweeping, all those things. We

Passing on the culture: Aboriginal elder and child. Photo by M Young.

made sure that the girls didn't go running around, they listened to what we said. Now I have thirteen grandchildren and twelve great-grandchildren.

In those days the Wittenoom asbestos mine started. Herbert worked there. Horace and Wobby, his brothers worked there. There was a big Aboriginal camp in Wittenoom Gorge near the mine, and all of those boys worked there. They were at that place before there was a mine it was like a holiday place. They had a bough shed there. And when the mine started, they started working there.

Station workers from Mulga Downs would come and go to the mine. And with others who worked the mine, they would go around with a hammer and chip, chip, chip, at the rock. They would fill up bags with asbestos rock. Horace used to be the boss and they would dynamite the rock. The working men would then go around picking it up and putting it in bags. They would work on the station for a few days and then go down to the mine, and work there for a few more. It worked like that. Ian Dignam was a whitefella at that camp but he lived with an Aboriginal woman. He was the son of the station owner. Herbert and I lived and worked at Mulga Downs. He was born there. I cooked in the station at the new homestead. I had my daughters Margaret, Marjorie, and sons Maitland, Slim and Guy. Two of the kids were delivered in the bush, Slim the other side of Mulga Downs at the holiday camp, at the windmill. And Marjorie was born at the station.

The time came when we left the Mulga Downs area. I don't really remember why, but I think it was because all the whitefellas came in to develop the mine and kick the blackfellas out. We went out to Marillana Station, there was no job except for poor wages. We took a fencing contract at Marillana and Wobby came with us. His wife was then Queenie, and she was with him. We had all the kids and one old fella with us, called Jonah.

After this contract we went to Roy Hill Station for more fencing. This time we went right to the eastern fence line out in the desert and were there for a considerable time. It was hard and we had to carry our water. The work could only be done early in the morning and late afternoon. It was so hot and fencing is hard work. There were five other workers with us on this job, and Wobby and his next wife Lola. Queenie had gone.

We moved next to Ashburton Downs Station over the other side of the Hamersley Ranges. There we were continuing to take fencing contracts. The last fencing contract we did was at Wyloo Station, near Ashburton Downs.

We continued moving west and went to Boolaloo Station. Here Herbert worked mustering with the big mob of station boys. We then mustered Mount Stuart and Nanutarra Stations. After the mustering was over we stopped at Nanutarra. Herbert worked as a station hand, and I was the cook.

When we were at Nanutarra, at holiday time we would get in the truck and go and see people at the station communities. We would visit all the stations back to Mulga Downs, talking to our people and having corroborees and singsongs. Holiday time would be the hot season after Christmas.

When we left Nanutarra it was to come to Onslow to live.

The treatment of Aboriginal workers on the stations was often very bad. At Mount Florence we were treated not like humans. They wanted us to help them but when it came to meal time we would get a tray of tucker, and have to go and sit on the wood heap to eat it. The same for breakfast. Most of the other stations were the same. We were never treated as human beings. They would give us tucker through the window, even when you were the one who had cooked it. And nothing changed when Lang Hancock was running the station. Even at Mulga Downs they did that, and you sit down on the wood heap to eat.

At Nanutarra it was different for us because we used to get our own rations and cook for ourselves. We had a house and a kitchen. When we worked for other stations as workers we didn't get rations. We got rations as fencers, and at stations when we worked as contractors. Food and clothes were part of the rations.

My Aboriginal name is Yaba and all of my education was in the bush, learning the culture and how to survive in the bush. But when we were at Nanutarra and even at Mulga Downs, my kids had to learn whitefella education and go to school. It was then made compulsory by the Government. They had to stay at the hostel when they were at Onslow school. I didn't really like them being away but accepted that they had to go, even though I didn't know what they would be doing.

Today's life is not as good as what we had out in the bush. We then went out, met each other, talked and corroboreed. We had no problem with the drink in those days, there was no drink on the stations. There was no drink till everyone got to Onslow town. Now we are tied up in town. That's when it started and it's gone from the big fellas to the kids now. If they go away I worry if they are okay or are in trouble. I do remember however, that when there were race meetings at Onslow or Wittenoom there would be drinking by our Aboriginal men, but it was only race times. Now in town our culture is going. The kids watch TV, learn nothing and get drunk. They should be learning about tracking, and getting kangaroo, and all those things.

WOBBY PARKER

Birth Date: Not Recorded
Birth Place: Munjina Station
Tribal Group: Punjima
Skin Group: Milangka

The hill near Marandoo, Mount Bruce, blackfella calls it
Bunurrunna, it comes from my great-grandfather,
grandfather and fathers, for our sons and grandsons.

I was born on Munjina Station (now part of the Karijini National Park
— KNP). That was on the other side of the ranger's camp (KNP
ranger's headquarters), the Five Mile we call it. Munjina was next to
Dignam's Station. The ranger's station is at Dignam's Well, a part of
the station, the place that Dignam's homestead was moved to. The
homestead was in a different place when Dignam first started. The old
place was down in the swamp the other side of Marandoo. This is my
country. It goes from the ranger's camp to the gorges, then right across
to Weano's Gorge and back to Dale's Gorge and up to Munjina Station.
This is Wobby Parker's country.

All my brothers were born down below in Mulga Downs station, I
was the only one born up on the range at Munjina.

My brother Horace he was born on Yangkalinha Station, the old
name for Mulga Downs Station. That's his country, in the Fortescue.
They shifted the homestead from Yangkalinha to where it is today, at
Mulga Downs.

My brother's country runs along the bottom of the hill, in the area
of Yangkalinha and Wittenoom Gorge. The homestead where
Horace was born was Kunangkawanjarrinha.

The top side of Hamersley Range we call that Karijini. It's the hill
that runs right through to Weeli Wolli Creek, and across the top
there from the Ranger's camp to old Munjina Station. It goes to Rio

Tinto Gorge, from there it goes to Millstream, but that part is not called Karijini.

This part of the Hamersley Range in your language, we call Karijini. We call Karijini it's the name of the hill. It's the same as that hill near Marandoo, you call that hill Mount Bruce, and the blackfella calls it Bunurrunna. That comes from my great-grandfather, my grandfather and my fathers, to our sons and grandsons.

My father was Sam Coffin. My mother and father were Punjima. They lived at Munjina and Yangkalinha Stations. There were lots of our people here working on the stations in those days. My mother and father worked at Munjina station where I was born. My grandparents lived and worked at Munjina also, Tommy Tucker and Sam Coffin. And old Jacob the oldest one of grandfathers belong to me and Brian Tucker, he was there.

My uncle is my mother's brother. Doris and Lola are my cousins out of my mother, and uncle's father belong to Madaway's sister old white head. These two, their father Cookie Cutacross, that's my uncle.

Our people used to work on the station in this country before we

Dignam's well, or Birdi Birdi. Now the site of the Karijini Park Ranger Station.

were born, Rocklea, Mount Bruce, Munjina. My old people working there have all passed away now.

When I was a young fella I was a station hand at Mulga Downs and then went to Marillana and Roy Hill Stations. Mulga Downs was owned by Fred Nelson, who also managed Marillana. I was a young fella then, and at Mulga Downs I worked with brother Horace. But he also worked on Cowra Station, forty miles from Mulga Downs, and towards the Marillana.

I worked around White Springs Station with old Johnny Walker of Roebourne (respected elder). We drove sheep from Yandeyarra Station to Hooley Station, near Tambrey Station. Rufe King was the manager. That was the war time. I drove sheep on a long, long run to Mulga Downs Station. That's when Johnny Walker got shot through the arm. He was working for the manager bloke from Wolli Station. In those days we had a .303 gun, and he had the safety catch off his when he rolled it up in the swag. Then he grabbed the swag and chucked it into the ute and, bang, it went off and shot him through the arm. Lucky for him, he could have been killed.

Robert Lee Steere owned Ashburton Downs Station when I went there. He sold the station to Peter Madden who also bought Rocklea. I worked for Peter Madden at both stations as a musterer, station hand, fencer and horse breaker. In those day we had no Land Rovers, and no planes to muster cattle, we did it with horses. We'd chase the cattle with horses and bring them in. I used to work with a saddle and bridle. We used to chase the cattle and throw the bull down, or any cattle, with the horse. The boys on the back would jump off and grab the bullock when he fell down, or jump off the horse and grab him by the tail and throw him down. You'll never see that again. Then we'd earmark the station's mark, with a pocket knife.

Today they've got Land Rovers, planes, motor bikes, and helicopters. And they've got walkie-talkie to listen to the planes who tell them where the cattle are. We had to find the cattle. Today there are no horses and no blackfella to work for them. Only white people work on the stations these days.

There was a big mob of us worked for the stations then. They'd cook the tucker at the station and we've got to go with our plates and a fork and sit down in the wood heap or somewhere to eat. Not like sitting down with a knife and fork at a table. No blackfella has sat with the squatters, at his table, in these stations. We sat outside to have our feed. Today we can sit with knife and fork in the kitchen, or the boss might sit there and we'll have a feed together.

In the days of old-time money the squatters wouldn't pay proper wages, my mother and father worked for them. When the wages changed they sacked the boys. Today some things have changed, my child and those of others have been to school. They are educated like the whitefella. But we were sitting under the tree before and our kids are sitting under the tree now. Looks like nothing has changed. Whitefella never think nothing about the blackfella.

We used to work at Wittenoom for Lang Hancock in his mine, and Broadhouse, a Hancock partner. Wittenoom Gorge was part of Mulga Downs Station. We used to go to Wittenoom when there was no town, no pub, there was only a mine, and that's where we camped. They shifted us Aboriginals when there was a town there. Hancock still owned Mulga Downs and Hamersley Stations. We used to work for him in both stations. He sold Hamersley when we all left the area.

But after the Wittenoom asbestos mine started in Yampire Gorge, everybody shifted to Roebourne, to the reserve there. Some others went to Onslow. After that Hamersley Iron is mining all that country for iron ore and took the stations. We all shifted out from that country. They reckoned that the asbestos was a poison, killing people, and they (Hancock) moved us. When we all moved away from there they started mining the iron ore.

I believe that the result has been that our people have been pushed from our country. You can see the stations have gone and instead there are mines. We don't live on the stations any more, we live in the towns like Onslow and Roebourne.

The land from the Yandicoogina iron ore mine right through to the Weeli Wolli Creek belongs to us. That is Punjima country. Aboriginal people have got their blocks of land like the stations. They have boundaries, rivers, hills. I own the land to the gorges up to Mount Bruce.

I've been up on that Wakuthuni block near Tom Price that belong to Lola and Doris Cooke. John, the Rocklea boss, had a meeting with

Wakuthuni and he has given them land. They wanted to get Mirwida, the area of the Government Well that belongs to old Mirru George. It's the country where Mirru was born but they're using that so he's getting this land up near Tom Price instead. They can see Doris' grandfather's hill from there and that makes them very glad. That is called Wakuthuni.

Mount Bruce's Aboriginal name is Bunurrunna. Mount Meharry is Wirlbiwirlbi, that's on the south side of Rhodes Ridge. The Kungkanhawarra Hill belongs to Lena Long's father of Roebourne, his name was Kungkuna, my uncle. It's just out from Newman, and from Juna Downs Station.

We lost our land. My mother and father owned the land, and my grandfather Tommy Tucker on mother's side, and Sam Coffin on my father's side. His father died at White Springs Station. In those days our people would marry into other tribes, those on our land boundaries. My grandfather was a Punjima. My grandmother belongs to this mob related to Doris and all them, Yinhawangka. Doris Cooke's father is my own uncle, and they are my cousins.

Every year we have initiation ceremonies to celebrate the arrival of our young men to manhood. We do this even today. In days gone by all of our ceremonies and corroborees were held at Munjina, Dignam's, and Mulga Downs Stations in this area. We had the biggest ceremony ground at the new station.

Aboriginal people came from all around to visit us. They came from the communities living at Rocklea, Millstream, Jigalong, Yandeyarra Stations and such areas. They'd all meet up here for the ceremony, putting the young fellas through the law. Sometime we would go to them and we'd meet up at Tambrey Station, they called it police camp. There was a big law ground there too. It's the Yindjibarndi people's country but we were invited to go to the meetings. Same as they came to us from all those stations. Today you can't find any blackfellas around the stations, you'll find them in town, young and old. We used to work for twelve months in the station, we never went to town.

In the summertime we would get a holiday from the station and go out for our Aboriginal meetings and ceremonies. We would go to any and many meetings. People would say we've got some boys to put through the law, we're going to have a meeting and you're invited to come along for this ceremony. This culture belongs to every Aboriginal person, right across Australia. I don't care whose son, from the desert, Wiluna, or wherever, we all follow that young fella and put him through the Aboriginal culture. He belong to everyone of us. We follow ceremonies each year and attend as many as we wanted to. And they would come to our ceremonies.

You know sometimes we might go for four or five months with law ceremonies. We'd talk to the boss and tell him we wanted to go to the meeting. And we tell him how long we'd be before we'd be back working on the station.

We called the main celebration ground at Mulga Downs Station the Mullu ground.

If you have been promised to a woman by the elders, your grandfather, grandmother, or your mother, then you got to marry that woman. These old people talk for you to your father-in-law and your mother-in-law. You've got to sit there and listen to them. And they'd tell you you've got to marry that girl. In those days, if you were promised you had to marry.

It's up to you when you get married, and you could get divorced. If you cause trouble to the woman and she leave you, or if the woman causes trouble to you and you leave her, then that is something that is between you and your wife whether the marriage lasts. Nobody would interfere if you split up, that is our Aboriginal culture.

If you have been promised to more than one woman then you must marry both. I had three wives and nine living children. I married Lola Young and have six children: Johnny Parker, Rodney Parker, Cecil Parker, Mervyn Parker, Rhonda Parker, and Dawn Parker. I married Queenie Yuline and have a daughter, Susan Parker. I married Lena Long and have a daughter, Charmaine Parker.

MABEL TOMMY

Birth Date: 1927
Birth Place: Jirrirdinku, Mount
  Brockman Station
Tribal Group: Yinhawangka
Skin Group: Banaka

*I had four grandmothers ... and I walked with
all of them: Wilyinha, old Winnie, Makarli or old Jidi,
Yarnbanku and Biniyanku. I learnt a lot.*

My mother was born at Nyimirli hill next to Mount Tom Price. There is a spring there where she was born called Bimbanha. Whitefellas call that spring Maggie. People would call my mum Bimba Maggie. She was a Yinhawangka.

Father was Joey Kaybi, born at a place called Kajiwinha on the top end of the Fortescue River. That's Yindjibarndi country. He was a Yindjibarndi elder and his mob live in Roebourne. Though father was Yindjibarndi, we kids are Yinhawangka, we take our mother and grandmother's tribal line. My grandmother's name was Kurdakurda. All of my brothers and sisters had their Aboriginal name. Muyirdnha was called Amy. Kunkinna was Limerick. Injie had no English name neither did Coondy. Limbit was Jambu Giggles.

I was born in 1927. Amy in 1932, Jambu in 1920, Injie in 1924, Limerick in 1930, and Coondy in 1939. I remember these dates because our boss, old Jack Morris, he used to tell us kids how old we were. I remember him saying, 'Mabel will be six years old now.' I took note of this. I was born on Mount Brockman Station when William Morris was the manager. It may have been an out-station of Hamersley Station. My mother had two babies at Hamersley, Jambu Giggles and Injie. They moved on to Murimamba Station, between Hamersley and Mount Brockman. My brother Limerick and sister Amy Smith were born there.

We were all born in the bush. Only her sisters helped my mother.

52

From the one father, the man in the burdangka (burial tree), she had three sisters. Her father had two wives, Muminna of the Bloodwood family in Port Hedland, and my mother Bimba Maggie. Biniyanku was Listen Listen's (an Onslow elder) grandmother and Kurdakurda was my grandmother, we had the same grandfather, Bundaliny.

The grandmothers remained single women after they lost their husbands. They were strong, they would chop out the honey from the tree. From Murimamba we would walk to the rocky spring they call Wakulanha. Then we'd walk to Mirwida down where Mirru George (an elder) was born. We'd walk from here to Rocklea. We'd walk to the first waterhole at Mirwida, and we'd come to Kulandinha, that's the crossing of the Rocklea and Murimamba old road. These walks would often last for more than one day. I'd camp out with grandmother and we'd walk wherever she wanted. I started walking when I was six years old. I never bothered my mother and father.

I had four grandmothers, mother's side and father's side, and I walked with all of them: Wilyinha, old Winnie, Mukarli or old Jidi,

A burdangka, or burial tree, in the Hamerlsey Ranges. Only people of special status were accorded funeral rites of this nature.

Yarnbanku and Biniyanku. I learnt a lot about the bush with them. I was the only kid with the grandmothers in those days, the others always went with their father. They used to tell me to get a kajawari, like an orange. And a jilbukarri like a passionfruit. Jibulyu, those little ones, green ones in the spinifex country, like a gooseberry. And burdarbu are like mulberry, the same colour in the season. They'd say, 'put a sheet or something under the tree.' And they'd shake it until all the ripe fruit fell.

When we went walking we'd take flour, tea, sugar, and we would find the rest of the food from the bush.

When I was little, about five, I would go with my parents in the bush when they had their holidays. They worked on Hamersley Station, then Murimamba, which Mount Brockman may have been called in those days. Holidays were taken as soon as the cattle mustering was finished and the cattle driven to Meekatharra for sale. They'd send two mobs to Meekatharra just before Christmas, and buy supplies for the station to bring back. Then we'd all go on holidays.

On the holidays Dad used to take us down the Murimamba Range. We'd go out with grandmother fishing, and looking for bush honey, jandaru. Grandmother was from my mother's side. She was the same one that had been married to my grandfather Bundaliny, who was buried in the burdangka. Bundaliny was a Kurrama, and Wirndawari's son. This burdangka is not far from the Karijini National Park. His father, Wirndawari, was one of those men sent in chains from his country to Rottnest Island where he died in misery. It is an honour for my people to be buried in a burdangka. It usually means that they are gifted people. Bundaliny was a great hunter.

The springs down from Murimamba had beautiful water, down in the silver grass place. That country was really rich. In those days my grandmother and old uncle used to take me along the hill to show where the waterholes were. We came down the range to the water at the end of the top creek, Kardajirri, or Duck Creek.

In those days at Hamersley and Murimamba there were the biggest mobs of our people. There were lots of corroborees, dancing at Hamersley and Murimamba. There were places just for dancing. Down near the Hamersley Gorge they had law grounds for everybody, Wirlumarra. They waited till there were enough boys to go through the law, and then held their ceremonies.

My father moved to Rocklea. He was an important man and made the meeting ground there. This change was not well accepted, at least not at first. Because of it, when he wanted to put his son Jambu Giggles through the law, my dad could get no help from his own Yindjibarndi people.

The Yinhawangka people wasn't strong at the time and Jack Biluri (an elder then) and others said they wouldn't give him a hand. So he decided he would go to Jigalong (Aboriginal community) and get help. I only ever remember one trip by our people to ceremonies outside our area, and that was my father taking Jambu Giggles to Jigalong. They put Jambu through the law at Jigalong. Jigalong people had their own law ground. But there's a straight line between the Yinhawangka lands and those of the people of Jigalong, their tribal boundaries come together and mix up. There was another law ground at Kanyjiyanyji and another at Kulkanjinah, near Mirwida. That's where my uncles and some other Yinhawangka went through the law.

My other brothers went through the law on my father's side. Mum and dad allowed their children to go through the law at law grounds from either of their tribes. My father helped put his son Jambu through at Jigalong, but his brother Limerick didn't want this. He wanted to go on top of the Fortescue River where he's in Yindjibarndi country. So they had it on the top end of the Fortescue, near Wittenoom somewhere. But the boy can't choose where he wants to go through the law, this is a decision only for the elders. The mother is the carrier of the boy and she has a right to say where the son goes through the law. The mother and the father will decide. They work it so that some kids go through the law at mother's tribal ground and the others go through at the father's tribal law ground, because the family may belong to more than one tribal group through the parents.

There was no school out in the bush and I and all of my family never went to school. I grew up running around in the bush. And when it was time the elders trained me to be a dancer. We learned corroboree at our Aboriginal school of life, and the songs. My uncle William Jiyalong was a famous singer, he was a son of the man in the burdangka. He would make up his own songs about what he saw. If he went to strange country he'd make up a song about it. People make up their own dances, but if the dance is about a song's story then they can show what the song means. Some dances are like that.

There was a song about this man who couldn't be still. He was always moving around, one minute going through a bush, the next up the rocks and then down again. He was everywhere. The story was good, and funny. But so was the dance, with the dancer jumping all over the place. I sang this song when we were walking with the tourists in the Karijini National Park last month, on the 'Karijini Walkabout'. This is something new that Karijini is doing. The song comes from my old great-grandfather, Dhurdangkaji.

He was the greatest singer in the Hamersley Range, before my time. He made songs about the first lot of whitefellas to come here. He mentioned all of the whitefellas' names in his songs. That's how I know whitefellas' names from before my time. I still know some of his songs, as we would sing them when we was walking.

I'll tell you about one of his songs. The story was about Dhurdangkaji and another teamster going over the mountain with a bullock team. The wagon got to the top and as it started to go down began to move very fast. They couldn't stop it. They saw great danger and needed help. They called out for someone to send Jack Barry, a noted bullock driver.

My mother and father didn't want me to get married with a young man. I already knew this from my old grandmothers. My grandmothers used to look after me and they kept me away from the boys. They would tell me, 'don't you go muckin' around with those boys, you'll start making trouble. Your mother and father don't want that.' I wasn't a troublemaker, and I took their word for these things.

My grandmother badly wanted me to stop with old Tommy, Kunkurrnardi. He would have been about fifty. My grandmother would say, 'you've got your uncle William, Bundaliny's son, you must take his advice.' Tommy was a good man. When he was young he'd been through the law, but he had to stop another two years before he was allowed to get married, after he'd been initiated. They'd say, 'you've got the best man, he'll look after you. That's why your mum and dad want you to go with this man.' And they would remind me that I would be punished if I didn't accept their advice. Nor could I flee. Grandmother would say, 'when your mother wants you to stop, you stop, don't you run away.'

We went for a meeting up along Turee Creek, and they wanted me to stop with that man old Tommy. I thought to myself, if I run away I know I'll get a hiding from my uncle, I'll try and stop with him.

And then he went bush with two other old people, and my old brother-in-law took me out with them. This was my honeymoon time. I used to get frightened and I would sit away from the fire. My old husband would cook dinner and I used to sit a long way away, frightened. And when I came to have dinner, I would wait for him to go out first, then I'd come in and eat. My old brother-in-law, Bonny Tucker's grandfather on the mother's side, he used to see me do this and be frightened, and he said to my cousin sister Ngalirinku, Amy, 'why don't you explain how you have been. You must explain the Aboriginal way.'

I would sit with this old fella and he would say, 'don't you be frightened. See this one sister of yours, she been like you when she was small. I been reared her up to be my wife.' And he would tell me these things and I would feel better. This happened in about 1940.

My husband was a good man. He could get bush tucker. Those were hard times to get flour but he could get some. And he would go and get some dingo and sell the scalps for money. Dingo pup time was best time to get money. We'd go to Turee Creek Station area when old Dwyer was boss. My husband knew all the bush tucker and wild potato (kulyu) in the kulyu country. He would dig them up and fill up a bag for me. Fill up the billy can with wild honey. We would cut a big tree and get the honey there. We didn't take it all, just a billy can, and we'd leave the rest to keep the bees happy. This was on the other side of my place, Bellary Creek, on the way to Juna Downs Station.

There was a group of us travelling together. Me, Kurdakurda, and my husband Kunkurrnardi, Spider Kunyika my brother-in-law, Ivy his wife Ngalirinku, Limerick's uncle old Jimmy Daji, and his wife Diana or, Binbirrnha.

My traditional country is the area around Turee Creek. It used to be really rich. I was very happy there. We lived on kangaroo and bush potato, and never worried about damper. My husband could cook. He would make a little hole in the ground and put some stone in it and fire, then put in a dish with sweet yellow vegies and small carrots and any other tucker. He would cover it over with hot sand. And somehow he knew how long it would take to cook. When he pulled that dish out there was no dirt, it was all clean.

Nyimirli, the hill that belonged to Mabel Tommy's husband, Kunkurrnardi.

I am the mother of Julie and Roy, the twins, and my other children Nancy and Moira Tommy. Mum was working on Minderoo Station near the coast, and staying at Ngaandawanna Windmill, as a musterers' cook. I was at Ashburton Downs at the time and heavy with child. Minderoo had a pedal wireless set, and when the station manager put it on he heard the flying doctor plane go overhead towards Ashburton Downs. They told my mum and she reckoned that plane was going to pick me up and take me to Roebourne Hospital. Mum made a song about the birth of Julie and Roy. She gave the song the name Warlkangka Kawurrbarndi Walkayinya Julie.

I'm a grandmother now. Nancy has four children. Julie's got three, and Roy's got three. Moira has one. That's eleven grandchildren and they all have Aboriginal names. I gave them the names used by the old people way back.

Old Tommy worked at many stations in the old days, Turee Creek, Ashburton Downs, and Hamersley. Also, he was the man that helped the people start Bellary Station. He drove a wagon carting Miss Aldersmith's building materials and furniture there.

When they moved to Rocklea he moved them there from Bellary. On Rocklea old Tommy worked with the well sinkers. All those wells have an Aboriginal name given by my husband, Nyimirli. This was before my time. When he lived with me, he was getting his pension. I think he was born long time before 1900.

The first station him and me worked together was Ashburton Downs. We moved there because there was no job at Rocklea for my old husband. A lot of Yinhawangka people moved there, too. He was a stockman and he taught me to muster sheep. That's when I was twenty. We'd stop out at the seven mile at shearing time pushing the woolly sheep into the race. At times we'd stay out there for six weeks because the boss could only trust one man, my husband, the best man. He'd ask the boss, 'How many sheep?' And the boss would tell him, 'Tommy, we want twelve hundred sheep from the paddock.'

We'd muster out in the bush and he'd tell me, 'put them sheep together.' We had two dogs and I'd put the sheep together. When we brought them into the holding yard I had a long stick for the count. The boss would say to me, 'you put a cut on the stick every time I yell out.' 'Okay,' I'd say. And when the sheep were counted through there would be twelve hundred. That's where I learned to count and that's why they liked old Tommy.

Nancy Tommy was born in 1950 when we were at Ashburton Downs. I had all my kids at Onslow while we worked at that station. That's when I took over cooking. I started at the mustering camp and when that was finished, cooked at the station. Fifteen years I cooked there. When I started Bobby Knowles was the boss. That's when I was mustering. He was going blind, poor fella. He had been the manager for twenty-five years. Then they got Les Hill to take over and I started cooking. The last manager was Billy Hughes.

When my kids started going to school in Gilliamia Hostel in Onslow, my old husband stayed in Onslow and I stopped out at Ashburton Downs. At holidays the kids would come visiting the station. My husband had his pension and lived in a tent where the old reserve was, now Bindi Bindi. He told me, you're young and I'm getting old, you might want a young man and I want to stay with the kids. He was happy. He was really good and straight — no man was like him.

I worked sometimes at Mulgul and Mount Vernon Stations after I left Ashburton Downs. They'd ask me to go cooking for the musterers. They told me they knew I had a good record at Ashburton and so would ask me to come out and do some cooking, and go riding. They knew that I liked riding and chasing the wild cattle. I had a good time.

I came to Onslow and had another husband, Daji Limerick's brother. I had a bit of work at the hostel doing the laundry. I didn't want to stop in town, so I went to Yarraloola Station and worked. I started living with Algie Patterson and we've been together for about twelve years.

I live at Bindi Bindi but we're thinking about what to do. I want to go to the Yinhawangka block of land they've just got at Bellary (near Tom Price). And Algie wants to go to the block in his country with Gordon Lockyer (Pannawonica). We don't like Bindi Bindi.

We lived at Warramboo Station, but the house was blown over by a cyclone. So we've got no place and have to put up with Bindi Bindi. There is a flat there. We hate that place. People are drunk, and the kids go through your room and steal your things. Things that you really want to keep and have kept for years. They'd go through the cupboards and take anything. They go through the freezer and take all of the food. Nobody stops them, no mother stopped them, the fathers are busy drinking and don't look after the kids who just go anywhere. They always make noises and the big people have no feeling for the old people. They make a lot of noise, they never think the old people have to rest. Night and day they go, drinking and music going full bore. Nobody stops them, and that's why I'm always growling at people at Bindi Bindi. I tell them, you fellas drink and don't know how to look after your kids. I never did any of these things, we'd have got a big hiding from our old people. These people don't respect our culture, nothing.

These are the reasons we try to get homes away in the bush. They can't look after their houses, so they shouldn't have them, but should just sleep on the ground. They need strong people living there to stop these things, but they're not on the committee there. It's really bad, broken glass and lots of kids, and dogs.

I think things are getting better with Hamersley Iron mining. They're going to have a big corroboree on Bellary organised with one of the elders, Peter. He's my nephew. Hamersley are to put up the toilet block. They will only talk to the boys and not to the women. My old nephew made things bad for us when he was talking around the back with miners. I used to have a row with him all the time about this. The same thing happened in the National Park at Marandoo. They always used to say that women were rubbish. I would say, 'Why are women the rubbish? Women are the starters.' I would tell them straight.

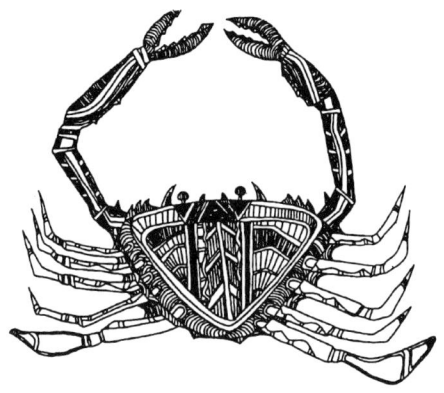

QUEENIE YULINE

Birth Date: 1935
Place: Nullagine
Tribal Group: Nyiyabarli
Skin Group: Burungu

*I was a 'give away' in those days, it was the
tribal law. My brother made a man of him (Wobby),
and so they give me away.*

I was born in the bush on a station in the Nullagine area. My mum
was Jesse Paterson married to my father Banjo Paterson. They were
on a station behind Mount Newman, Weelarrana I think. I grew up
in that place, with my family and a lot of working boys.

My father, mother and me used to work there. I helped by
washing up dishes and working in the house. We used to get paid
with clothes, little small clothes, and tucker. No money. My mother
and father got low money in those days, just a couple of bob. And
rations, tea and sugar, a bit of clothes, flour, and tobacco.

I had two brothers but they've passed away. I have two sisters,
one in a nursing home in Hedland. Me and my brothers and sisters
never went to school. It didn't happen in those days.

Wobby Parker and me met at Mulga Downs. I was a give away,
tribal way. In those days it was the tribal law. My brother made a
man of him (Wobby), and so they give me away to Wobby then
under Aboriginal law.

Under Aboriginal law I became his wife. It's supposed to last
forever, like white people properly married, but didn't last too long.
He took off. Later I was legally married to Gordon Yuline's young
brother, Dick Yuline, from Marble Bar. We were legally married by
white law on Peedamulla Station, Onslow.

I've had two Aboriginal marriages and one whitefella marriage. I don't know why I married him by wajala (white man) marriage. I don't know. Silly! But that police sergeant Ian Blair came out to Peedamulla station, where we were working for Colin Yuline, and we got married.

We worked in Mulga Downs, me and Wobby. We went on a holiday, where the bee farm was going all round looking for honey. We went round there to Juna Downs Station. And that place in the Karijini Park with the date palms, Minthacoogina.

Another time Ginger Parker and his wife, Horace and Olive Parker before they had kids, and Winston and Peter Parker, Wobby and me went on bush holiday from the station. We looking for goanna, honey, wild honey. We were hunting in the Mulga Downs country; kill a kangaroo, or goanna. We'd go on the weekend.

You can't get much bush tucker now, this time all finished. You know quandongs the big round one (fruit), we used to go out and get them. And sweet potatoes, wild orange, from round Wittenoom country. And the big green fruit and little green berries they got them from around the Tom Price place. They got big mob round there.

I been living here with Sue Parker, my daughter, for eight years. She's Wobby's daughter. She been with me six years in Karratha, but she also lived with me in Wickham and Roebourne. Before I came here I lived at Mulga Downs. I lost my husband there and I had another old fella, Brendon Lockyer. I was with him, he had that asbestos. He passed on. I never lived in the town of Wittenoom, but Sue did, and all my family did.

So Brendon worked in the mine. They worked Mulga Downs Station over there for eight years, and he lived in the town of Wittenoom, before I met him. I've seen asbestos tailings on the driveways there, flaky stuff.

The fishing party. Beadon Creek, Onslow.

JOYCE INJIE

Birth Date: Unrecorded
Birth Place: Hamersley Station
Tribal Group: Yinhawangka
Skin Group: Karimarra

> *I tell my grandchildren, you might not want to go to an*
> *Aboriginal dance and not want to talk our language, but the*
> *whitefella still calls you Aboriginal.*

I was born sometime in the 1920s. Mabel Tommy, my sister-in-law, told me that my husband was born in 1924 and I was younger than him. I think I was born about 1927. I was born in the bush not too far from Hamersley Station, Marlumarlunha Springs. It was clean water. Mabel (Tommy) was born not far from there, the same creek we call Jirrirdinku. My great-grandmother was a Yinhawangka and I am Yinhawangka. My great-grandmother, Jarrdu, was married to a Kurrama man and so were her two sisters, Waya and Kiya. They used the Kurrama language, like the man buried in the burdangka, he is their cousin brother.

My grandmother was auntie Kumbi Gladys Bennett. She came from the Tom Price area, and I was born in Hamersley country, that's my country. My Aboriginal name is Marlumarlunurri. They used to call Mabel (Tommy) Jirrirdinkurri in the country where we were born.

I had no brothers or sisters, only cousins. My mother's name was Ada, Mulli in my language. My father's whitefella name was Toby and his name was Divin. His father's tribe was Yindjibarndi and his great-grandmother was Punjima. When I was a little kid I didn't speak Yinhawangka, even my mother didn't learn. Her mother used Kurrama words. The Yinhawangka lost their language a long time ago, maybe around the time my grandmother was born. I've been speaking Punjima and today everyone uses the Punjima language.

My mother and father used to argue about whether I should stay at Hamersley with them or go to Rocklea and start married life. One of the arguments used was that if I didn't go then the police would come and take me away the same as those who had already been taken to Mogumber. They were determined that the police would not take me away.

One day the Native Welfare lady came with her husband named Don. My father saw them coming to the holiday camp where we were staying. He said to me, 'You'll have to run or they'll catch you up. And if they grab you they'll never let you go.' When she came close I ran and then she started to run after me. My mother and father said 'You'd better hurry.' I ran — not to let her catch me up. It was about sundown and I ran a long way. She never caught me, but made her intentions quite clear. She told my parents, 'I'll get the police on to you. You won't have that girl for too long, I'll report you. She's got to go to the settlement.' She did report me. But we moved to Rocklea Station. While we were at a meeting there my father heard of a job as a station hand at Wyloo Station. He got that job and I got a job there doing housework. One day the police came there looking for me, but the station manager said, 'She's all right, she's working here, we'll look after her.' So finally the police left me alone.

Within a few weeks I had my cousin brother and sister picked up from Mulga Downs and at Mount Florence. Ronnie Mills, his sister and cousin were taken away to Mogumber. They were younger than us by perhaps four or six years. Native Welfare picked up another two kids from Hamersley. They were the younger cousin brothers of Nelson Hughes (an elder). They never returned to their home country.

I was married in about 1942 to Injie, whitefella name Joe. We were given away to each other by the old people. In about 1944 I lived with him. He was working at Rocklea mustering sheep and I was at Hamersley with my mother and father. I was working on the station since I was fourteen. I did the housework, cleaning up, mopping, polishing. When I was at Rocklea with my husband I learned to ride. We had no kids, then.

In 1946 at Duck Creek Station in the bush I had a girl, Effie. This was the first survivor. My husband and father were cattle mustering there. I had Darren's (Injie) mum, Colleen, in the bush at Duck Creek in 1949. I had Stuart in the bush at Mount Stuart, and June at

Boolaloo Station. After I was sitting down in the bush with June they told me I shouldn't have any more in the bush. So I had Ken, Lorraine, Tina, and one that we lost in 1968, and Warren. These were all delivered in Onslow Hospital. After Warren the doctors said that I shouldn't have any more as I could get sick and might die.

My mother's life from Hamersley to Wyloo Stations was being a washerwoman. She never used a washing machine until the 1960s in the village at Onslow, and I first used one at Minderoo Station after I had had all of my kids. Every Tuesday she would hand wash the sheets and every Monday the clothes. My mother would have four tubs. One for washing, the next one for washing that was a bit cleaner then rinsing water, then the blue water tub. And my mother was so fussy, you know. She would see if there was any stain and rub to get it really clean. Everything was boiled in the copper the same as we do now. I worked in the Gilliamia Hostel in the 1970s and we boiled the clothes there, too. She only worked for tucker, she got nothing, the same for me. My father would look after sheep and the windmills. He only worked for tucker on Hamersley and other stations.

We worked at Hamersley Station and Rocklea Station. I lost my first child, a little boy, there, at about two weeks. We left there and came to Wyloo, because of this bad luck. My husband, father and mother were working there. At that time the Leonards were in charge of Mount Stuart, Boolaloo and Nanutarra Stations, and they made it clear that they didn't like Aboriginals, and were not keen to employ us. We came to Onslow in 1959 to live. Up to that time my mother, father, Joe and me were living and working together. I became a bush cook, roasts and dampers. I'd kill and skin the sheep if the men were busy, cut it up and cook it. We never came to Onslow until I lost my father. He died in the bush at Duck Creek when a horse he was riding fell. And we came here then because when we had been working on the stations we'd been to the Onslow races and had liked the place. We started to do our shopping there, to get stores. Sometimes we'd visit for the weekend.

We lived in Duck Creek when my father was alive and had never been to the Waluruk Springs camp. Our family's livestock consisted of six dogs and two goats. My father also had a truck. He worked for the stations, and so did my mother, while I sometimes would set a trap to catch a dingo. We were all going to move to Waluruk.

That morning my mum and I set out from camp. I remember we'd had a pancake breakfast, and we carried a billy can and a knife. Sometime later we see a bull coming across the paddocks. My mum said we better run, he's following in our tracks, he's coming for us. So we ran. Ran down to the river and we lost the dog. The dog had gone looking for kangaroo. This is what we had told him to catch, the kangaroos. We were singing out in Duck Creek, calling the dog's name. We could hear him in a cave now, crying out. My mum told me, that's a junakerra, a featherfoot. We were afraid and didn't know what to think, what were we going to do? We decided that we had to keep going to Waluruk.

We were walking all day from Duck Creek Station to Waluruk Springs. As we got close mum said she reckoned that the men were not there. There were no horses there, and we could hear no horse bells ringing. We came to an old fire and mum put her hand down flat to feel the ashes. They were cold. She said they went yesterday. We had no tucker, no blankets. We had to sleep in a bough shed that had been built a long time ago.

We slept there with the two goats. Next morning we go again, we must have been in a gorge, nothing to see. We thought, where have they gone, Boolaloo? We didn't know anything about other stations in this area besides Duck Creek. Mum said we'll have to camp at the first windmill we come to.

At the windmill I found a piece of meat on the ground. 'This is good,' I said. 'No, no,' my mother told me, 'that is a bait, it's poisoned.' This was our second night out, I was that hungry. After two nights I was starving. My mum went to the tank and I grabbed that meat and I put it down my front next to my chest. I ate it quietly. She saw me and said, 'What are you eating?' I said 'I've got a piece of that meat, cooked one.' She said, 'Well, give me some because if you are going to die I'll die with you. I'll have some.'

We came to Mount Stuart then. But nobody was there. We still had to find the men, we had to keep going. There was flour, tea, jam there and I started cooking. That was the first food we had after four nights. We had damper and tea. We camped there. But we thought that the men must be in another place. I'm tellin' Mum, 'Those cattle were being driven. We saw their tracks and wee there. They might drive them all the way to Boolaloo Station from Duck Creek.' Mum said, 'We'd better camp, it's getting dark. The men must be camped on water somewhere.' We slept with no swags again, under a snake-wood tree, murruwa.

We got up early in the morning and there were bells everywhere. We had found the camp, but they'd be off without us. But Mum was finished, she was tired, sore foot, she could hardly walk, and just managed to get to the tank. We had made it to Urandy Station, not far from Boolaloo. There she told me, 'There's the motor car there for the boss, he might be going down the road, halfway to Boolaloo, you know.' He had gone riding. I wasn't sure that I could find him. But Mum was telling me, 'You got to go, because if you've got to walk again they might get going and leave us behind again.'

I found the boss. He said that they were concerned because they had taken off when we were not around. This had caused us to become separated from them. They were going to Boolaloo. He would tie the two goats in the back of the truck where the swags for my husband, father and another worker were. He said, 'I'll leave you fellas here, the station is just down the hill. We'll just put the cattle in the yard. And away he went.

When he went to the station, he never told my father and my husband we had caught up and were there, on the top of the hill. And those two were running round while we were lying down near the rock, tired out. My father came along and saw our goat from Duck Creek. You could see his puzzled look. Then he saw us, what! I could see his expression. As he came close. I tell Mum, 'Dad's coming.' And she sing out to him then.

We had no clothes, no soap or anything. We brought the goats with us all the way like dogs, no matter where you go, they follow you. They eat your clothes. When we went back we stayed for the shearing and the manager went back to Duck Creek with a mardamarda bloke and shot all the cats, and he tied up all the dogs. We stayed there a couple of months and went back in June. That's when I had my daughter.

The boss told my husband, 'I'll have to buy clothes for your wife, in town.' He said, 'I'll just get a couple.' When I got to Boolaloo I had to wash the clothes I was wearing and put them on wet. I only had a petticoat to put on while I washed them. My Mum was sick then.

When I was little the main person to teach me our culture was my father's father. My grandmother was there too. My grandfather on my mother's side passed away when I was little.

In those days young girls would not go near their father, you don't talk to your father unless your mother was there. Even your brother, he'll hunt you away and say, 'Don't you come near you're my sister.' You are not allowed to sit near your brother. It was against the law. These days people talk to their brother. Our law allowed the youngest brother and the oldest sister, thurdu, to talk.

Boys and their mothers talk to each other. Jambu Giggles and Amy were Mabel's brother and sister. Amy told me that when Jambu came to Onslow he never used to let Amy come near him and he used to hunt her away when he was at Rocklea. Only lately brother and sister talk.

You're a mother-in-law you're nyirti. You can't talk to your son-in-law, you've got to call him nyirti, and a manyka, that's a son. I can't talk to my son-in-law. If I want to come close to that boy somebody has got to take me. And you must blow into your hands to show that you are intending to come close. And if you want to say something to him you have to ask another person, who is not barred by the law, to talk to him on your behalf. Where it is a woman she can talk to her mother and father in-law.

We've also got to have skin groups to control relations between all people. You can't go free, and mix with anyone. By our law we can only marry people from certain skin groups. These days the law is breaking down and some people do anything. Some have married their uncle, or a skin brother married his sister by skin grouping. In the old days the people would tell you not to marry this way, and if you did you would get a good hiding. In other places things are mixed up, and brother and sister even walk together.

But if you go to Yandeyarra, (Aboriginal community) you've got to be able to call people properly, people expect a proper greeting. And they keep the culture strong in Woodstock and Warralong (Aboriginal communities). The nyirti cannot come near in these communities.

Birluba means the one they give away in marriage. You've got to marry that person, right or wrong. If you don't marry then he picks you up by himself. He'll come and the mother and father will leave the room. And if you stick with the mother, then at bedtime he'll come and get you and take you bush for one month or more. The mother will give the man room so he can get that girl. My mother had been like that, too. Still, she gets used to that husband. Young Aboriginal women found marriage difficult in these circumstances, they were shocked. Of course their husbands were usually older men as was required by law, and the girls felt that the men were too old for them. But the marriage laws were also part of passing on the culture. My mother and aunties were all given away to older men. In my days the give away was often to young men. Injie and me were both young.

I visited many more stations. At Christmas holiday we would visit our relatives at the station they worked on. And we'd have dances, singing, and meetings. My father had a lot of songs. He made a song about the train coming from Carnarvon, and that song went from Rocklea to Carnarvon. He made that song when he was at Wyloo (Station).

I still eat bush tucker, kurrumanthu, a goanna, and bunku, that's the little one. Another is yankuna. Then we eat jankurna, emu. But I like it cooked properly, some of them just cook it and in a few minutes it will be gone. We regularly have kangaroo, bajarri the big one. I'm getting lazy, I don't cook it in the ground like we used to, but in the frying pan. There is a plains kangaroo we call the bajiwana, because he has long arms. The little one of these we call jarndu. Marndamalu or big plains turkey. We eat all of these types of bush tucker.

They want to start teaching Punjima and Dhalanyji in the Onslow school like at Woodstock, only for a couple of hours. They want a couple of elders to teach. The kids here don't know the rules of their culture. And we say come to the bush and we will let you know the medicine plants, and animals. We've got four types of lizard here. Kajardi is a little one, another is the Karlikarra that's the one that runs very fast, the bulina is a big one. The old people used to kill him and have his eggs too. The other one is the muntha, the one that waves with his front leg as though he is calling you to come to him.

When the rain is coming we say barlkanu. When it is raining we say barlkanu bunthalku that means the rain is falling. The lightning is kanaji. Kanaji binbaku? Is the lightning flashing?

In those early days, the 1950s and 60s, some of our women were still frightened to use a bra. Too shamed! My daughter one day, when she grew up tell me, 'You better use it Mumma.' All the old people still don't want to use it. Too shamed, we not used to this one. They don't want to use it. We can't change when we been grow up without it. Some of them little ones wear a man's long sleeved shirt, instead.

I never went to school, but a lady at Hamersley Station wanted to teach me a little bit. But my mother and father didn't like that. All of my kids went to school. But two of them were big. When we came to Onslow we found no school. Some of the welfare people said 'You want to put those four Aboriginal kids in the school.' There were my two kids and the other two belonged to Maudie Dowton. We said we haven't got a home. They said if you fellas have got a tent we can get a toilet and bathroom for your mob, till the house is built. We been talking then with Maudie and her husband and they said if you fellas go bush we look after the four girls in town, let them go to school here. They were the first four Aboriginal kids at school in Onslow. After this many families come to live at Onslow from the stations. My husband used to work at Red Hill Station, Minderoo, Yanrey and Nanutarra.

I was working in the pub and at those little houses when I first come here. Two dollars a day I got for cleaning up, and bathing the little girls. I did the washing, and the woman showed me how to use that washing machine. That was the first time I used this machine. How to put clothes through the wringer, that's the one I learned first. I was really frightened of the wringer because sometimes the clothes would get tangled up and the top of the machine would fly up to release the clothes. It really frightened me. Each day by six o'clock I would leave.

I finished working in Gilliamia Hostel, washing till 1981 when I retired. They told me you can't get a pension. They said you not the age and not a sick woman. Then June, my daughter, got a supporting parent's pension. She was the first of my mob. They said you can't get it because your husband is getting it, $80 a fortnight, he was a sick man. In 1982 my husband died. Then they gave me the pension, the widow's pension.

It's like when we got rations. In 1959 they started on rations here. We got these from Ian Blair, the police sergeant. He used to give out the government blankets, jumpers and all that, every Tuesday. My mother got a little bit of pension in the 1960s, $30 a fortnight.

This is December 1993. Tomorrow, I will go out to the Cane River, for this is the time for the initiation of the boys. There will be five young boys from here and after that there will be some from the Roebourne side. They will start a burndurr. They had this dance here last year. My grandson is going through the law this year. I have to look after my daughter and son, this is a karnku. I have to make sure that they have tucker and things, so I see that the shopping is done, because my boy's parents have to stay out at the law ground.

After Saturday the parents are free to go. But the boys might be out there in the bush for months, it depends. I think it better if they are out there longer, for if you bring them back early they go drinking and cause trouble. Then they get cheeky to the old people, and get punishment.

Most of the people around Onslow will go out for the law ceremony. Some will stop there, others won't. The burndurr is a dance and people will stop for it. But others don't know how to do it, yet they have grown up in Onslow, they saw it when they was little. They are too shamed to dance Aboriginal dance! When the disco comes to town they go there. And I tell them, my grandchildren, you might not want to go to an Aboriginal dance and you might not want to talk our language, but the whitefella still calls you Aboriginal, I don't care how you act like the whitefella. You are still Aboriginal, you can't change that. Some of those whitefellas they don't like blackfellas. I never go near whitefellas, I stop on the one side.

PETER STEVENS

Birth Date: Unknown
Birth Place: Hamersley Station
Tribal Group: Kurrama
Skin Group: Burungu

> *You can't just throw a spear at the kangaroo ...*
> *allow for them to jump one way and throw for*
> *that spot. That way they jump on to the spear.*

This is a story from my country. It's about the seven sisters, they call them Kurri Kurri, who were chased by three men. To get away the seven women went up into the sky, to Yilykarri. If you see the three stars in the sky it is the three men called Wanaki (the handle of the constellation others call the 'pot'). The three men wanted to build up their tribes by catching the seven sisters and be their husbands.

The women were sitting on the little pinnacle of Mount Bruce, called Nganuwirra. This is not the big one, that's Bunurrunna. Nganuwirra, that's where those three Kurri Kurri stopped. The three men were on Bunurrunna and they then sang a song to the Kurri Kurri telling them of their needs.

The sisters were scared and saying, 'We've got to go now, we've got to go to the skies,' and they ran away up in the sky. Today in the sky, you can see the seven stars and the three stars following, that's the seven sisters and the three blokes chasing.

I don't know my age but people reckon that I'm about sixty-five years. My name is Nyimiliny. I was born on Hamersley Station. That area is called Jilkuwanna. It is where my grandmother and my mother were born. My mother's name was Jessie, Wilgi was her Aboriginal name. Marlumalank was my father, and he was a Kurrama from the area. My mother and my grandmother were

74

Kurramas. My great-grandmother was a Yinhawangka. My skin group is Burungu.

My father was one of six sons of Wirndawari, who was taken from the Pilbara to Rottnest Island in chains. There he died. My father was born in Jilunnhu, a waterhole on the road to Marandoo. He died in Roebourne. His oldest brother was a famous hunter, Bundaliny. He was born at a waterhole between Hamersley and Mount Brockman Stations called Bundinha. He was buried in a burdangka (tree burial) near the Karijini National Park. Tree burials were only given to people who were special, like they were good hunters.

Another old brother was buried in Jabikal on Ashburton River. Wungina, another brother whose white name was Doug, was buried at Marndiwindi, down from Jigalong.

My grandfather named Winyjukundi was born in Hamersley Gorge. Hamersley Gorge's name is Minhthukundi. Nhadi, Wirndawari's brother, was born at Minthi Spring, at a place called Marlakan or horseshoe. Another old grandfather was buried at a place called Wandika, a Hamersley Station out-camp, that's where they used to have dances and all that (ceremonials).

Bundaliny was born at Bundinha, that's in his country, between Brockman and Hamersley, Jilywanna. So we name people after the land and places or things where they were born, but change it a little bit. My grandmother's name was Mulkunnaddi, she was born under a snappy gum tree. The name for snappy gums is milykan.

I grew up in the bush and was taught the law. All of our elders teach the kids our culture. The old fellas show the men, and the women teach the girls. Girls learn how to make digging sticks, walking sticks, yandis for seed collecting, and anything to do with collecting and preparing food, and women's business, that's their culture. But we all learned such things as the names of trees, for example, the sandalwood we call burradu, and winya is a fruit tree, while the seed for grinding to make flour, we call kalbari.

Traditionally Aboriginal law was decided in councils of men and they decided matters of the land and its boundaries.

My father and uncles taught me about our boundaries, where they meet up, and where the other tribes come in. Minthi Springs that is a boundary for the Punjima and Kurrama tribes. Pelican, or wirlimarra in my language, is a creek near Camp Anderson. That is the

Coppin Pool (Dharlibiri) in the Karijini National Park.

boundary of the Yindjibarndi and Kurrama and another of their law grounds. Having law grounds on tribal boundaries enables people of both tribes to meet together without crossing other people's lands. For this reason there were always some law grounds on their boundaries. At Marrina Spring, near Camp Anderson, there was another law ground. Yindjibarndi and Kurrama met there for the law. That is where my father went through the law. If the meeting is of one's own tribe then it is held at any convenient place. And when people from other tribes were going through the law they would have the ceremony at the joint boundary.

You follow all of the ranges and hills, they're often the boundaries. You can see gaps in the ranges, we call wilga. It's through these that there is a pad along which we go to meet the people in the next tribal area. You follow the river it's the same, a boundary. If we go to Coppin Pool (in the Karijini National Park) we call it Dharlibiri, that's the river that runs into the pool. But as soon as you get to Coppin Pool the name of the river changes, it is now called the Turee. The different tribes have different names for their stretch of water. Like the one that runs through Rocklea they call it Yandiwogka. When you get to Carbery's camp they change the name to Burlinkarnu. It's the Ashburton River then. The Ashburton coming down from Mount Vernon to Turee Creek they call it Kabawarra. When it comes to Sport's Creek they stop and call it Minderu. The name always changes when the river reaches a new boundary. There are a lot of names in that country, all of the hills, springs, rock holes and waterholes have names. They are important to our people, and have been for a long time.

At Bimbanha Springs, between the pipeline between Tom Price and Marandoo, you can see that the water is just about finished. There have been a lot of cattle there. It is now dirty when once it was always running. It has stopped running now. This is on Hamersley Station. And Bimbanha never used to go dry, that was the old people's main camp. Now it's dry, finished. There's lots of carvings there, too. It is an important place. You can see where they used to grind them seeds all over the place.

Those carvings can tell you many stories. They can tell you what food is in that area, and what you can eat in that land. The same things happened down not far from the Channar mine near Paraburdoo. The mud springs there was a permanent source of water. It is now finished, all dry. There was also a night spring there which would run every night; it's finished, too.

These two springs have gone dry since the Channar mine started operations. The mining is sucking away all of the water from these natural springs. The springs were never properly protected from the cattle and this made the springs dirty. But the cattle will be finished now it's dry, because there is no water.

All my family was born at Hamersley Station. When the man buried in the tree passed away, we all moved to Rocklea Station. I was reared up at Rocklea and worked there until I went through the tribal law.

From that year I followed that law and the next year my uncle went through the law, Peter's father Limerick (Injie). I followed that law right through to Mulga Downs then. At this time my brother-in-law and me were told that we were man enough to talk, we had passed the law.

When we came back we started the meetings at Wyloo. My uncle Paddy Williams (passed away now) had a big meeting and dance when he went through the law then, him and old Johnson, brother to Nelson Hughes (local elder). We are looking for that dance now, called Nhaddiwah. It is forty years since we had that dance. It hasn't been danced since then and we want to find the sacred thing and bring it back here to Tom Price.

The pattern for the dance was laid down in the form of a frame. Usually the frame would be made out of sticks, every year. But this time we made it out of metal rods, so every meeting it was there and didn't have to be re-made. We just used it with other sacred things for our ceremonies. I have been to ceremonies all around the place, Yandeyarra, Woodbrook, Yangkalinha (communities).

I'll tell you a story about the bird you call the dove. This bird we call a kaarbun, or kalidah. He always complains. He wants it to be summer all of the time, he doesn't like winter. One time he was a man and he went with a spear looking for emu. He sees that there is an emu not far from a bathara, a plum tree. But a jidarka (fruit bird) is singing out about there being a lot of fruit in the plum tree. The kaarbun yells out to him, ssh, wangkawili, wangkawili. Stop that noise!'

He tried to stop the jidarka from frightening the emu away. Finally in anger he turns and spears him in the chest, and knocks him on the head. As the jidarka was dying he said, 'You bathara manhubanu,' meaning that you'll always be here at the fruit tree taking the fruit. And that's why you can always see that bird in that tree. He said, 'Jidarka kaarbunki' which means he has to wait for the summer all of the time.

The procedure of initiation is men's business, this has nothing to do with the women. But when the parents are from different tribal groupings they will decide between them where each child of theirs will be initiated and at which tribe's law ground. Like my old man he was a Kurrama but he went through Burndurr, that's the Yindjibarndi's law. So the parents share the young fellas. My old man went through the law at Marrina Springs, they call it Marrin. I've never been to that place but I'd like to go there sometime and have a look.

When there are law meetings for initiation, the starting procedure is for the ceremonies to start from the centre of the law ground. Say you've got a son to start the meeting, you must stay within the law ground boundary and start the ceremony there. If you go to the ceremony, you can't leave that law ground until everything connected with the initiation process is finished. As a father you are not allowed to go anywhere. All the fathers must sit there throughout the ceremony.

The preparation for the ceremony starts with one boy going round to the communities bringing all of the mobs to the law ground for the opening. And this young boy and the others who are going through the law with him will come back to the centre of that law ground.

The traditional method was that two boys at a time would go through the law together in accordance with their skin grouping, and in a relationship of skin which cannot be mixed up. These boys are said to be yarlbu to each other, which means that they have gone through initiation together.

These days, with the loss of traditional land and culture, there is a lot of mixing up of skin grouping at these ceremonies, everybody is yarlbu now. Traditionally boys who were yarlbu were said to be like brothers-in-law, gumbarli. At the end of this meeting and when the ceremony is over, the people will decide where the next ceremony will be held, which law ground, and when.

The old people taught us how to track, where the waterholes were, and hunting skills. When you are a young fella you are not allowed to go and kill emu or any animal until twelve months after you have been initiated in the law, except for one kangaroo as is needed for survival. You are not allowed to come near the girls until after the twelve months, that's when the law is run properly.

I went through the law at Wyloo. I never came near my family but had to stay away. I wasn't allowed to talk about women or anything like that. And I went through on my own without a yarlbu. There was no one else there, in that year.

When they put you through the law you have got to follow that law all the way until you have finished. All the dances and songs, those things have to be learnt, and about the sun and the moon. So when they finish the law that year, the next year you have to follow the law, you keep learning about that law until you have finished. You're not allowed to dance or sing when you start. This is only at the last part.

When you are being shown the dances their meaning will be explained, what the animals were in the early days. The songs and dances associated with initiation are ones that go back a long way in our history. They have been made up a long time ago. These are traditional sacred dances and songs. At our corroborees you can make up a song or a dance, but these are different. We do this all the time for corroborees.

So initiation is just the beginning of learning the law, which is a long process of looking, listening and doing things. You may have to go out every day to catch kangaroo after the first twelve months period, supplying the needs of the people. At the end of the process you will be shown sacred things and that signals the end of the learning. These objects are strictly men's business and no male is allowed to handle them until they are have been through the law.

But everything we are doing as kids is leading towards the time when we will be initiated and must carry the law. So, as kids, we were not allowed to look at the full moon or the sunset (darraru), when the sun has just gone down. The boys, mullalu, must lie down facing the way the sun comes up, not towards the sunset, that is the law.

And though I never went to school I walked all over that country with my old man, and I rode a mule sometimes when I was a little fella. Later, when I had grown up, my old aunties, three of them, used to take me around Minthi Spring. We used to have horses and packhorses. The three old girls would walk from camp to camp. And we would go walking all over the country. They'd be teaching me about bush honey, and digging bush tucker, and those things. We'd be living on the bush tucker. It was another important part of my education.

Here is another of our traditional stories, this one is about two birds. One is a grey looking little bird that always sings out 'godgie-bira-biroo' at the night time, and a Willie wagtail (jirtijirti). The night bird said to the Willie wagtail that its eye should be on its knees. 'Have a look at your knees and you will see two round hollows below the knee caps where they should be. The wagtail said, 'No, no, you can't put it there, you put it up on the head.' The night bird said, 'If you put it on the knees you got to die as soon as they are old.' 'Nonsense,' said the wagtail, 'you can't do that, you must put the eyes on the head and live forever.' And they had a big fight about it. The night bird won. He told the jirtijirti to put the dead body in a kurrajong tree so that it would stink. This way he would never come back but would be gone forever.

When I was young all of the stations down in that country were sheep stations, except Juna Downs, Mount Vernon and Turee Creek, which had cattle. Paraburdoo used to be a sheep station, too. I worked on Rocklea Station, Ashburton Downs, Mount Stuart, Duck Creek, Boolaloo, Wyloo and then Carnarvon. There I worked as a butcher. I worked at Gifford Creek Station, Mount Phillip, Wanna, Wandagee, Meeragoolia, Maroonah, Yanrey, Urala, Kooline, Hamersley, on the railway from Dampier to Tom Price.

I was on the railway for twenty years, truck driving, and labouring. I worked at Tom Price for seven years and had a house at Wittenoom. I only went to my house at the weekends. So I camped at a Hamersley camp through the week. There was plenty of asbestos there at the time. Later I lived at Karratha.

I married Julie Malcolm, a sister to the policeman recently from Roebourne who passed away. She was a Yindjibarndi woman. She was Milangka skin group. We were married straight. She was a give away woman and so we were of the right skin groups. Her mother was Topsy Malcolm. We had eight kids, seven boys and one girl, Fabian, Wayne, Rex, Tanya, Jason, Quinten, Peter, Guinness. Most of them live in Roebourne.

Have you heard the story of the eagle hawks and the crow? The eagle hawk was a man, wadirra, and he had a brother. They got a wallaby and were chucking it into a cave to eat. Along came a crow, wakurra, who said, 'This is no good, you should go further into the cave and eat in peace.'

They accepted his advice and went into the cave out of sight and commenced to eat. As soon as they began to eat the crow blocked the cave entrance. The eagle hawks were trapped inside. Wakurra then went and took the eagle hawk's woman and made off with her. They went to Wanmala, further north.

The two brothers sent a little feather, a waluku, it moved and went through a crack in the rock and they sent a mabarn, a powerful spirit, through that crack and it busted the rock and made a hole for the brothers to escape. They got outside and saw that wakurra, the crow, had gone. They went up to the top of a hill, made a fire and cooked a kangaroo.

They then lay down for a while. They sang a song. They saw one of those hawks who fly around when you make a fire, they call a nirdi. These two brothers were Burungu skin group. They then went somewhere out near Jigalong.

Later, they were coming back with a mob now. The crow was there and he had that woman with him. They went back to their own camp and as soon as the sun rose, they were back at the wakurra's camp. The wakurra is saying to the hawks, 'Uncle, uncle,' crawling to them, but they pushed him away, and speared him. The eagle hawks told the woman that the crow was a scavenger, as soon as we left our camp, he came there and picked up the woman.

I've been making artefacts and weapons since my father taught me. I used to go with him and watch him spear kangaroo. I couldn't spear kangaroo, I tried but I wasn't good enough. He was more powerful with the spear than me. Also, he was very good at telling which way they were going to jump. You can't just throw at the kangaroo, you must allow for them to jump one way and throw for that spot. That way they jump on to the spear. He was very good at judging this, that old fella in the burdangka, he was the best one with the spear.

I'm trying to make knives now. Women and men carried knives. The women used to put their knife into the end of their digging stick and carry it. The men carried theirs in the woomera, they put it in the wax of the woomera and have it ready for when they want to cut the meat up. They have marking tools and carving tools, and they put these there as well.

I make these artefacts: water pannikins or mirrudanku, jurna or waddy (diggings sticks), punishment spears or makurndu. When you make trouble you get one of them. Sound sticks are little jurna. Tips for hunting spears are yunu. Mirru or spear-throwers, they call them woomera, too. Boomerangs are wirra. Kininkra is a stick that shows that initiation is finished, and is worn in the hair at the back of the head. Yandis are used to sort out seeds, before grinding.

Fighting spears and ones for emus, they are very sharp. The emu spears are longer and the hunters wait in a tree near a waterhole. When the emus come to drink they sit or kneel down in the water. You can spear them from the tree. They call the emu spear a winda.

There's a story about making songs and naming 'country'. My old mother's father was born there at Minthi Springs in the Karijini National Park. He was that grandfather who was the youngest brother to Wirndawari. His nephew was born up on the tablelands at Kuralanha Springs on the tablelands of the Bilbuwarra, that old fella's country. And he found his nephew, Bluey, was building a yard there so he sang him a song.

The song says that Bluey was building a yard where the old fella was born, the old fella in Jubbigul. And down from Minthi there is the Blue Hill, Muddaka urla muntha. When he went back there, he saw a big mob of crows, they are called kwarnura. That's when he decided to go back to Marlakan, his country, and leave Bluey to build the yards. They were a sign.

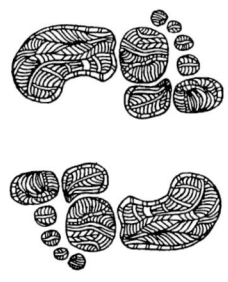

ALICE SMITH (Auntie Alice)

Birth Date: 1928
Birth Place: Rocklea Station
Tribal Group: Punjima
Skin Group: Banaka

> *I didn't want to have my kids in hospital because the doctor is a man. Out in the bush you don't have anyone but a woman friend to help.*

My father was a white man named Alex Stewart who used to cart all of the food stuffs from Cossack and take it out to the stations. At one time he lived out at Rocklea Station with his own wife.

My mother was Maggie Johnny. She was married three times. Johnny is the first husband belong to my brother's father. My brother who died in Onslow this year, 1993,(an important elder) was a son to Johnny. In those days the Aboriginal people had only one name. Her second husband was named George, he was my father, and he was Mirru George's (respected elder and uncle of Doris Cooke and Lola Young) father, too.

My grandmother Kudjibunghu, a Punjima, she was my mother's mother, had two children when she was first married, my auntie and my uncle, not my mother. The husband belong to my grandmother went up to the top of Mount Bruce. He died there. Grandmother lived on the other side of Mount Bruce at an out-camp. She left there with the two children and went to stay at Hamersley Station. She found another husband, my grandfather, Bindima, a Kurrama man (George).

My mother was born then, at the out-camp called Hamersley Windmills. Her name was Yallumarra. That's the name for the windmills, too. Whitefellas name her Maggie. When she grew up as a teenager she married this Johnny and they went to live at Bellary Station near Rocklea. She had three kids with him. My brother

Jukari, the first one, was born at those date palm springs near Paraburdoo airport. He is the one who passed away 1993 at Onslow.

Later when she married George, she had another two children, my sister Jessie and me. My brother Mirru George was born after me and had the same father, but by a different mother, my auntie.

We moved to Rocklea and lived there until we were grown up, that's our home. My father died and my mother died, and I was still there when my mother died. We used to work in the station. Les Smith, the father belong to my husband, worked there. And when we finished work we all used to go out bush. Sometimes we'd go to Juna Downs Station and all around Turee Creek. The old people would be having a meeting. Sometimes we'd go from the station down this other river, Turner River, and we'd have our holidays there. Sometimes we'd go right up past Marandoo to that palm spring, Minthacoogina. That's my nephew Roy Smith's country. I had two of my nine children in Juna Downs Station, Camus and the one who died.

I got married to Jack Smith in 1942. We didn't get married like white people, we are given away to one another. The mums gave us away. We had nine kids. I had five of them in the bush and only four in the hospital. Des was born in 1944 at the station out-camp at the windmills near where Paraburdoo airport is today. My husband was killing dingoes and selling kangaroo skins, that was the only way we could get money then. We had no money from Child Endowment or Social Service those days. We had to work for our own money. Eva Smith was born at Rocklea Station. My husband brought me back from the out-camp because Eva was due. He dropped me off there and he went to a meeting at Mulga Downs Station that was putting one of the boys through the law. So Eva, my sister and the brother who died at Hedland were born at Rocklea. Camus was born at Juna Downs Station. Marshall, my son, was born when we were travelling back to Onslow to get some food, because we couldn't get enough food at the station. He was born at Medawandy Station. Marshall's Aboriginal name is Madawandi. Angus, this last one of mine, he was born the other side of Pyramid Station, out in the bush. That was in 1967.

I didn't want to have my kids in hospital because the doctor is a man. Out in the bush you don't have anyone. The mother got to sit down by herself, and a woman is there just to help. She don't do anything I got to do that myself. And that's why I like it out in the bush. None of the women used to go to the hospital. I used to have bush medicine all the time. If they get sick we know what tree to get, and to boil it or whatever we needed to do. This was nothing to do with the whitefellas' medicine. So having the kids in the bush was better. Because all Aboriginal people have their children out in the bush, my parents, my grandmothers, great-grandmothers, were all born in the bush. And I was born in the bush myself. I grew up in the bush and never had a tablet to fix me. When I was a baby my mother got bush medicines for me when I was sick and I did the same for my mob, none of them went to hospital. Only one, Nina, she had a funny sort of sickness and she was born in the hospital. But if I'm very sick I may go to hospital.

I lost none of my kids. I knew how to look after them, same as my great-grandmother and grandmother. They tell us how to look after the baby. We couldn't do it ourselves. I was young when I had Des, only sixteen, but we used to get the right stuff to keep that baby well all the time.

In the early days Alex Stewart used to give a lot of food, bullock meat and things, because no money in those days. He gave bullets for the gun but the policemen didn't like that in those days. Police didn't like Aboriginals having the gun. My brother Archie, a whitefella, he was at Rocklea when Alex Stewart lived there, and I used to go and play with him. My father died in Onslow. The mother and my brother then went to live in Sydney.

My father George, he's the one that taught me all the Aboriginal ways, you know. My mother and him. And all the law, we going to stick with our own law. You're not going to be married to wrong one, you've got to be married straight. There are four different colours, or skin groups. Mine is Banaka. My husband was a Karimarra. My kids from me are all Burungu. A Milangka man will be the brother-in-law to my kids, their kumbali. Once an Aboriginal knows a person's skin group then they know their relation to that person, their obligations, and how they must be treated.

In tribal law you are not allowed to go over anybody's place, their country. You got to wait for people to come and tell you where you can go in their country. When I come to Roebourne in 1969 I didn't go and tell the Ngarlumas what to do, this is their country. I've got to wait for them to tell me where I can go. That is the proper law.

Jukari, a respected elder and brother of Alice Smith, at Bellary Creek.

We had ceremonies every summertime. We'd go out meet people, they might have come from Mulga Downs or from Turee Creek, or Ashburton Downs, Wyloo or from Mount Vernon Station. There'd be a big mob for the ceremonies putting the boys through the law. They'd have a big corroboree dance and all go back to the stations again when it was over.

I never went to school but learned of things in the bush as we went out hunting for food. We would get marla, a sort of carrot. We would dig it up. And kajawari a green orange, and jilbukarri like a passionfruit we would pick. We got wild onions, too. We would fill a wooden bowl that the men had made and we'd store them on a shelf in a cave in our camping area. We call this onion ngarlku. Men made wooden cups for water also.

Men caught goanna and porcupine, jinkajibuka, there were lots of them. You don't hunt them in the day but in the night, at full moon. You find them walking in the bush around the spinifex. You'd throw a rock at them and they'd stop, knowing something was there. A man would then turn them upside down and knock them on the head. The kangaroo they would get with a spear. Sometimes if the children were really hungry the women would make a fire at the end of a gorge and the men would wait at the mouth of a gorge. The kangaroos would come out one after another and be speared.

My husband was born on Mount Brockman. I was born at Rocklea, that is my country, though really it is where Mount Bruce is, that is where the tribe came from. Horace Parker, the Punjima elder, is on his right country at Mulga Downs. There are two Punjima groups. They have languages that are a little bit different. Horace's group calls the kangaroo widjina and our group says badjeri. There are other little differences, too. The other Punjima's country comes up as far as Dignam's Station, and we are right up to Mount Bruce, Juna Downs Station and back to where Lola and Doris Cooke are living near Tom Price. They are living between Kurrama and Punjima country. The Yinhawangka country is on the other side. Really Yinhawangka country is Turee Creek area up to the other side of Coppin Pool. Joyce and Amy Injie got a great-grandmother from that area, that mob.

I was born in 1928. I had my husband here at Roebourne and I kicked him out. He was doing the wrong things, going with the other women. We were living at the woolshed at first and I told him we'll have to get a house in town. I was doing something for my kids. When we were here we had a big fight and I kicked him out. I hit him with the wood. He thinks he can do those things and come back home. But he don't know what I was thinking, I hit the woman first. I got the police to put him in the 'cocky cage'. Then me and him had a fight. Angus was three at the time. I had six children at home then and I told him you're not allowed to take those kids. I let him see the kids after twelve months on the school holidays.

I never got Supporting Mother's Benefit. I used to work in the shop there, the Four Square. I got Supporting Mother's in the 1980s. But son Des worked for the Shire and daughter worked at Weeriana Hostel. We used to save everything we had. Now everybody got a lot of money and they can't keep the money. They start drinking now. In the old days nobody was drinking hardly. It was good. When the free things came that's when it started. Drinking fit to kill now and people are dying, just over that drink. Free money and free drink. The blackfella could go into the pub now. Only one of my kids started drinking and he got off it himself.

All of the kids went to school. When my husband was working around Wittenoom we put them in the hostel for schooling, so they were in the hostel and we were working on the stations. When we came to Roebourne it was a chance to get all the kids back together with us. Four of the children have been to Perth for high school, Marshall, Ken, Charlie, and Nina. All of them have found employment and are now working. But places like Roebourne are in the highest need of jobs for Aboriginal people.

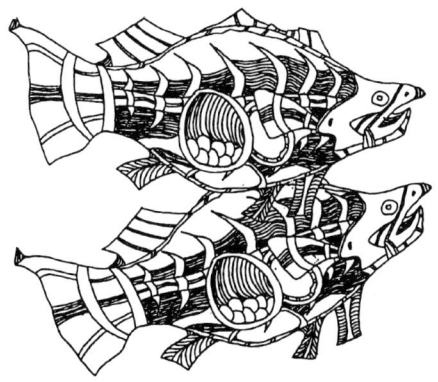

GREGORY TUCKER

Birth Date: 8 May 1953
Place: Carnarvon
Tribal Group: Punjima
Skin Group: Banaka

> *They had taken me and my brother from*
> *our parents. Now we were a burden, they*
> *didn't know what to do with us kids.*

The date of my birth has always been a mystery. The old Native Welfare Department's records have my birth recorded as 1 July 1952 and 8 May 1953. They had my brother Archie's birth as 2 July 1954 and 3 April 1954. The Department of Social Security, when I was going to school, believed that my birth date was 8 May 1953. The Nullagine Mission records show me as being born on 1 July 1952. Last year I applied to the Registrar of Births, Deaths and Marriages for registration of my birth. The office investigated the matter and found that I was born on 3 May 1953. This information was found in the log book of Winning Pool Station, Carnarvon, where I was born. This discovery has made me ten months younger.

I suppose they didn't know the date of my birth when I was taken there to Nullagine Mission. They didn't know where I was born, but could easily have found out. It seems that they weren't interested in these things and so had a bit of a guess, and put down that date. I lived at the mission until I was fourteen years old.

My mother is now deceased. She was a member of the Punjima tribe from the Mulga Downs Station area, just outside of what is now called the Karijini National Park. Her name was Blanche Tucker. She was born at Mulga Downs Station and worked there. But she had a wide experience of station work and worked at other stations like Giralia at Carnarvon, and Juna Downs and Boolaloo in the Pilbara.

She ended up at age fifty on the Aboriginal Reserve Onslow,

destitute, in the mid 1970s, and died in my arms at the Ngurawaarna community in 1986.

My father is European. My mother told me his name. I then made some investigations from the elders from Mulga Downs area. I went to Onslow and they told me about who was my father. He worked on the station next door to Winning Pool. I then made attempts to see him, I wrote a letter saying as much. He replied saying I was wrong and that I should ask a certain elder from Carnarvon. This I did and he told me that this same white man was my father.

For those fourteen years that I was at the mission, I was separated from my mother. At no time did the mission people tell me who my mother was or where she was. The mission made me do some schooling but I wasn't really concentrating on school. I didn't like it. And though there were local Aboriginal people on the reserve there, we weren't allowed to join in with them, we couldn't mix. We could only mix with those Aboriginal people who were on the mission but not others.

So I didn't study very long or very hard. You see all those years I didn't know who I was. I had fair complexion compared to some other Aboriginal people. Was I to be a European? Was the mission trying to make me a white? I knew I was a bit of an outsider but nevertheless they were trying to educate me in the ways of the white man.

The time came when the mission was told to close. They had taken me and my brother Archie, he was three years younger, from our parents years before. Now because they couldn't get their act right, we were a burden, and they didn't know what to do with us kids. One of the white missionaries decided that the thing to do with us was return us to the parents.

I had never seen my mother in my life. My life in the Christian mission completely cut my ties to her. It did not even let me know who she was, let alone tell me if she missed me. I did not know that my mother was an Aboriginal mother.

Never mind, they took us back to Mulga Downs Station where she lived. There was a reserve at Mulga Downs where the Aboriginals lived. It was separated from the white people. So off we went, me and my little brother Archie, to go to Mulga Downs and the white European homestead. But they didn't take us to the homestead. They stopped at the reserve and told us to get out. I was speechless. Then they pointed to an Aboriginal woman and said, 'That is your mother.' And I went, 'Oh-oh,' I could not believe it. No one had prepared me to understand my past. 'No,' I said, 'she's not my mother, the skin is different, darker, black, not the right colour.'

It was a big shock, first time I ever see my mother.

I think it was a shock for her, too. She knew who we were. But she was really waiting to see what we gonna do.

Well, I cried. I didn't want to stay there, I wanted to go to the homestead. Archie was the same but there was nothing we could do, we had to accept it. That was our mum and that's where we had to stay. I was fourteen years, I had to learn all my Aboriginal culture. I knew nothing. I didn't know about Aboriginals. I didn't know about the culture, colour of skin, nothing whatever. I had to really learn.

In fourteen years at the mission I had learnt nothing about my own culture, I had been taught little in the white education matters. But we had to say grace before every meal, prayers at night, and attend Sunday School each week.

Of course me and Archie soon accepted our mother, our uncles and aunties. We had a big mob, the family. We just learned from them, learning slowly.

But that is not the end of this story. It was only about twelve months later that the native welfare people came and took us away again, this time to the newly established mission school at Marble Bar. It was run by the same people with Pastor Dave Stevens (of Roebourne) old father in charge, as he was at Nullagine.

We came back to Mulga Downs for holidays. We stayed at Marble Bar for about two or three years and then in the 1960s a hostel opened at Roebourne. We were taken from Marble Bar to Roebourne for school, and to live.

I didn't like schooling there either, there were more Aboriginals with all mixed colours there. There were three different schools, I attended the new primary in the first term. There were three different schools then. The Aboriginals who were considered to be 'full bloods' had to have their own school. The 'half castes' and the 'whites' had their own school. And then they opened the primary school to take in all children and they all became one school. We all went there. We were allowed to mix in with the others, the station children, too. That was what it was built for, so we all moved into the Weeriana Hostel.

From Roebourne we sometimes went for a holiday and saw our mother. I used to see Mack trucks going up and down the road, carting asbestos from Wittenoom and we used to sneak away and get a lift. They would dump us off at the turn-off. We used to walk into the station ground, it was about thirteen kilometres, to see Mum, and stay for two or three days.

This was when I was old enough to leave school, or when I left anyway. I didn't like it, got fed up and left. I went working at stations with my parents for soap and tea. This was in the sixties and us Aboriginals were still on soap, tea, clothes, blankets, etc, as wages. By this time my mum had married Jeffrey Long.

These marks on my body are initiation marks. I have been through the law. Actually my grandfather put me through the traditional culture law around Jigalong, called bush culture.

Then one day I knew I had to go through initiation. They picked me up and took me to Jigalong to start the process of initiation. Later they brought me back so that I was initiated in my mother's country. I was at Jigalong a couple of weeks and came back and they put me through. I've been following the culture ever since.

You see that land at Jigalong was once our land. Those people there came out of the desert and had no land like us, so we gave them that land. So we have a good connection with those people.

My grandfather told me before he died, 'Now you are a man you follow our people's culture in the Pilbara.' My grandfathers were Percy and Raymond Tucker, they had planned the initiation. The law grounds were out there in Wittenoom at Mulga Downs. The initiation ground there was a bush sacred site.

My grandfathers died of asbestos disease.

Then came the free citizenship period. The citizenship started about 1967 and that's about the time when all the Aboriginal people from the stations weren't wanted by the squatters, so we came into Roebourne. There was a reserve across the river, especially for the ones who couldn't work any more, the old people. This meant that part of their traditional culture was again dead. They couldn't live in their home country because this was not their land. A lot of old people who died, could not handle their separation from their land and the conditions of reserve life.

In that time there had been lots of Aboriginal people on stations like, Mulga Downs, Hooley, Mount Florence, Urala, Nanutarra, Rocklea and Hamersley are just a few. All of those stations had Aboriginal communities until the late 1960s when the pastoralists kicked us off.

I worked on nearly every station in the Pilbara, at Onslow, Port Hedland, South Hedland, Wittenoom. I've been fixing windmills, fencing, and mustering cattle, riding horses, all those things. It's not surprising that when I got to my twenties I was a reckless bloke. I used to get drunk and get into trouble with police. I did a bit of time, assault, assault police, domestic violence, drunkenness. But when I finished I helped old Woodley King to establish Ngurawaarna as an alcohol rehabilitation centre. I worked there for five years as coordinator, bookkeeper, and general caretaker. Ngurawaarna was up and running, with transport and accommodation and a shop. But I was tired and needed a rest.

In recent times I have been working as an Aboriginal Liaison Officer with the Education Department at Roebourne. I've been there for seven years.

My school work is to assist the communication between Europeans and Aborigines. To try and encourage kids, especially high school kids, to concentrate on their studies, not like what I used to feel. Nowadays you get paid to work. Try to explain that to them. And the better you get, the better chance to get jobs — in a time when there aren't jobs.

LOLA YOUNG

Birth Date: 14 January 1942
Place: Rocklea Station
Tribal Group: Kurrama
Skin Group: Burungu

> *Up at three in the morning, 'way you go', gotta dress nice,*
> *shoes on, clean. Oh, we really worked ... riding horses,*
> *mustering sheep, everything.*

I'm fifty-one years old. My mother was a Kurrama and my father a Yinhawangka. Their traditional country was the Rocklea Station area, on the south side of the Karijini National Park.

I was born Lola Cooke, the eldest kid in the family. I got four brothers and one sister, Doris. They are all still alive and live in the Pilbara. Colin Cooke lives in Hedland, Kevin Gilba lives here in Karratha, then there is Brian Aquinas at Hedland, and Nick Cooke living at Roebourne. My brother Nick, sister Doris, and I were born at Rocklea Sation, not far from Paraburdoo.

My father was a great stockman, well known in the Turee Creek area of the Pilbara. When they mustered cattle he was the one who bulldogged the calves for branding. His name was Kurrubunha, a Yinhawangka. Born on the Hamersley Station area. He worked at Rocklea, Juna Downs, Ashburton Downs and Minderoo Stations breaking in horses and doing stock work. His whitefella name was Cookie Cutacross.

Father was also a drover. When they were married he and Mother worked on these stations, and we lived there with them. We were always moving around because my father was a drover for the station, droving cattle all the time. The cattle would be mustered and driven to Meekatharra to be trucked away. We were doing this kind of work for poor wages. This was before there was new wages for Aboriginal stockmen after the 1968 pay award. It was a bag of flour, tea, clothes and maybe some meat.

When we left there I was still a little girl of about nine years. Must have been in the 1950s. There was only me and brother Nick, and we moved to Onslow. When we got there we started work. We had no choice as Dad was in hospital. He was sick all the time then. I think he had ulcers in the stomach. My mother kept us when he was in hospital, and we had to work to help with our upkeep. Nick used to work in the butcher's shop to bring the meat in, and I used to work in the bakery. A Malayan couple used to have it, friends of Mum and Dad.

Father was buried somewhere in the Hedland area and members of the family are now trying to find exactly where.

Onslow wasn't much of a town then. We were the first lot of Aboriginal people who came here from the Hamersley Range area. We camped on some land before there was a reserve. This was down near where the old reserve was later situated, now Bindi Bindi. We used to stay there by ourselves, although there were some of the traditional Aboriginal owners of the area living near the spring, a couple of hundred metres away from our camp, towards where the hospital is now. We all used the same spring for water.

I remember an old man called Claude Bell Jack lived there. That old fella would come and visit Mum. There were also some station workers who used to come and go. We would also get our water from a soak down from where Onslow is now situated. We did our washing there.

Me and Nick used to get out early in the mornings and go off to our work. The butcher used to come and pick us up in his little sulky, so I got a ride with them and jumped off at the bakery. The bakers gave us bread and made clothes for us in exchange for my work.

Then we moved. Mum got a job on Ashburton Downs Station. My old uncle Jack Smith came down and picked us up. He was Marshall's (Smith) father. Mum's job was cooking. I got a job there as house cleaner. I was a big girl by then and stayed until I was thirteen or so. It was a pretty tough life. I'd get up at three o'clock in the morning, 'way you go', gotta dress nice, always shoes on, clean. Oh, we really worked there. It was riding horses, mustering sheep, all sorts of jobs, everything. We really learned a lot about life there, then. At this time my sister Doris was a little girl. Too young to work. She was one of the lazy little ones who used to walk around all day.

But all of my life on stations was spent working. Not just mucking around like these days. We had no time to muck around stealing and getting into trouble. We had to be on time at work. Get up early and get into it, cleaning, washing and ironing. Mum cooked. I used to just wash. And oh, do all the housework. You have seen the old movies where there is the Aboriginal waitresses, waiting on all the other people having a banquet. That was me. Standing up with a white cap. And for all of that work I got just clothes, no money. I didn't know money. We never saw money. Oh, Mum used to give us something when we'd go to town. But we were never given money for our pay.

Then Wobby Parker came and picked me up. I was a give-away wife to Wobby. I was about fourteen or so then. He came over to Ashburton and I went with him up north. Then we came back here and finished up working on Mount Stuart Station. That's where I had Roberta. She was my first daughter, and I was eighteen. She lives today at Hedland.

Then we moved up to Nanutarra and stayed. I had all my other children there. I had seven kids but lost two, one at birth and the other in a car accident at eighteen.

Our people practised all aspects of culture. They would hold a big meeting on the Turee at a meeting camp. They called it Karlkatharra. They'd have dancing, talking, corroboree and horse dressage contests. Who had the best turned out horse. My father always got the first prize, and what he was given were spears, boomerangs, mirrus, and whatever people had. Some of them would bring a jurna (waddy). He had lots of spears and things. They made these things specially for this contest. They held these types of gatherings about fifty years ago.

In those days my father used to use spears to hunt. As a kid I could not touch the little sharp mirru tip. I was not allowed into the bough shed in case the spears, and other gear touched it. This was when we were living at Cobbore. He speared kangaroo in those days. He'd sneak in on one with its head down drinking in a soak.

Sometimes they would use the spear or boomerang on other people. My mother and father were married according to the Aboriginal law, they were promised to each other by their elders. My father was bad tempered, and my mother told me that he speared his brother through the leg, just because they were having a fight.

We eat a lot of kangaroo and goanna, these are the best meats. The plains turkey is all right, and the emu we eat, only when we want to eat him. When we eat emu we cook it up and ask people to come and get their piece. They've got to come to my camp that is the law, and when we eat it, we must sit down. These are customs based on our culture. It is a rich meat. We would get its oil and use on the skin in treating sores.

Another custom is that when some relative dies, we must stop eating one type of meat. We decide which kind, but we don't eat that for some time. It's a mark of respect. Also there is the custom that when a person passes away we will either move from the house in which they lived to another, or we will have the house smoked. This is to remove the spirit from the place.

In addition to custom, there is our language and its differences to that of other societies. Our language uses different names for our different grandparents. Like this, mabuji, that is your mother's father. Mayali is your father's father. Kabarli is my father's mother. My kantharri is my mother's mother.

In our family we show particular respect to the grandfathers on our mother and father's sides. Both have places named after them. Our mabuji was Wakinbanku (Wakin), a Kurrama, who foretold the fate of that hill next to Mount Tom Price. We believe he owned the hill we call Wakuthuni. Our mayali was a Yinhawangka whose place was Nyirrimba, the head of the Turee Creek.

I think there is a lot that non-Aboriginal people could learn from Aboriginal people. You know, the non-Aboriginal people named the biggest hill around here, at Tom Price, Mount Nameless. They didn't ask the Aboriginal people here if that place had a name already. And it had. Its name for thousands of years has been Jarndunmunha, there's nothing nameless about that. I think it is a matter of respect of cultures.

So you can see that our family believes in our Aboriginal ways and culture, and that we do our best to keep them alive. The old people passed the culture to us and to do this they would take us bush and teach us, all the time teach us. The grandmothers would teach us. They would take out all the girls and the boys. We learned the culture things, the bush medicine, bush tucker, the stories, all of it. And all the time when we were small we would go to corroborees.

Even now I go out bush to initiation ceremonies and other meetings. It has always been a part of my life, and part of my culture.

We were taught our skin group so that we would know who we could relate to and who we could not. I am a Burungu, I am straight for a Milangka man, all of us. Burungu women are sisters. My father was a Karimarra.

When we go bush we have a great time with other people. We see the young people come into the law. I'm trying to teach the young people these days, my grandchildren. I just hope they keep it in their head. This is why we are trying to get back to the land to teach our grandchildren our own culture. We always tried to teach them but they get a lot of other things, space invaders, video games, and all those things. We can't get them out from the house. We can't sit down and talk to them unless we've got a place to go, a place of culture, our country.

We try to take them back to our own country, out under the stars to enjoy it. Where all of us can sit around the camp fire. Then the children will listen to you. Every long weekend we need to get and teach them. If we teach them from outside of our land we get no strong inside feeling from them. You can feel it really strong when you are talking from your own land. I really enjoy it, everybody enjoys it. We had a bit of a corroboree out there this time last week. There was a big mob of our people from our group, the Wakuthuni, that went bush. They're all tradition people from Tom Price area. Some came from far away. They all came because they want our group to get some traditional land. When they got to the camp they started straight away singing the old songs and teaching all the little fellas. They were songs from that country.

We've got to keep that Karijini Corporation strong for us to get some land. That is its main problem to get our land. That is the burning need of the people. We are going to go out there on our land and survive the way we used to survive if we have to. To live off the land. Kill kangaroos and everything else needed to survive. We don't worry about the shops, as long as we have the basic stores. Some of our young people are keen to do this too.

You know, getting away from the town will ease a lot of our problems here in town, drinking and carrying on. The youth don't even take the time to come and visit us any more. They have got plenty of time but don't make the effort to come and see their

A bough shed on the Wakuthuni Aboriginal Corporation's block, Tom Price, 1994.

relatives. If we want to talk about our land I've got to go and get them together. And I go around and around looking in every house. Oh, he's not here, he's gone somewhere else.

I think they're losing the culture.

Neil Finlay worked for Bell's Transport at Roebourne, and I worked at the pub doing the laundry five days a week. We developed a relationship. Then I wanted to go to Wittenoom where my mother was living. She wasn't well. So we both gave up our jobs and went there. He got a job with the CMM Company on rail construction to Tom Price.

We lived together for seven years. Neil said that if I wanted to get all my kids back together he would look after them, so I started to do this. I had eight children. All, except Dawn, were in the Gilliamia Hostel and under the control of Wobby who was working on a station. Dawn was schooling in Perth with her grandmother. Apart from Dawn and Roberta, I had John, the ranger in the Karijini National Park. Then there was Mervyn who lives in Roebourne, and

Cecil who's in Carnarvon. Rodney works for the Community Health Department at Roebourne, and Rhonda lives at Hedland. I lost one. They all came back to Wittenoom, except that one, and went to school there.

This time was the late 1970s and then there was a lot of asbestos lying around in that place. The Government moved us out, and I came back here to Wickham. The Government reckoned the asbestos was bad and we were breathing this in. So they moved us out and gave us a house at Wickham. I was in Wickham for eleven years in the one house. We were the first Aboriginal family to get a house there from Homeswest State Housing.

Now it's the end of the year, 1993. There's a small group of the Wakuthuni Group living on our traditional land, an excision from the Rocklea lease near Tom Price. We've gotten out of town life. We look forward to a new start in life for our young people. We look forward to a better future.

BONNY TUCKER

Birth Date: Unknown
Birth Place: Bonny Downs Station
Tribal Group: Punjima
Skin Group: Karimarra

*My mother reared me on a horse ... I would ride up behind
her clutching her waist. She loved riding and would go
chasing cattle with me up behind her.*

My name is Bonny McKenna. My father used to work for this white
bloke McKenna, a station owner at Mintina the other side of
Nullagine. I was born at Bonny Downs Station and that's why I'm
called Bonny.

My mother's side of the family was Punjima. My mother's father
belonged to the Wittenoom area. My mother was Fanny McKenna,
and her father was Harry Yilbinna. My mother's name was
Kijiyamba, the white people named her Jonah. She was a Nyiyaparli
and married a Punjima man, same as me, see. My grandmother came
from Yandicoogina, where that new railway line is now going and
the new BHP mine is being built.

My father was Snake McKenna, he was a Kartujarra. They came
from Nullagine, Jigalong, their traditional country. The Nyiyaparli
were staying at Marillana, Warrie Stations, and all around
Yandicoogina. Marble Bar is traditional Nyamal country.

I never went to school. The only schools for Aboriginal kids were
at White Springs. That was around Woodstock, Yandeyarra and
Wathinkinha way, right on the highway that goes to Mount
Newman. Another one was in Carnarvon. They were Catholic or
Christian schools. I wanted to go to school but my parents told me,
'No they might take you away for good.' And they ran away in the
bush, and we went hunting for gold. But the Native Welfare were
only looking for mardamarda kids, not full bloods.

My family worked on Bamboo Springs Station. That was like their base and they would go from there to wherever shearing, mustering or other jobs were done. This was not far from my father's country. Most of my family stayed at Bamboo Springs, my mother's sister, my father's sister, other near relations. There'd be a big mob there. I used to work in the house, set the tables for the boss wash dishes, sweeping, make the beds, washing clothes, ironing, and my mother would cook there, making home-made bread in the oven, cakes or whatever.

My father would be a stockman, ride the horses, check how the stock were getting on at each windmill. My mother and father used to get say ten pounds, that was the price for those two. I never got wages, just soap, dress, blankets, cool drink in tins, and condensed milk. Sometimes the boss would ask if I wanted to go mustering and I grabbed the chance. We'd go after cattle and sheep. I loved to ride horses, my mother reared me on a horse. When she used to ride a horse I would ride up behind her clutching her around the waist. And she loved riding and would often go chasing the cattle with me up behind her. I would have been about seven.

The family were strict in practising the law. My mother taught me most of the important things like skin groups, relatives, bush tucker and so on. I never saw my grandparents, only my old aunt on my father's side, Minbanha. The family would also go to the big ceremonial ground on the Shaw River up near Hillside Station and Coongan River at Marble Bar. The people could come from all around to talk and meet, and find out what's been going on around the place. We'd stay up there for two months and have meetings.

I was a promised bride and married Percy Tucker Aboriginal way. But long before I was given away my mother told me, 'We can't have our daughter here lying around, you're past your teen age. We're going to find you a good husband to live with you.' I was twenty-six at the time and I think my parents were happy for me to leave. You see in those days the father wouldn't sit with the daughter, that's shame. Not like these days. Then the father was not allowed to sit with the daughter, only the mother or auntie. These days you hear them, 'Eh, sister come on over here and have a drink.' And you are not supposed to talk to your brother, even your cousin brother.

At some stage I was told who the chosen husband was and I knew him, but we never spoke. One day we went to the Wittenoom races, probably their first race meeting. The father belong to Slim Parker, my uncle, asked me, 'You like this nyuba?' or true love. 'You've got to live with your own nyuba from around Mulga Downs, not those long way ones,' meaning from far away. He was strong for me to marry into the local Punjimas, as our family had Punjima people on both parents' sides. And he said, 'I'm going to give my boy away for this girl now.' He was there too. My uncle had asked my mother before if he could raise this question with me.

I went back to Bamboo Springs and the next time I went to Mulga Downs was to live with him. Later my husband, when we had some kids, took me to the Wittenoom police station and we were married whitefella way. This had been urged by the welfare mob because as they said, they'd know I was Mrs Tucker, then. My husband was frightened that they might take away the children's entitlements.

Margaret Parker was schooling in Nullagine at the time I believe. My uncle went to Nullagine to pick up their schoolkids and they came my way to pick me up and take me back. The Parker family worked at Mulga Downs then.

Everything was all right for me, I wasn't worried. Besides, my mother's family were there. However I did take on my husband's family, three children under the age of six years. He had been married but his wife left him. They were Gladys Tucker, Wadu they call her, Sue Smythe of the Aboriginal Language Centre (Port Hedland), and the other girl she's passed away, was murdered by two white men. At the time of my marriage the kids were at a hostel in Nullagine but they came down to Mulga Downs with me.

My husband was much older than me. In those days you can't get away, it was very strict. These days anything goes, you might marry a relation or something. Now you can see them, kids having kids.

At this period my husband was working on the asbestos trucks of J D Tsakolas. He would call in at Mulga Downs every few weeks for a break. I lived in a bough shed out in the bush with my sisters-in-law Ivy and Elsie, and my old brother-in-law Raymond. I worked at Mulga Downs Station, in the house setting tables again, mop the floor, iron the clothes for the boss. I did some mustering — sheep, and my husband would drive the truck loaded with camping gear. And I'd cook for the musterers.

We went back to Bamboo Springs when we left the Mulga Downs area. I had my first two babies, Brian and Rex, in this period. They were born at the Lock Hospital, Port Hedland, now the Mulgunya

Hostel. We both worked. He had finished with Tsakolas and became a station hand. He worked for the Agriculture Protection Board (APB) as a dogger on Bamboo Springs as well. We went together, it was a good bush life. We went right over the other side of Roy Hill Station, Noreena Downs Station, Balfour Downs and Ethel Creek, not far from the desert past Nullagine, back to Marble Bar. We went through Corunna Downs Station back to Hillside and right down to Cowra out-station. We go for six weeks sometimes. We had an old Land Rover and a tent in case of rain. We go around tracking the dog, and keep moving. Westen was born in the bush at Mulga Downs in this period. And when we worked at Coolawanyah Station Carol was born. I had Beverley when we were at Bamboo Springs. These last two were actually born in the Port Hedland District Hospital.

After this the old fella went back working in the tin mine at Shaw River, driving a truck. He got sick of this driving and we came back to Wittenoom and he was dogging for the APB. We lived in a house across from the police station. I had Charlie at the hospital here. By this I had all of my kids.

We kept on the move throughout our life together. A lot of this was following work, but some of it was mixing with his relatives and my relatives. You know, Aboriginals say when they get sick of a place, 'let's go back to our own country.' And later, when they get sick of that area, they'll say, 'I'll go back to the husband's country now.' Not like the days when we're in here, the town, all the time.

Sometimes they travel like in holiday style. A group would start from Marble Bar and travel to Hillside Station. Along the way they might hunt kangaroo and camp, or something else, and get to Hillside whenever they want to. After they've been to Hillside they move on to Bamboo Springs Station. Perhaps they go fishing on the way and stop the night, or two. Then they get to Bamboo Springs and might stay a day or so there, talking with the people about how things are going. Then they leave and go out to Warralong Station near the Shaw River. If something catches their fancy they will camp a while. They might then go to Bonny Downs station, Roy Hill Station, Ethel Creek, and end up at Jigalong. Always enjoying the country and doing the things they wanted to do to survive. And they would return to Marble Bar the same way. The next time they would perhaps move in a different direction, say toward Marillana, and then other different places. That is the way our people have moved. You can see that in this process they passed information to different people.

Me and the old fella next moved when the APB sent us to Onslow. We lived in a house in Cameron Street. He was dogging on the stations of the Onslow area, Red Hill, Yalleen Station and right back to Roebourne. But he didn't want this job any more and went working at Yarraloola Station as station hand for twelve months. Then he was offered a job putting tags on dingoes by Peter Thompson at Fortescue River, he took it. By the time this job was done he was feeling really crook.

We had a holiday and when it was over Peter Thompson came to him and asked whether he wanted to tag more dingoes. My husband said, 'No, I'm not feeling well. I think I'm going to see the doctor.' He went to the visiting doctor from Carnarvon, at Onslow. He couldn't see anything wrong. So he waited but was getting worse, and the Carnarvon doctor sent him to Perth.

He came back from Perth and said to me, 'I gotta tell you because you're my wife, I don't think you'll have me too long.' I said 'Tell me, tell me what's happened.' He said, 'I've got that asbestos in the lungs, and they're infected.' He was in hospitals, Sir Charles Gairdner, Onslow, and Exmouth and I spent time with him in each. The doctors said, 'I can't do anything about it.' Finally, I said he must stay home at Onslow for the kids. They never went to school for two months. He passed away at Onslow Hospital.

I have six kids. These are their names, their order of birth, and where they were when their father passed away. Brian (Pundulmurra Aboriginal College) and Rex (Hedland High School) were born at the Lock Hospital, Port Hedland, now the Mulgunya Hostel. Westen (Hedland High School) was born in the bush at Mulga Downs. Carol (Hedland High School) was born at Wittenoom Hospital. Beverley (Primary School Onslow) and Charlie (Onslow Kindergarten) were born at Port Hedland Hospital. I supported them on benefits when the old fella passed away. I stayed home and worked to support them. Two sons and three grandchildren live with me now. I now have seven grandchildren.

My kids are grown up and mostly live in Onslow. They have been taught their culture but if you ask me what is their tribe it's hard to say. They were taught language but now they can't speak Nyiyaparli or Punjima, the parents' languages. They understand what I say in those languages and will listen, but can't talk. If you take our tradition when we talk of carriers of the family line, my kids would be Nyiyaparli. But they probably believe that they are Punjimas the same as me.

GUY PARKER

Birth Date: 22 February 1959
Place: Roebourne
Tribal Group: Punjima
Skin Group: Burungu

> *Wittenoom is our traditional country but it has*
> *been polluted. I hope that the State Government*
> *will be able to close it and save lives.*

My family area is Mulga Downs and that part of Karijini National Park associated with Wittenoom. My parents moved from the Wittenoom district into the Ashburton district prior to my birth. My father had taken up a position as a leading stockman at Nanutarra Station. This was the late 1950s and we remained there until mid 70s, then moved into Onslow. There he set up the Noualla Aboriginal Corporation as an Aboriginal Resource Centre.

My schooling went to year ten at Karratha Senior High School. My primary schooling was at Onslow. My parents were very supportive. But during those days education in the white man's system wasn't a priority to my parents. The priority of education was to ensure that I had all the skills necessary under Aboriginal law and culture, and I am fully experienced in the law and culture system. That is important for the survival of indigenous people.

In our young lives we were forced to attend school. But all of our holidays and spare time out of schooling was spent with our parents. They were involved in station work. We went mending fences, mustering, repairing windmills and other chores. During the summer season we used to be involved in Aboriginal ceremonies. This meant living out in bush camps assisting our parents in ceremony activities. My old man was thoroughly involved in traditional law and these times and the activities were stepping stones to my later involvement at every level of Aboriginal religious and cultural activities.

I am employed as an Aboriginal Education and Training Officer with Karratha College. We look after Aboriginal adult education throughout the West Pilbara region, assisting to develop programs appropriate to the needs in the community. I've been in the job for two years.

The communities I work with are Roebourne, Karratha, Onslow, Tom Price, Wickham and Paraburdoo. Very few Aboriginal and Torres Strait Islander people live at Tom Price and Paraburdoo. However the others are major centres for delivering courses to Aboriginal and Torres Strait Islander people.

The focus of my work is on adult education, targeting people in the range of school leavers to adults. The main aim is to ensure that our people get the appropriate skills and certificates to get jobs. Without certificates they are not acceptable as employees in relevant areas. There is a large number of Aboriginal people who have no access to skills training. If you live down at Onslow, a small isolated community, you have very little opportunity of employment and you have very little opportunity of future education. But many Aboriginal people like to reside in their own communities and will not leave there for skills training.

A major problem in my area of work is that despite the College's training activity there is no guarantee of anyone getting a job. Most of our courses are targeted towards unemployed people, just giving them skills from basically nothing to something. Then maybe they can take bridging courses, build up their academic self esteem, and become self motivated to learn new skills or trades. There were ninety-five Aboriginal and Torres Strait Islander students enrolled at the College from 1992. In 1993 we have sixty-two from the whole area of the West Pilbara. They range from sixteen to thirty years of age. The current level of unemployment in the Pilbara is very high. I think about seventy per cent of the Aboriginals living in our area are unemployed.

There is a possibility of an employed future for young people if they can achieve a basic academic level and skills of the standard needed to be employable. At present there is no way that Aboriginal people would be employed without a better academic scale of education. If we don't obtain that there's no way that our people in this country are going to be recognised. But this is vitally necessary to develop employment prospects for our people. And while we

Karijini bush meeting with government officials.

believe in the necessity of Aboriginal community development in our homeland, this does not mean returning to the old skills of hunting and gathering and ignoring modern society's skills. No matter which way lies the future, we have to ensure that our children have an education and the possibility of getting employment. This means that our responsibility, as parents, is to make sure that those kids get the required education and training certificates for their future employment.

I am a member of the Karijini Aboriginal Corporation which has been very active for the people. It represents a few hundred Aboriginal people from their traditional homeland in the Hamersley Ranges. It has played a big role in trying to overcome obstacles to allow the Yinhawangka, Wakuthuni, and Ngudarra Punjima people to live back in their homelands.

It has also been concerned to ensure that there is full environmental protection of the Ranges and surrounding areas. That's why Karijini's involvement in the joint management plan for the Karijini National Park with the Department of Conservation and Land Management (CALM) has been welcomed by our people. We are looking for an equal partnership with CALM. We will not be used as mere tokens. The venture may ensure that we have direct association with the mining companies who want development in the area. Aboriginal people need to make sure that they have thorough and direct involvement at every level of any form of activity in their homeland area.

The main problems for our Aboriginal people are unemployment and to make sure we get our land. If we don't get our land, we haven't got any security of living rights, despite our traditional ownership. If we get some land back it will give our people something to live for and enhance our kids' futures. We live for our land. Money isn't everything. Land is certainly a thing that our lives are traditionally tied around, and if we had our land we can develop on that.

The name Karijini is our traditional name for that part of the Hamersley Ranges where the Karijini National Park is located. I mean we are Punjima people and we make a stand and get recognition as the traditional owners of those places, together with the other tribal groups in Karijini.

Some people say this area is going to become a central tourist area. Tourism can be a great thing for us. It is new to Aboriginal people here. We need to be trained on how to take advantage of this situation. Tourism can be a great opportunity for Aboriginal people, providing Aboriginal people have control of their culture. It is our own enterprises that need to take advantage of the opportunity. Aboriginal people can have a career in the tourist industry as original Australians with knowledge of the bush and its creatures. But more, we are the only carriers of Aboriginal culture.

I mean, just look at the Karijini National Park: if Aboriginal people had a tourist enterprise out there it could be of great significance to the tourist industry. Aboriginal people could provide the information, show their culture, sell their artefacts, and in this process develop their Aboriginal economy and provide work.

Mind you, there are some parts out near the Park that are not good for tourism. It is my family's view that we don't want to get involved with Wittenoom because that place has killed a lot of our people and· they are still dying. We still feel the asbestos there is not safe. Even driving past the place, on the outskirts of Wittenoom as well as on top of the soil. Wittenoom is our traditional country but it has been polluted by European society's industry. I hope that the State Government will be able to close it and save the lives of other people.

I recently went to the funeral at Roebourne of my uncle who died of mesothelioma, which is the worst form of asbestos disease. There have been many cases in the Aboriginal and non-Aboriginal community. My uncle had contracted the disease as a child. It was several years before he got confirmation of his condition. That's years down the track too late.

There is no set program or project to offer or provide a service directly to the people who are ill from that disease. There are no basic checks on people's health even when they have been associated with Wittenoom. I mean the Health Department hasn't set up any program to look into it. Individual requests through the families have been directed through a medical practitioner. Yet the deaths continue, silently.

TREVOR PARKER

Birth Date: Unrecorded
Place: Mount Florence Station
Tribal Group: Punjima
Skin Group: Burungu

*In 1966–68 the rights came and equal wages ... the wages
went up and our people got kicked off the stations.*

My mother is a Ngarluma, but there is Punjima on her mother's side.
My father was Yindjibarndi. So according to Aboriginal law I would
be a Ngarluma, because we follow the mother's side in deciding
tribal descent. But tribal law has been disrupted in many ways since
we were pushed off our lands.

Mother married Slim Parker's father, a Punjima, I grew up with
the old stepfather, and took his name. I am a Punjima, the law and
all, like the rest of the family. From a young age I was introduced to
our law and its customs. And I've always followed it and so have my
children. And I'm proud of that.

But today our culture is under threat from mainstream society and
we need help to maintain it. Our decision to establish the Karijini
Aboriginal Corporation was a necessity, it has helped to coordinate our
efforts to protect our culture. But without land our culture won't
survive. We can't teach the young people without our land and it's no
good the Government helping us to get any land if it's not the country
where our old people were born. So we've been fighting for our land
out near the Karijini National Park, that's where we come from.

I've worked on stations all of my life. I lived with the parents and
when I turned twelve or thirteen, I was doing work with them, like
fencing and things around Mulga Downs Station. Then they decided to
send me to school. I was about thirteen or fourteen. That was my first
time at school. It was at Nullagine. I went to school late, I think,

113

because the old people were concerned about Native Welfare taking half caste kids away. They were hiding me in the bloody scrub, until they stopped taking these kids away. This was 1958. I did three years schooling there, then I went to Onslow School. The Gilliamia Hostel opened up there in 1961 and I lived there in 1961, 62, 63, and left then.

I worked on Nanutarra Station with the old man, and also worked in Onslow town for a little while at Old Bill Clark's garage. I worked at Urala Station. Then I went to Maroonah Station for three years.

The Government purchased Peedamulla Station for the Aboriginal people in this district in the early 1970s. Peter Salmon, me and a few other boys, were the first ones who worked there. After a couple of years I left Peedamulla and drove a taxi in Onslow for two years.

Mulga Downs was always a lively place. And when there was a bit of break from work on the station, like a holiday, then the old people just travelled. One time in 1956 I remember the old man had two trucks, two Bedfords. We travelled all the way from Mulga Downs, doing corroborees, and going by Hamersley, Rocklea, Wyloo, Ashburton Downs, Mount Stuart, Nanutarra, Minderoo, Yanrey and to Onslow. The two trucks took mainly the whole family, Mum's and the old man's. We would stay a couple of nights at every station, then push on. From Onslow we came back along the coast to Roebourne. The round trip would take two, or three months, maybe.

It wasn't a one-off thing either. The old man saw this as a role he had to play for the people, and he did it often. Couple of other times we did trips around I remember. The old man would work on Nanutarra Station to get a bit of tucker and fuel money to get home in a couple of weeks. Or he'd do some fencing and that got us back home, and maybe a look at the country.

When I was a kid there used to be corroborees all the time. Now we only have one or two a year, maybe. But in those days, about 1955, 56, 57, there was a corroboree just about every night. There would be a corroboree on every station. We'd meet up with each group of people and all wanted to have corroborees.

To travel by car was a normal thing in those days. Before that the people used to do it on foot, then they got horses. I remember the old people use to say we travelled to 'that spring', or to 'that camp', and did corroboree there, and we'd go and do another one 'over there'. And then the motor car came out and we just travelled round in the

114

car, doing the same thing. This was the way our people communicated with each other.

These were occasions to show different dances from different people, or different groups, or tribes. These corroborees were expressions of the old people, which showed that their own culture was still alive and developing. There would be new kids, new members every time watching new dances and participating in it. The culture was being passed on.

The Aboriginal people on those stations would be from all Pilbara language groups of the area, Punjima, Kurrama and Yinhawangka. When you come down from Mulga Downs, you got the Punjima on the Fortescue there right down to Hamersley, then you got the other Punjima, the Rocklea Punjima. Then you start mixing up with other people like the Yinhawangkas, and then you go right down to the Bailyku mob. And this was going on at every station, which meant that there were many communities of our people living here.

Now this has all changed. The communities have gone. The change started in 1966–68 when the rights came out and equal wages. Because the wages went up, they said they couldn't afford to pay them and our people got kicked off the stations.

They had a manager and three other hands when I first went to Peedamulla. They'd be fixing windmills, fences, etc, just station work. The next time I went to Peedamulla I stayed nearly twelve years. I'm still there now, as manager.

At one time there were forty or fifty thousand sheep running on Peedamulla. They reckoned it was overstocked back in the forties and fifties. In some places there is bad erosion, down on the coast side. When we got it there was still sheep and a few cattle. We brought in five hundred head of cattle and ran them on the place. They built up to over fifteen hundred, over the years. Then the Agriculture Department told us to get rid of the bloody cattle, go more into sheep. They said it wasn't cattle country, that it was more sheep country. Well, we did that in the last three or four years. Now, the wool price dropped last year and this year is worse. At the moment you can't make any bloody money out of wool. We've got about ten and a half thousand head. All of this has made Peedamulla a difficult economic proposition. I'd think of selling half of the stock to the live sheep market. But we've got to decide about our future direction.

We would like to see Peedamulla under the Karijini umbrella as an enterprise capable of earning tourist dollars. If we could do this then we may be able to give Peedamulla a new lease of life which can link into the tourism industry. We could have a little business there. There would need to be decent accommodation.

Peedamulla is for all the Aboriginal people of Onslow. It was bought for them as an enterprise. I argue, why don't we use the place to set up some other things rather than having it solely as a pastoral lease? We could have an artefacts shop, a soft drinks shop, a kangaroo stew, damper and billy tea outlet to bring in some money. If we were on a tourist route we could advertise horse riding and things.

At that 1992 Karratha conference for Aboriginal Self-Determination, Cultural Respect and Economic Development, the bloke from the ATSIC Development Council, Peter, spoke about the loop system they developed in Central Australia for the tourism industry. There the tourist bus goes to the stations and the gorges. The same could happen here. It could go to Peedamulla Station and to the Karijini National Park and around the gorges. Peedamulla is close to the highway and could be a place for people to stay overnight, if it had the facilities. Or tourists might stop here for teas and snacks.

MAITLAND PARKER

Birth Date: 1 October 1952
Birth Place: Roebourne
Tribal Group: Punjima
Skin Group: Burungu

*There is a need for more Rangers to do more interpreting,
talking to tourists and visitors about the natural features,
cultural heritage of the park.*

I started schooling at Nullagine State School and I stayed at the mission hostel there. The family moved and so I finished primary school at Onslow. I lived near the school at the Gilliamia Hostel (before it was called Gilliamia). It was used for Aboriginal kids, whose parents worked on stations, who were schooling in Onslow.

I can still remember some of the kids who were at the hostel then. There were boys and girls dormitories. The manager was Mr Angel and he was a good fella. But we had a change of managers after my first year and some were very strict. There was a big mob of kids there who were my relations so I was never lonely.

I finished primary school here and went to Derby High School for two years. It was my first time flying, first to Hedland and then to Derby, in the old DC3s. The only times we came home was for Christmas holidays and for the Onslow races. I used to ride in the gymkhana run at the same time.

I grew up in the bush and worked with the old man from the time I was a kid, handling stock, riding horses and every kind of station work. After I left school my first job was as stockman on Nanutarra. In those days there would be at least ten other Aboriginal station hands on stations like Nanutarra on this side of the Ashburton River, Minderoo and such like. I worked there until 1980 and left because wages were too poor. They weren't paying me the award rates.

I came to Onslow and was interviewed by the Community Health Department for a job as health worker. I got the job and worked there until 1985. My job as an Aboriginal health worker meant going to the community on the old reserve where Bindi Bindi is today. The people were living in the old-style reserve houses, two bedrooms with kitchen/dining in the middle. The laundry and toilets were outside and were communal, for men and for women. We did a station run every six to twelve months. I was the only Aboriginal health worker. The hospital staff made up the rest of the health crew, a matron, nurse and casual doctor.

Hedland was the headquarters for community health in our area then. A nurse in Onslow was in charge of me. I did various health training courses like Sexually Transmitted Diseases (STD), Infectious Diseases. I'd make sure people took their medicine and the correct dose. We would weigh kids. This was a full-time monthly job keeping all their weights and measurements. We'd check them out for sores. And if there were sick ones we'd take them to the hospital and get the names of those to see the visiting doctor. We would then make sure that they were seen. Visits to the school to inspect kids for sores and treating these was a big part of the job. I liked the work, it gave me an insight into the health scene and its problems. A lot of it was band-aid treatment, but it had to be done.

There was a lot of talk in 1984 about the Department of Conservation and Land Management (CALM) starting an Aboriginal Ranger Training program for the National Parks. CALM started to take an interest in which tribes were the traditional owners of the park areas. The Millstream area is Yindjibarndi country and the Hamersley Range area is the country of the groups who are members of the Karijini Aboriginal Corporation. And so CALM started to get in touch with the right people. I was interested and went to a couple of meetings called by CALM. In 1985 I put my name down to be part of the trainee program. There was a three-month trial selection period at Millstream for six Aboriginal workers. Only four would be selected to be trained as Rangers, two for Millstream and two for Karijini. Cousin Johnny Parker and me were Punjimas. Bruce Woodley and Robert Cheedy were Yindjibarndi. We were selected to train as rangers for the two parks. This selection was consistent with our tribal areas.

In 1986 we went into full-time training for twelve months, based at Millstream, with Steve Szabo as training officer. CALM guaranteed that at the end of the training period we would be housed in the park and have a full-time job. John and me are still with CALM at Karijini, but the two fellas at Millstream have left. Robert Cheedy works for Robe River Iron at Pannawonica and Bruce lives at Roebourne.

I think the course was good. It concentrated on what park rangers do in the parks and their administrative work. We did field trips in other national parks in the south-west to see how they operated and also CALM's role in the forest industry. CALM was concerned to promote Aboriginal culture but I believe that the National Parks and Wildlife Service (NPAWS) had a lot of input into this course and had promoted it actively.

The Aboriginal trainees who left Millstream have been partially replaced by one Aboriginal worker, Kempsey Coffin, who is to be trained as a Park Ranger in the future. I think the Millstream Aboriginal Rangers had a problem with their administration and that is why they left. I have enjoyed every year of working at Karijini. The Ranger in charge there has been involved since the word go and we get on really well with him. This job was a stepping stone to me going back to work in my own country. This was a tremendous thing.

I believe there is a need for more Rangers in the Karijini Park. There are four Rangers now, two of whom are Aboriginal. I think there could be eight, with four Aboriginal at least. There has been an increased role for Rangers in the period since I've been there. More could be done but we don't have the staff. We would like to do more interpreting work, talking to tourists and all visitors about the natural features and cultural heritage of the park. At the moment we can't do enough of this because of the staff situation. We need to be able to get out in the park more and give talks to school groups and coach-loads of people. We believe that when the mine construction workers at Marandoo commence to live in the park there will be great need for more Rangers at Karijini to protect the east of the park, as well as to interpret it.

In previous years we have had our ups and downs with tourists but I can see we will have an increase of tourists in the park because of the improved roads that are in an advanced planning stage. There will be a link road from Marandoo into the park and this will have a huge boosting effect on tourism. To date there has been an increase in tourist traffic, both private car and caravans and also coaches. Private operators from Tom Price and Wittenoom (who pick up tourists at Auski Roadhouse) are bringing a lot of traffic to the park.

The most popular place to go is the gorge system in the north of the park. The Dale's Gorge area is the main place and contains the Fortescue Falls, the Dale's Gorge Look-out, Circular Pool and the Fortescue camping area with all facilities. The other attraction is the western area, or Weano end of the park. This is at Oxer's Look-out, where the four gorges meet, Weano, Hancock, Joffre and Red Gorge. It is spectacular. There are camping facilities here also. Between these two areas there are other significant gorges.

People who come to the park express their admiration of the natural beauty. Many are overseas visitors from Switzerland, Germany and many other countries. This gives us a good feeling and in return we give them the Aboriginal history of some of the places. As soon as they see Johnny or me and our Ranger badge, they want to talk to us. They ask me all sorts of questions including those which show that they are uncertain of whether I am an Aboriginal. All of this supports our view that there is need for more Aboriginal Rangers in the park.

Visitors who are genuine tourists are good users of the park. They clean up their litter. It is those who come from the towns close by who make the greatest mess, the local yobboes, they are the worst.

I grew up respecting our Aboriginal culture. We were taught about it and its practice by all the relatives, but mainly the mother and father and grandparents. I don't have much of a memory of my grandparents but on my father's side I do remember my grandmother called 'white head'. She was a Punjima. I don't recall the grandfather. On my mother's side the grandmother is Daisy Moses who lives in Roebourne, she is a Ngarluma like my mother. She would be in her late eighties. A grandfather on my mother's, old 'Clucky' Moses helped me a lot to learn our culture. He was an uncle to Mum in non-Aboriginal relations, but in the Aboriginal way he was a grandfather. I would go bush with all of these people and they would teach culture. The first thing you learn as a kid is, of course, your own language. I learned to speak Punjima and I still use it today.

As you get to your teens, as a male, you are put through men's business, or cultural law. The elders decide what form your initiation will take, and in my case they decided I would have 'free law', but I had to go through the process of development to manhood as required by our law. The learning covered such things as what you can eat, what you can't eat, what you can kill, what you can't kill, what you can track and how to tell what tracks mean, what fruits are, what is this tree, what are the medicine bushes or plants and what are their uses. In addition we had to know the structure of skin relations, proper manners, respect and the significance of our land and its sites.

When we went bush as kids we basically lived off the fruits of the land. We had our flour and tea, but the rest came from the bush. We'd kill a roo, or a goanna (kurrumanthu), or scrub turkey (tharraki), or emu (jankurna). We'd cut wild honey (jandaru), too. It depended on supply what we actually ate. We'd be talking as we go about these things but looking for signs of tracks. The bird tracks, animal tracks and insect tracks and what they meant. You had to know how old the tracks were so that you could decide whether they were worth following, in order to catch the animal, or food.

Tracking is an art-form for the indigenous people. Our Aboriginal trackers have been exploited for years by this society. They are asked to solve complicated problems of finding people in harsh environments and in the end are given a 'thank you', at most. Money is never mentioned. As experts they should be paid appropriately. The non-Aboriginal society has to stop this exploitation of our skills.

All of my training in the bush skills of our culture helps me tremendously as a park ranger. I believe as an Aboriginal I see the bush differently to people of a different background. I think that I am constantly looking at and through the bush, looking for signs and automatically interpreting what I see. It's an automatic coordination of my facilities to interpret the bush. On this basis I can tell people what is happening in the fauna and flora of the bush.

It's the same with bush orienting. Our constant studying of the environment enables Aboriginal people to get to the place they have set out for without getting lost. Our people historically always described their land on the basis of identifying landmarks. We set our direction in the same way. Our lands were described by hills, trees, rocks, creeks and such natural things. Each tribe stuck to their own boundaries unless given permission to enter the neighbouring tribe's land. If they didn't there would be trouble.

MARGARET PARKER

Birth Date: 1 June 1951
Place: Port Hedland
Tribal Group: Punjima
Skin Group: Burungu

*Living in the town is breaking our culture, we want
to run our lives the way we want, and slowly, not
in the pace of the white man who is fast tracking.*

I was born at the old Port Hedland Lock Hospital. That's where
Aboriginal mothers had their babies, at that time. It was once used to
confine Aboriginal leprosy sufferers, but converted for other uses
with the reduced incidence of leprosy. They had a hospital in
Roebourne but my mother was sent to Port Hedland to have me. My
mother came from Roebourne, from the Ngarluma tribal group. My
father is Punjima from the top end of Karijini National Park, near
Mulga Downs area. He was a well-known leader for the Aboriginal
people who respected him as a role model.

I first went to school at Nullagine. I was there with Trevor my elder
brother for a couple of years, and our cousins Winston and Peter
Parker. That was the closest school at that time for us, the Riverdale
Mission. My father was working at Mulga Downs Station and in the
Wittenoom mines. The Parkers were the first people to work in the
mines there you know, old people like my old Uncle Ginger Parker
and Uncle Horace. They were the ones that worked with old Hancock,
old George Hancock, with that asbestos.

My father talked about the effect of mining at Wittenoom and in
changes in the Wittenoom area. They even barred Aboriginal people
from the town. So the Aboriginal people starting scattering, going,
some went more towards Marble Bar, some came to Roebourne,
some come here to Onslow. That mining at Wittenoom caused
dislocation of our people.

Later, my family moved down to the Ashburton district and worked on Boolaloo Station and then Nanutarra Station. My father did station work nearly all of his life. Mother looked after the kids and was a musterers' cook and did station cooking.

I then came to Onslow for my schooling and stayed at the Gilliamia Hostel when it was opened in the early sixties. From here, I completed my primary school, I went on to Derby High School and stayed there at the United Aboriginal Missions (UAM) hostel. I did two years up there and I enjoyed it, but was missing my family, you know. I had a really close network with my family, very close. We used to come home on Christmas holidays, but for the other holidays we would go to Fitzroy Crossing.

I'm the elder sister in the family. They have to respect you as an elder sister and then also it is the other way around, you have to respect your youngest as well. I had a big responsibility in my family. With my brothers and sisters, we'd sit down and talk about things. It's just been hard in this last few years, since our dad left us in 1985. You know, we were sort of lost really.

He was a powerful figure and his going has left us with no one to fall back on as a father. We've got two next fathers, like Uncle Wobby and Uncle Horace. But they have their own families and their own problems within their own families. We had no sort of back to lean on when we needed support. Uncle Wobby is really our backbone, but the other old fella, he is really stubborn headed. He likes to just play his own role.

One reason for my father to move from Mulga Downs, where he was born and worked all of his life, was so we could go to the school. Onslow was our closest school. And they made it compulsory to attend. When my father shifted from Nanutarra and came and lived in Onslow, he started having a lot of input into the Aboriginal affairs. He attended meetings and he was in the National Aboriginal Conference (NAC). He was the first member from the Pilbara to be elected to represent the Aboriginal people. He attended a lot of meetings with the Aboriginal Legal Service (ALS) and the Advisory Council.

He wasn't home most of the time, but was out on the run travelling to other towns. Everyone was looking for him. He's on the run, when he's not tied up at meetings. He's on the road visiting all the Aboriginal communities, seeing what they want and getting all the information from the community and then he would take it to the meeting.

It's different now. People just go and put their own issues to raise from their own individual groups. Whereas he used to go and visit all the communities right up to Jigalong and back again and getting all the information. So he was a real spokesperson for the people in the whole of the Pilbara.

When I finished school I came back and worked at the District Hospital in Onslow. I got a job there and boarded at the Gilliamia Hostel. I only stayed here for about eight months, working. Because of the freedom that I wanted to have at my age, I couldn't have it because my parents were really strict. They didn't want me to go out after nine at night. I was sixteen or seventeen years old and to have to come at night by nine was tough. A couple of times I came home to the hostel after nine and it got back to my parents. They reacted and just came in, picked me up and took me out to the station. They took me out to Nanutarra and I worked out there as a house girl, doing cleaning duties and doing the washing and everything for the boss and the missus and looking after their little ones.

Then I met this school boyfriend that I had at that time. He came out there for a little while and stayed with me. But it was only for three months and it didn't work out with us. We broke up and my dad and mum agreed for me having this other bloke, Peter Salmon. He's the father of my daughter. He came one day and picked me up at Nanutarra and took me to Glenflorrie Station. That was in 1969.

It wasn't really an Aboriginal arranged marriage from when I was small, it was just my parents decided. He came a couple of times to try and see if it would work, but I was sort of frightened of him. And then one day he came and just picked me up and I went with him.

My parents were very strong for the law. They believed in arranged marriages but in some cases it happened and some it didn't. I don't understand why.

My marriage wasn't arranged, we weren't forced to marry, but Mum just came up one day and said, 'Oh, we would like you to get with that boy you know.' It sort of was a shock to me because he's much older. I thought to myself well, he looked very attractive at that time and was a working man.' So I thought, to please my parents I would get the man they want me to have and looking at his

124

background he's been a worker all his life. So I went along with that and stayed with him. We had our ups and downs but I enjoyed the life that we had together. Then I ended up being pregnant and had my daughter 1971. Only the one child we had.

It was no good in town. For some reason we came back and lived in Onslow and then everything went haywire for us. He ended up being the first manager of Peedamulla Station for many years then and I was up and down from Peedamulla and into town, up and down and gradually we split up then and I went my way.

My brother Maitland, he was promised to Margie and I thought that wouldn't get off the ground. But, you know, they are together still and have been since leaving school. They have got three daughters and a couple of 'grannies' (grandchildren) now and they are still together. They're happy. My other brother Slim is married into the same family, to Margie's younger sister. He's happy and got six children.

Most of our culture ceremonies take place at Cane River and also at Hancock, since moving down here from the Wittenoom, Mulga Downs area. Aboriginal people moved from the stations there, with the majority coming from Rocklea Station. The central town became Onslow. They all got together and talked with the elders from here, like old Jack Hayes. He's from the Dhalanyji group, they're the traditional owners of this Onslow area. They had to get his permission to have ceremonies on Dhalanyji land. He said it was okay for them to start up the law camps out at Peedamulla Station at Cane River. So they went along with that.

So, people that came from the Hamersley Range area like my father's mob and others, started to practise their culture in the area that they've moved to, as well as going back to their home country. Yes, we got to practise our culture somewhere, we've got to pass the culture to the young ones. We still go back and visit our homes, our traditional home and we go back and visit places in the National Park like Coppin Pool, the Five Mile, the Stone Hut, some other springs and the gorges. We've had corroborees in the Park area and I know there have been ceremonies at Mulga Downs, Bellary stockyards, Minthi Spring and Bee Gorge.

Those old people were keen on us young ones learning the law. By sitting down talking to us in groups and round camp fires. They always used to tell us stories about how the old people used to be, what they used to do. They got us all interested, sang corroboree songs for us. The kids all would get up and dance. We just used to sit down and have a big yarn about things.

My father used to tell us about our kinship ways, how we should be married, who we should be married to and also he used to tell us about our tribes, about Mum's side where they come from, because I really never knew anything about my mother's side of the family. When I was very young I never had that talk or anyone really sit down and talk to us about my mothers' side, even Mum. All she used to say was that our grandmother and our uncles and aunties are in Roebourne. Never gave us any background history. When I went to live in Roebourne I found out from some of my old grandparents, my grandfathers there. And they used to tell me how I fit in with my families there in Roebourne. But I never ever grew up knowing about my mother's side of the family. I always used to know only my father's side.

My grandmother in Roebourne, old Daisy Moses, my kantharri, she is my mother's mother. My father's mother is called my kabarli. Mum and my other old grandmother on my mother's side, old Kerry Andrews and my old grandfather Jack Andrews, when they were out at Nanutarra, they used to show me the bush medicines and things. I used to go out with them on a picnic, or down the river, we used to go for a walk, they used to show me which is the medicine for colds and other medicines for sores. They used to show me about three or four medicines that were on the river. When we went out on the runs they showed me the gum medicine that you can boil and drink. These other ones you boil up from the side of the river bed. Also, the young shoots of the gum trees, you can boil them up and that's a medicine, too. I still use a few of these, but I haven't been out to collect any lately.

A cultural practice of our people of great importance relates to our attitude to death in our families. Like when we have someone passed away in our families and not even our own close families, the family belongs to us all, you know. The whole community gets together and shares that sorrow within the whole community. It don't have to be a close family. We say it is close because of our kinship ties and that means it's family. We all get together till that funeral, till we put that person away. So every time someone comes in to town whom we haven't seen, that could be two or three days after we get the bad news, we all get together and meet that person, we have to drop what we're doing and get together.

We have to cry, in sorrow, share our grief by crying and that's how we break that, by sharing together as a community. This is an important aspect of our culture. And this is how we are brought up. I see it is lacking in a lot of other towns where we go. We go there to meet people and to share our sorrows and the white way of living in the town is breaking our culture.

And a lot of towns you go to for funerals, want to do their own little individual things, instead of dropping what they're doing to get together to meet the people coming in from out of town. The family has to sit in one house, or one area, so people know that they have to go straight into that place and meet up. We go and pay our respects. You supposed to just sit down and meet, eat together, share, until that body is put away, you know. Afterwards, we do whatever we want to do, after we leave that certain family.

Nowadays, people just come up and shake hands, want to shake hands all the time. To me it's hurting, because we all know and we grew up in our culture system and that means we should embrace others to share the sorrow, men and women.

We still practise our culture. We still tell our kids that when we meet up with other people they have to sit with us and meet. You see a lot of our children sit on people's laps. This is wrong except where they are babies. When we meet we embrace and keeping kids on the lap stops this cultural practice and it does not encourage the kids to embrace like they should. They are learning that people don't have to practise their customs any more and this is wrong.

Now, we haven't really got our own land to live on. We live on someone else's land, in someone else's house and with the day-to-day conflict of two cultures. If we had our own land back alcohol won't be so bad as it is here in town. Alcohol is a big problem here in Onslow and Roebourne, it is a big problem because it is so easy to grab hold of. We have health problems because of the food we eat in town and buy in the shops, it isn't the food of our land.

The quicker we get our own land back, our grandparents' and uncles' areas, where we belong and where we come from, the quicker we can go and live on it and run it the way we want, instead of white man telling us how to live. Someone is over us all the time telling us how to live and run our lives. We want to run our lives the way we want out there and slowly, not in the pace of the white man. Keeping up with the way of the white man is fast tracking. We need to live from day to day and build up our own self-esteem and confidence back on our land, instead of doing things for other people in other towns. That's the way to go.

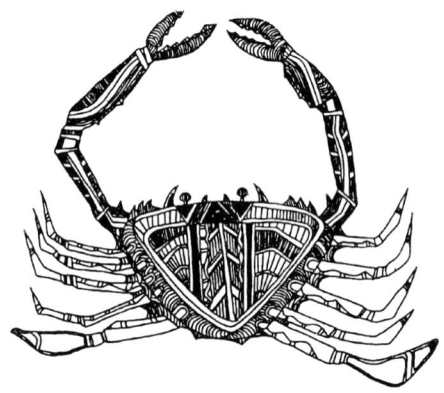

MARJORIE PARKER

Birth Date: 1 October 1953
Birth Place: Mulga Downs Station
Tribal Group: Punjima
Skin Group: Burungu

There is nothing for Aboriginal patients to make them feel supported in their cultural, spiritual being. Sometimes treatment needs to go further.

I was born on 1 October 1953 according to my mother's citizenship paper but there was no registration of my birth. My brother has the same birth date but of the previous year 1952, so I think my birth date is a rough guess. I did all of my primary schooling at Onslow and three years of high schooling at Derby.

I stayed at Gilliamia Hostel when I went to primary school. I fitted in the hostel scene okay, I just did as I was told and lived by the bell. At the hostel I got woken by the bell, had breakfast by a bell, got ready for school by the bell and went off to school by the bell. At school there was a bell to start school, a bell for lunch and other breaks and a bell when these finished. Again at the hostel there was a bell for tea and another at bed time.

We did cleaning work at the hostel on a roster. We washed up and dried, swept the dormitories, cleaned the toilets and bathrooms. We peeled the potatoes and other vegies and set the tables. I had my circle of friends there, mainly my cousins, Eva Black, Tootsie Moses, Wendy Hubert and others.

When I was doing high school way up at Derby I would get homesick, but I would write letters, lots of them, to the people at Nanutarra Station. The only time we would come home would be for the August races and the Christmas holidays. But there were a lot of kids up there from Roebourne, Onslow and Port Hedland, Pilbara kids. The hostel we stayed at in Derby was for Aboriginal kids. The school was for all kids but more than half were Aboriginal, I think. I sat for my Secondary Certificate at the end of year two and passed. Then sat for my Junior Certificate at the end of third year but didn't get it. 1969 was my last school year and I then went out to work.

When I left school I wanted to be a nurse but was too young to be admitted to the nurse's aide training program. I had to wait until I was seventeen. So I worked at Nanutarra Station as a housemaid for twelve months. At the same time I applied to be admitted to the training program through the Department for Community Services.

I started training as a nurse's aide at Mount Henry Hospital, Perth. It was a public hospital for old people. It was a training hospital and all enrolled nurses first went there for three months and were then sent to country hospitals. I was sent to Collie District Hospital and spent eight months there until I became qualified. It was freezing there.

I went to Carnarvon District Hospital in 1972 on probation for over a year. I was boarding at the Church of Christ Hostel there. After the probationary period was over the manager and his family asked if I would go with them to Marble Bar Hostel funded by the Department for Welfare. I agreed and was there for twelve months.

I came back to Onslow in 1974 and did odd jobs at the kindy near the caravan park and bookkeeping at the Noualla Aboriginal Centre. Then a job was available at Community Health. It was a field worker and I took it. We did ear, nose and throat (ENT) health clinics, school visits and visits to the old people to check on their medication. It was band-aid treatment for the Aboriginal people. We went out in the field in those days to see people. We would go to Bindi Bindi on house-to-house visits checking people, mainly the old people. We did station trips once a month. This was good, we could end up out at the mustering camp giving the musterers tetanus injections, updating their immunisation. When we visited the school we would check the kids for sores, trachoma and nits. We would see them a class at a time. I finished the job at the end of 1975.

In 1976 I joined a survey group, going to many towns doing surveys of Aboriginal people. This was called a medical audit. The research teams consisted of a doctor, registered nurse, male field worker, myself and a lab assistant. They would give people a thorough medical and get all required information written down and put into a computer. We started in Mount Magnet, then Cue,

Meekatharra and then they went to the Kimberley.

I didn't go to the Kimberley but stayed in the Murchison–Gascoyne region having formed an important attachment to one of the locals. I got a job at Mount Magnet with Community Health as a field worker. This didn't last as my friend lived in Cue and I got sick and tired of travelling between towns.

I went to Cue to live and got a job as a cook in a kids' hostel. I knew nothing about cooking and spent much of my days walking around with a cookbook in my hands. I remember burning the custard the first day and the kids refused to eat it. But it got better and so it should, as I was there for a couple of years.

We came back to Onslow for a holiday and went back to Cue and bought a house. They were selling cheap as the price of gold had dropped and people were leaving the area in 1978. I started work as a domestic at the hostel. I left Cue at the end of 1979 and went to Perth to do a Hostel Senior Assistant's Course. It took twelve months.

I went back to Roebourne, Weeriana Hostel. The Fields, who had been managing at Marble Bar, were now at Weeriana. I stayed a year. I went back to Perth and worked in the head office to liaise with all Aboriginal hostels in the Perth metropolitan area for young people from the country going to school in Perth. There were hostels at Subiaco, Mount Lawley, Bentley, Hamilton Hill and many others. This lasted only three months and I went to manage Bentley Hostel for Girls for a short period. I then worked as a relieving manager at Cue and then went to the Port Hedland Moorgunyah Hostel as senior assistant. My work involved a fair-sized group of high school girls.

I applied for a job at Onslow Hospital and worked at Moorgunyah until a vacancy occurred. In October 1982 I started at Onslow as an enrolled nurse and have been here ever since, except for short breaks, like transferring to Kalgoorlie for six months. I've enjoyed travelling around meeting people.

I prefer working with the old people. I love the old people. We need to spend more time with them, it's no good looking after them in the hospital situation. They need to have their own units or whatever, out in the community, like they've got those Health And Community Care (HACC) Programs set up now. This provides for carers to give the old people support, help with their washing, or with a shower, etc. Once you take the old people to hospital they just fall apart, just vegetate. They must be cared for in the community. In the hospital they have no stimulation. We had an old fella patient in hospital and as usual we had plenty to do. The only chance to talk is when we ask a patient if they want to use the bottle. This old fella must have got really upset with me and said, 'You only ask if I want to kumbu, kumbu, kumbu (urinate). It's the only time you talk to me.'

So his message was that he was not being given enough attention from the nursing staff, it was not enough that he be only asked if he wanted to urinate. This is the situation of all old people who are taken away from their home situation and put into institutions.

Looking after the children is not as rewarding because you don't have a one-to-one relationship with them, there are too many of them in a hostel. You couldn't give them that individual attention. Kids are all showering at the same time, wear identical clothes, their personality doesn't come out. Looking back the same thing happened to me, we were treated like animals. You wear this, you eat that, you don't do that and so on.

I enjoyed community health at that time. But I could never go back to community health now because it's all changed.

I come from an Aboriginal family that is very supportive of our culture and there should be more cultural education of health workers in all parts of Western Australia. I don't have the time to teach this when I'm on the job. It should be part of the training. There is a little bit now but it's just scratching the surface.

In hospitals they should have Aboriginal videos, playing culture for the people. There is nothing for Aboriginal patients to make them feel supported in the cultural, spiritual being. The hospital staff don't take into account the spiritual well-being of the Aboriginal patients. It's all medical treatment. Sometimes you need to go further. Some patients have requested treatment from their own culture, from medicine men. Hospitals do not recognise the legitimacy of treatment that traditional healers can give and this is wrong. They think it is voodoo stuff.

One time an old lady, who didn't appear to be very sick, but felt that she wasn't going to last the night, wanted to go home to her family. She was just wailing and wailing. I said to the sister, 'We can't keep her here, it's cruel we must send her home.' The sister said, 'But the doctor's orders are to keep her here.' And I said, 'Yes, but the doctor is in Exmouth and this poor patient only wants to go home and be with her family. I believe that she spiritually feels that she is not going to survive the night.' I thought that if this is what she believes then she is entitled to be with her family and to die wherever she wants to, not in this environment.

I said to the sister, 'I must go to Bindi Bindi village and see the relatives.' I suggested that if she was concerned about the doctor's orders she ring him up and tell him what I'm doing, and of the patient's distress and calls to go home. If there is any backlash I will take care of that. So I got the orderly and took her home. She was very breathless and life was dim. Yet she spent the evening with her family and passed away that night. This is but one example of the cultural-based requirement of nursing and caring for Aboriginal patients.

Recently I attended a meeting at the invitation of the Puntukurnaparna (Western Desert) Women's Council out at Well Thirty Three Community, about five hours drive from the Northern Territory border. This was a very significant event in my life, especially as it took place in September 1993.

I went because I believe that in the Year of Indigenous People this was a great way to celebrate our culture. Women went from everywhere to get together and exchange our culture. I felt very privileged to go there. Seven of us went in our women's vehicle, a four-wheel drive with trailer. Three vehicles went from Roebourne and others from Port Hedland. People came from many other places.

We left on Sunday and with permission of the Jigalong women camped there that night. They also gave us permission to travel through their country as far as the Cotton Creek Community. We did this on Monday, by this time we were a convoy of ten four-wheel drive vehicles. After two and a half days drive from Cotton Creek, following some of the Canning Stock Route, way out in the desert, we reached Well Thirty Three.

SLIM PARKER

Birth Date: 1956
Birth Place: Mulga Downs Station
Tribal Group: Punjima
Skin Group: Burungu

*Town life doesn't completely stop us going bush, taking the
young ones and showing them, teaching them names of
places and their significance.*

My father (Herbert Parker) now deceased, was born on the new
Mulga Downs Station, Kunangkawinghadetha. My uncle Horace
was born at a place at old Mulga Downs Station, near Wittenoom.
My father was a respected elder of the Punjima people. My mother
Jukari Parker nee Wedge is a member of the Ngarluma group, born
on Sherlock Station, near Roebourne.

The old man worked on Mulga Downs, Roy Hill, Marillana, Abydos
and White Springs Stations. He finally left that area in about 1957 and
worked in the Ashburton district and then came down to Nanutarra
Station. He stayed there for almost twenty years, working on the
station. The old man moved away from his traditional tribal land for
work and also because of compulsory schooling. That's really how we
came to be in Onslow. That's what happened throughout the whole
region with Aboriginal tribes. People like the Yindjibarndi mob, they
moved from the Millstream area and eventually camped into
Roebourne. The Nyiyabarli and Bailyku peoples, who also worked
around the same stations, finally moved into Marble Bar.

Nanutarra and Onslow are hundreds of kilometres away from
Mulga Downs, my traditional country on the Fortescue Tableland.
The family always goes back to see our country. Our people had to
change their meeting places, places of culture. We had meetings at
Nanutarra but most recently they have been held at the Cane River.

I've just come back from a week's trip with Mum and the rest of the elders looking at our sites. The old people like to see them and take comfort from them. I've been back to these places with the old man when he was still with us. He showed me a lot of places significant to us. In his days there were ceremonial grounds at Rocklea Station, Wyloo Station and Mulga Downs Station. The main Punjima law ground was at Mulga Downs. There was another place on the Turee Creek called Karlkatharra, where corroborees and traditional ceremonies took place.

I remember my father talking about the big ceremony at Buuminyjinha, the Yindjibarndi law ground on Tambrey Station. There they celebrated the first joint law meeting between Yindjibarndi and Punjima people and where the Yindjibarndi Budira Burndurr was performed with the Wardirra laws. The time of ceremony is a time of joy when our young men become men. It is a time when relations from all over the Pilbara and beyond, visit and take part in the ceremonies. We go to other places to attend these ceremonies organised by the other tribes.

Initiation into Aboriginal law requires that candidates show a certain level of understanding of our culture and custom before it can be complete. It was out at the Cane River, not the main site, but at the Cattle Camp, where Donnie Hicks, Tim Parker, Stuart Injie and I went through. Tim and I went through the process called 'free law' or Wamulu law. The other two went through the initiation ceremony. Both forms of passing through the law are as old as antiquity. I was seventeen at the time.

Our young people are still brought up in the traditional ways. We try to make them respect the law and our culture. I believe the more you respect culture the more people respect you. But you cannot demand respect, you have to earn it. Once there is respect for culture it helps to achieve the unity of communities throughout the region.

The main feature of the Aboriginal law and culture is respect for land, it has to be. We've got our traditional bush tucker, medicines, waterholes, soaks and life support systems in the land. We also have all of our personal histories and those of our tribes, in our land. There are our ancestors and spirits there. We must protect the land to keep alive our own identity and for our children's future, so that they can follow the traditions. The importance of land to us is shown in the practice of initiation. There are heaps of things that boys need to be taught. The only way this can be done is back in their own country. There they can be taught the use the land has for all of us. It's the same with the girls. They are taught their own matters, Traditionally they were gatherers of fruit and vegetables and so they go bush to learn about bush food and bush medicine. But the woman's social role is far more complex and so is the learning process.

We also greatly respect our deceased. The way we address each other is very important. Proper behaviour to each other at funerals will show that we respect each other and especially those who have passed away.

It is unfortunately true that we are losing respect for each other as we are confined to a town-based lifestyle. Without our land we do not practice or promote the physical cultural things. Daily practice keeps us fine-tuned in the relationships we have with each other culturally and this is a bonding for our communities. The families aren't getting together and sitting down talking about the law and the culture like they do in the bush. We do sit down in our town backyard, talk and sing songs, even corroboree a bit. But the whole community isn't doing it together.

Town life doesn't completely stop us from going bush, we're out there at every chance. We still go to the same significant places for us like Minthacoogina Spring, in the Karijini National Park. This used to be a place where people from different tribes, like Yinhawangkas, Punjimas, or Kurramas, would stay for up to two months, dancing and making corroborees. We still go back there taking the young ones with us showing them and teaching them names of places and their significance.

In this great country which was once ours, we hunted for food and visited people over vast areas without any maps to guide us. There weren't the fences, roads, power lines, or railways that you see today. What our people used was the landmarks of the country. They knew all features of that country and the names of those places. For instance, some landmarks are Jarndunmunha (Mount Nameless), Bambajinha (Mount Whaleback), Minjiyanha (Mount Meharry), Bunurrunna (Mount Bruce) and others. About each one of these there are stories, songs and dances, which our people have created and which have been performed over and over from one generation to the next. All Pilbara Aboriginal people shared this cultural heritage and respected it.

Then there used to be a walkabout circuit around our country from Minthacoogina, to Milli Springs, to Coppin Pool, to Palm Springs and to Kardakarli at Rocklea. These places are important to us and we take a mob out there now and again. Everyone loves it.

This is why today people are involved in the homeland movement. It's an area that the Karijini Aboriginal Corporation is involved in, because of the interest shown by the members. The younger ones are very keen to see this happen. And the elders, every time they go out on a field trip to their country, they just come back full of beans. But it's still going to take time to set the rules that build a framework which enables us to regularly practise and to teach the young ones.

Respect for elders is another very important aspect of our culture. Elders are the physical vehicle for our culture. They carry it and pass it to other generations. They carry the Aboriginal law. They are

Pilbara conference involving Aboriginal people, pastoralists, miners and the tourism industry, organised in 1992 to discuss land use and Aboriginal culture. Then Federal Minister for Aboriginal Affairs, Robert Tickner, at left, Karijini chairman Slim Parker, right, with Karijini Elders.

rightly respected and honoured. Only some young Aboriginals, or others who are affected by the weaknesses of white society, fail to honour our old people and it's very sad. Our elders speak for our traditional country. They know where the boundaries are of each one's country. They know who was born here and who were their parents and relatives. The real elder of the Punjima people is of course Uncle Horace Parker. Then there is Uncle Wobby (Parker). He is Horace's brother. Uncle Horace is the second eldest, then there was my old man, then Wobby is the youngest of the brothers. The eldest was old Uncle Ginger, deceased.

We have a real and great wealth of knowledge in the collective memory and wisdom of our elders. The Punjima, Nyiyabarli and Bailyku people are very close. There are a lot of Nyiyabarli and Bailyku people who know where the Punjima people's boundaries are because of the long history of their relationship. I'm not just talking about Punjima people, but the Kurrama people and the Yinhawangka people also. All elders have that knowledge. It's been taught and it's been shared.

For this reason at our Pilbara Conference on 'Aboriginal Self Determination, Respect of Culture and Economic Development' in 1992 we were proud to introduce our elders on the stage to everyone. It is sad that so many are passing, but the following were some who were available last October, their tribe is in brackets: Jukari Parker (Ngarluma), Yilbie Warri (Yindjibarndi), David Daniels (Ngarluma), Jukari Solomon (Ngarluma), James Solomon (Ngarluma), David Stock (Nyiyabarli), Gordon Yuline (Nyiyabarli), Ken Jerrold (Yindjibarndi), Daisy Moses (Ngarluma), Jambu Giggles (Yinhawangka), Lennie Stream (Nyiyabarli), Mabel Tommy (Yinhawangka), Joyce Injie (Yinhawangka), Alice Smith (Punjima), Amy Smith (Punjima), Dulcie Condon (Yinhawangka), Gladys Walker (Punjima), Carrie Monadee (Yindjibarndi), Anita Fishook (Yindjibarndi), Dora Solomon (Ngarluma), Jukari Cox (Yinhawangka), Woodley King (Yindjibarndi), Wobby Parker (Punjima), Arthur Cox (Yinhawangka), Bobbie Scott (Wongi), Cookie Gardner (Nyiyabarli), Laurie Walters (Nyiyabarli) and Ken Jerrold (Yindjibarndi).

There was a time when we would all get together at a ceremony. Maybe a new baby would be taken there and everybody would say, 'Eh, what's this baby, where was it born?' Then the mother and father would say, 'He was born at that place.' Everybody would say,

'Oh, that's his country, we all know his country.' That's how everybody knew your country, the place where you were born. This was information that was shared together. So there is a real big wealth of knowledge out there.

The Nyiyabarli people's country is around Newman and across to Punjima country and back to Marble Bar. Today they live around Nullagine and Marble Bar. The elders that speak for those people are Gordon Yuline, David Stock, Uncle Lennie Stream. I call these men my uncle even though they are not of my tribal group. This is because of the relationship that we Aboriginals have through our skin groupings. All Aboriginal people have a skin group which tells us who we can relate to and what are our obligations to others. Always there was interaction between the adjoining tribes leading to marriages. So there have been definite relationships built up between tribes and their members, which can be as close as family. This is how our extended family works. It extends into other tribal groups quite naturally.

I first got involved with Aboriginal Affairs in 1972. The system for Aboriginal communities to raise issues with government then, at a local level, was called the North West Aboriginal Affairs Committee. It was in the Department of Aboriginal Affairs (DAA) days. Two members from each Aboriginal organisation were elected to attend and represent the people. I was elected to represent the Noualla Group of Onslow.

There was also a state consultative committee which was made up of chairpersons of the local consultative committees, which formed the State Advisory Committee, through the Aboriginal Affairs Planning Authority (AAPA). I was chairperson of the North West Consultative Committee and therefore a member of the State Committee. In 1973 the Commonwealth Government formed a statutory Commonwealth organisation called the National Aboriginal Consultative Conference (NACC), which later became the National Aboriginal Conference (NAC). The NAC members were elected from each region in each State and Territory. The elected NAC members automatically became members of the local consultative committees. My father was elected for three terms as the NAC member, over ten years. The NAC took up issues from the grass roots level through the local consultative committee to the State Advisory Committee, through the Aboriginal Affairs Planning

Authority (AAPA) then on to the Commonwealth Government.

I believe this structure worked very well because it represented the people from the grassroots level and was a very powerful voice for the Aboriginal people, not only at a local, regional and state level, but at the Commonwealth level. That is why I find it hard to believe that the Commonwealth Government, back in 1984, scrapped the NAC.

The Aboriginal and Torres Strait Islander Commission (ATSIC) has since come into being with regional offices throughout the country. It has some good aspects, but needs a major structural change. It won't work until the Aboriginal people are making the decisions on the ground and at the time they need to be made. Only in this way can the Aboriginal community keep on developing and advancing. As things are, the whole bureaucratic system just holds it up and defeats the purpose for its existence, to give Aboriginal people control so they can implement self-management.

We've had some experiences at establishing local Aboriginal organisations. In the 1970s the Noualla Group Incorporated of Onslow purchased Peedamulla Station for the whole of the Aboriginal community in the area.

At that time the Seaman Land Inquiry recommended that old reserves should be handed back to the Aboriginal Lands Trust, or given back to Aboriginal organisations. The Onslow reserve was where the Bindi Bindi community is today. The Inquiry recommended that the reserve be either taken over by the Aboriginal Lands Trust or given to the local Aboriginal organisations. It was given to the Trust and today Bindi Bindi is a place of great suffering.

Me and my brother Guy fought very hard for Bindi Bindi not to be invested in the Aboriginal Lands Trust but in the Noualla Group. Noualla was structured as an umbrella organisation comprised of people in three different areas: Peedamulla Station people, the Bindi Bindi people and the town people. The structure didn't work and as years went by conflicts weren't resolved, but developed between the people. The structure just fell away.

The Ngudarra Punjima Group Incorporated (of Onslow) was established from the membership of the tribe. The name means 'we belong, we belong here and we belong there, that's our home and that's our country.' Punjima are traditional owners of an area of Pilbara land.

Karijini members discuss Aboriginal employment in the mining industry with mine workers' representatives.

In 1984 the group became involved with the Department of Conservation and Land Management (CALM). In 1989 we started to discuss a plan for the administration of the Karijini National Park together. We then started talking about the possibility of joint management. We got other tribal-based incorporated organisations involved, the Yinhawangka and the Wakuthuni. The park is situated on our traditional country of the tribal peoples of these organisations.

In the course of this process the three groups established an umbrella organisation to monitor the park in an organised way and meet with CALM to work out the process of joint management. In this way there would be one authority for the three incorporated groups and the public.

The organisation formed was the Karijini Aboriginal Corporation. The Joint Management Plan for the Karijini National Park was finalised by the beginning of 1993. It now sits on the shelves of the new Minister for CALM and Aboriginal Affairs. I'm not too sure when he is going to release it to the public.

Our discussions with CALM ranged widely and included the promotion of Aboriginal Park Rangers. We've had a regular training program with two men working out there, my brother Maitland and Uncle Wobby's son Johnny. They are employed as full-time rangers.

From a different perspective we've visited other parks, looking at existing models of joint management and what traditional ownership means to managing a park. Getting the title to the National Park has been discussed with the previous minister, Bob Pearce. We put the Government on notice directly and through CALM, that Karijini wanted title to the park and would enter into a lease-back arrangement, similar to Uluru.

There is some opposition from non-Aboriginal sources in the area, to the Aboriginal traditional owners becoming joint managers of the park. The reasons are too complex to work out, except that there is a fear of Aboriginal people controlling the land, even if in the name of all of society. There are forces who don't want that parkland to be administered from an Aboriginal conservation viewpoint. Some of the opposition comes from some members of the local Shire. Then some local community members of Tom Price were also concerned that Aboriginal people speak about this land, as if they owned it, when these townies believed it was solely theirs. There are many rednecks out there. Tom Price as a community has only been in existence for twenty-five years. I point out that Hamersley Iron destroyed a cave habitation site at Marandoo in 1992 that was 19,000 years old. That is proof of how long our people have been in that area.

Times are changing and such people have to accept their recent citizen status.

The name Karijini is our Aboriginal word for a part of the Hamersley Ranges where our traditional land is situated. There is a barlkabi (song) about that hill which my old grandfather, Mayali Paddy Long (deceased), a Nyiyabarli, sang and which is still sung today.

The Karijini Corporation was set up with the assistance of the Aboriginal Affairs Planning Authority. It is now resourced and has five employees. We first started with a part-time secretary and a coordinator, Noel Olive. He was the first Karijini coordinator and was with us during the time of the Marandoo dispute.

The Marandoo mine is on land excised from the National Park and on our traditional land. Incidentally the word Marandoo means goanna but not in Punjima, Yinhawangka or Kurrama, but in Nyiyabarli, whose people don't come from this area. So you can see how the whitefella uses other tribal language in our territory without consulting our people, the traditional owners of the area, or understanding the culture.

We fought very hard to ensure that Hamersley Iron, the major developer and the Government took account of our heritage and culture and were prepared to ensure it was preserved and protected as required by the Aboriginal Heritage Act. That is all we asked for. We didn't want to do deals and sell our culture: that is not for sale. On the other hand, neither the Government nor the miners offered compensation for the destruction of our heritage. Instead we were accused of land grabbing, holding up resource development, taking away jobs from workers — what about Aboriginal workers we asked? But we did none of these things. We fought to protect our country from forces who want to destroy it and bury our culture and heritage.

In the past there was no real consultation with our people, others just took our land for these purposes. This situation must change, we are entitled to speak for that land. The process of sorting out the competition for land use does not have to be hostile or aggressive, providing others recognise our legitimate Aboriginal interests. On this basis it can be a cooperative process to resolve the land use problem. I'm hoping that the people of the three tribal groups get back to their traditional land as a result of the Mabo decision. But we know that we have to compete with miners and pastoralists for our land.

The Karijini National Park is surrounded by a lot of vacant crown land. That land is within our traditional lands. I believe that this should revert to the Karijini people as traditional owners in the form of Native Title Land.

DOREEN JAMES

Birth Date: 21 July 1958
Birth Place: Onslow
Tribal Group: Yinhawangka
Skin Group: Milangka

My family were the 'station people'. They would come to
town for the races. These times many people were in town, it
was a good time for corroborees.

My parents come from the area of the Hamersley Ranges known as
the 'tabletops', it's in the Rocklea Station area. My mother lived at
Rocklea when she was a child. My father's people came from the
Meekatharra area. Mother's tribal group was Yinhawangka and my
father's were Binikura and Kurrama. They worked on Rocklea
Station. My old man was a dogger and would travel by horse and
packhorse. That was the only way you could get to the springs in the
hills of the Hamersley Ranges. He travelled right back to Wyloo and
Ashburton Downs Stations.

If you wanted to survive in those times you had to follow
wherever there was work, so when the dogging finished, they came
down to Kooline, Nanutarra, Wyloo and Mount Stuart Stations to
work. Finally my father went to work permanently as a stockman at
Glenroy Station, later renamed Urala.

I was born in a tent on the old reserve at Onslow, where the Bindi
Bindi Community village is now situated. My family were what was
called the 'station people' and they would often come to town for the
races. They'd stay for a week or two and then go back to the bush.
These times many people were in town, big mobs, so it was
especially good time for corroborees, singsongs and dance. I was
born at such a time. All of these great Aboriginal gatherings were
held at Bindi Bindi. I am the second youngest of five kids in our
family. I lost my eldest brother and a little sister when she was a year

144

old. But today I have two sisters, Roma and Patsy. Patsy lives in Onslow and Roma lives in Adelaide, she's finishing her training as a teacher. Her husband comes from Adelaide. I don't see her now ... too far away for me.

My first experience at school was at Urala Station. We had a couple of teachers from the 'School of the Air' come out there and live with us from time to time. There were three kids, me and two non-Aboriginals from the station. I went to school in Onslow till grade seven. Then, as we had no high school here, I had to go either to Port Hedland or Derby. There was no Karratha, or Karratha High School till the seventies. I went to Port Hedland Junior High School. The majority of kids were Aboriginal. In 1973 a senior high school opened at South Hedland.

I was at high school for five years. I repeated one year, but had completed Year Eleven before I left. There were only about eight of my Aboriginal schoolmates in the same class with me in Year Eleven and I think that only three Aboriginal kids completed Year Twelve in that year. Some kids dropped out at first year and some at second year. But I enjoyed my school and stayed. I made a lot of friends. In those days we didn't have TV, sport was our main amusement. We didn't sit in front of TV then, or get bored, we did everything. Of course we didn't take alcohol or drugs.

The subjects I liked most at school was maths, social studies and physical education. I also did woodwork. I was the only girl student out of twelve in the woodwork class. When we went to high school we kids from Onslow had to prove to the teachers that we had the brains to do the normal school work. We were treated differently to other students. We were never placed with the normal stream of students when we arrived. We were put into a Project Class. Aboriginal kids believed that this was because they had to prove themselves because they were Aboriginal. The class only took Aboriginal kids. There were about fifteen of us in the time when I went through.

This was in 1971 and I was there until 1973. In the Project Class we didn't do the full load of normal class work. We were out planting vegies, gardening, weaving, woodwork instead. We had our maths, English, science, social studies as our study subjects. History and geography were part of the social studies. I was in my third year of high school when I went back into the normal class. At this time there were about fifteen kids in the class, six of these were Aboriginal.

In some ways I think we were lucky in the 1970s because we didn't know about 'black' and 'white', everyone just mixed in. Occasionally we got a few whites who thought they were better than most of us. But I only really became aware of such things as discrimination and racism when I left high school and came back home to Onslow. At high school there were kids who called us 'boongs' but we didn't think that this was discriminating. We didn't call them names, but we didn't get upset at them either. I don't recall the teachers being discriminatory to us. Basically my school days were happy. My parents were keen for me to go to school although I only had one parent in my high school days, as my dad died in 1969. But they always made me go to school and told me to do the best I could there.

While I was at high school I stayed at Moorgunyah Hostel and after I finished with school I took a job as a domestic there. Then in 1977 I moved to Onslow and worked for a year at Gilliamia Hostel.

It was in this period that I met my husband Phillip Carey. Phillip's father really wasn't named Carey but Andrews. He had been a victim of the Native Welfare Department and taken away from his parents as a child and given a different name. There's not many Careys around this area and that's why. Phillip is from the Ngarluma tribe of Roebourne. We were married Aboriginal style though it wasn't an arranged marriage. I worked until I was seven months pregnant. We have three children, Ronwyn is the eldest girl at fifteen. Gayden, my son, is thirteen. Ingrid is ten this year.

After we were married we worked on Peedamulla Station, Phillip was mustering and I was a musterers' cook. We stayed there for five or six years. In this period the property was owned by Aboriginal people. In 1986 we came back to town for the sake of the children. They had to go to school. I started work at the Gilliamia Hostel as a senior assistant and worked there until 1989. I was then able to get a job with the Department of Community Development (DCD) and have been working there for the past three years.

I am a family resource worker. I work three hours each day of the week for DCD but my time is spread between the Women's Office, Bindi Bindi and the DCD Office. Bindi Bindi has funding problems. The activities that function are the nursery and probably the workshop. My main job is to go out in the community where I talk with parents and kids when they have problems. These may be why don't kids attend school? Or reports of sexual abuse. Mothers must tell us about any abuse. That is their responsibility. We can only help them if they want us to help. We will only intervene without such a call when we have the facts of a very serious case and it must be done. Then we will override the parents.

Years ago the DCD would just come and take away kids. No questions asked, just take them away from the family. Now as a result, people are trying to retrace their families. We don't do that now, but the bad of the past hangs around. As a result people don't look at us as the DCD, they still look at us as the Native Welfare. They still say, I'll go and see the Native Welfare, meaning the DCD Office.

We've had some success with our sexual abuse work. It's not mainly husbands or fathers who are the problem, but people you wouldn't think of, other relatives. We have to wait for the family, we can't interfere, or they get offended and tell us to piss off!

We deal with poverty situations, alcohol, no money and such things. Sometimes it's lack of understanding about money. Child Endowment is for the kids but there are parents who don't understand this and use the money themselves. Sometimes, on a money day, you see kids out there at the beach fishing, trying to get some food. This is because their parents drank away all the money. My parents were very strict. I never knew my dad to be a drinker and my mother only drank from the early seventies when my father died. I saw a lot of my school friends suffer because their parents drank. And now their kids suffer because they are drinkers. I like my drink but I drink only socially.

Today you see kids sometimes running around in groups of three or four, from age nine to fourteen. I think they do this to get attention because their parents are not giving them attention. We are emphasising with parents that some money must be spent on the children. There's no work around here for kids when they finish school. So we tell them that the better the education they get, the better their chances after they leave school of getting something.

I was lucky that I had parents who taught me about Aboriginal culture. Like who is your uncles and aunties, who you are allowed to talk to, who you are allowed to sit with and your skin group. Before we got married we learned the law side of it, your in-laws, the mangkalyis and all that stuff.

My skin group is Milangka. Phillip is a Burungu. We're married right by the law. There are a lot of people not married right. At times people may say that it's the young people who are breaking our law. But the way I look at it is that some old people broke the law before and provided the wrong role models for the young. It is their fault that the young cannot respect them. It is not much good to accuse the young of breaking the law when you have done it before them. Traditionally it is up to the grandparents to teach the kids the law, but the old people are dying out and our law is slowly dying. We must hold on to certain things for our culture and it's future.

When my son's time comes to be initiated, I will let him decide whether to follow the mother or the father. But on the mother's side he is a Yinhawangka. There are some differences in the ceremony between our mob and the mob over at Roebourne where his father comes from.

We set up the Yinhawangka group (incorporated association) in about 1985 to try to get our land back, my brother, his wife and me. We believed we couldn't stay in Onslow forever. That is the Dhalanyji people's country. Our old people only came here looking for work. Now they want to go back to their country and to show the younger ones our heritage and history. Originally we looked at Rocklea Station as the place to do this. The pastoralist wasn't interested. Recently the Yinhawangka group has taken a living lease on a block of land out near Tom Price called Bellary Creek. We are seeking funds to provide accommodation and infrastructure for some of the people on their traditional land, especially the older people. It's not big, just a living area.

The Aboriginal Women's Group started here in 1990. They were voicing their concerns on child abuse, domestic violence, alcohol, drugs and child care. They voiced their concerns at Yule River meetings (traditional meetings near Hedland) and social justice forums. I had started work with DCD and was given the job of coordinating this program as my responsibility, part time.

The group started from grassroots level. We sent out letters and voiced our concerns, especially to the Aboriginal Affairs Planning

148

Authority (AAPA), as we needed to set up a Safe House. After looking at the available houses we selected one, but it was in an area where the Onslow ratepayers were living.

AAPA agreed to support our project and to help by purchasing a house. We had to apply to the Shire of Ashburton for permission to use the house for the purposes as stated. The Shire rejected our application on the grounds that the ratepayers had objected to this use of that house. They claimed that there would be too much noise, kids screaming, men going around at all hours of the night, etc. Some of the objections upon which the Shire relied were made by people from as far away as Tom Price, Pannawonica and Paraburdoo. We had no option but to take the fight to the Town Planning Appeals Tribunal, in an effort to have the decision overturned. Well, we won and needless to say our safe house is the quietest house in its block.

In setting up the Safe House our men in town gave a hundred per cent support. We got no backlash from them. The husbands of the client women only go there when they have sobered up and to ask, could they just speak with their wife. Then it's up to the wife. We get a lot of clients using it. Some are domestic violence related and the women concerned are learning quickly how to use the Safe House. These women get away from the home or wherever before trouble has occurred. The women in town know it's there for them now and they go there without waiting for the worst.

We never set up the Safe House specifically for Aboriginal women, but for women across the board. It hasn't been seen this way, however. No other women except the Aboriginals have used it, yet we have seen other women bashed here. What can we do? We can't help people who keep this problem behind closed doors. If they can't say they have a problem to us women, then we can't help them.

I want to say something about the development of industry in the Onslow area. Now at the end of 1993 has seen the construction of a gas processing plant on the Urala Station land. The gas will be piped from the gas field offshore, be processed at this plant and piped to a location in the area for sale and distribution as LPG.

This is a big and important project and as a result there has been a great influx of workers into town. This has benefited the local shops and some other locals. But what has it meant for the Aboriginal people of Onslow, the majority? Today we can hardly get into the pub if we want a drink, when the workers come to town. For us women it's hard to sit down and relax and we can't play darts any more. The bar staff fall over themselves to serve the workers, so we find it hard to get service. Discrimination seems to have sharpened. The bar staff sometimes ask Aboriginal males to drop their money into their hands and not place it on their hand. I have seen this happen. And when we get change it is often dropped into our hands. Just like they are frightened the colour will rub off. Some of the staff insist that we Aboriginals say 'please' and 'thank you' or we don't get service. The whitefella doesn't say anything and yet they rush to serve him. The price of cartons of beer to the workers and to the locals is different, we pay more.

As far as the construction work, Aboriginals have not benefited. There are two Aboriginal men employed, Lester Drummond and Rodney Butler. Yet there are hundreds of other non-Aboriginal people employed there, mostly from Perth, but also locals. I think that it's good that these locals have got a job, but there should be more Aboriginal people. Considering the history of our struggle for Aboriginal employment in the Pilbara this amounts to discrimination against Aboriginal labour. If they have difficulties it is easy to go to the office of Aboriginal organisation in town and get help. But the companies never ask Aboriginal organisations here to supply labour. So much for the United Nations Year of Indigenous People, it looks like racism is part of company policy up in this part of the world.

'The Visitation', a rock formation in the Karijini National Park.

DORIS COOKE

Birth Date: Unknown
Birth Place: Rocklea Station
Tribal Group: Yinhawangka
Skin Group: Burungu

I hear every day white people asking, 'why don't Aboriginal
people get up off their arse and do something for themselves,
instead of whingeing and moaning?'

I was born on Rocklea Station, near today's town of Paraburdoo, not far from the airport. This is my traditional land where my old people come from. I don't know the actual date of my birth but it was forty-four years ago.

My mother was a Kurrama. She was born and grew up at Rocklea Station. My father was a Yinhawangka and he was born on Hamersley Station, but brought up on Rocklea. His father, my grandfather, named Dhurlja, was born, bred and buried in Rocklea. My mother's father was Wakin. The Yinhawangka people were the main tribe at Rocklea, but there were also Kurramas and Punjimas living there. My mother and father had worked together for many years on Rocklea and at Juna Downs Station.

I was very little when my parents moved from Rocklea to Onslow and then to Kooline Station out from Onslow. Later they went to work on Ashburton Downs Station and then came back into Onslow. I was about four years old. The family was living here in Onslow. My father got sick in this period and went to Hedland Hospital. Mother stayed around Onslow while he was in hospital. He came out to work on Munda (Mundabullankana) Station outside of Port Hedland, on his own. He worked as a horse breaker and was one of the best, so they tell me. But he had an accident breaking in a horse and died.

My mother was doing odd jobs in Onslow and when my father died she went back to Ashburton station. That's where we grew up.

She was the cook at Ashburton station for many years. It was difficult for Mum, who was pregnant at that time and had my sister Lola, brother Nicholas and me to look after. Then, on the way to Ashburton Station, we had to pull up at Kooline Station, that's where my brother Colin was born. Nick and I were the second and third eldest. Lola was the eldest, she was preparing to marry Wobby. They was promised by tribal law. Colin was next and then Kevin. They were too young for school at that time.

About this time my mother met my stepfather at Ashburton. He was a station hand. They lived together and went fencing. Brother Nick and me were sent to Carnarvon and put in the mission. That's when compulsory school started coming in. I was seven years old.

When we came home for school holidays Mum and Dad were then fencing. The old stepfather was a fencing contractor and fenced on Wyloo, Kooline. Every holiday we'd go to the fencing camp. We'd get sick of it and thought, 'Oh no, back to the fencing camp!' We'd help the old fella and Mum, because Mum used to help with the fencing. We'd run all of the wires for them. Of course Colin and Kevin can now build fences.

The parents used to come to pick us up only at Christmas for our holiday at Rocklea. They came in an old Ford truck. I remember one year they came to pick us up in a little old car. You know, those old ones with a dickie seat. It was not very high and had spoked wheels. When they came up I just jumped in. But Nick, he was embarrassed with that motor car. He wouldn't jump in with all his friends watching him. He reckoned it looked an ugly little thing. He told my mother and stepfather he was gonna walk back towards the road. They could pick him up there but not in front of his mates. Later when we came away from Carnarvon and went on the run out to the station he really loved it, he used to run beside that little car and jump in and all ... but he wouldn't let his friends see him jumping in.

I was well looked after at Ashburton Downs Station by a special person, Lucy Toby. Her Aboriginal name was Aji, but we called her Dido. She died at Wittenoom at 102 years of age. She was my mother's grandmother, a Kurrama woman. She lived around Hamersley Station, her tribal lands and was born in Boomanna Springs at the back of Tom Price towards the park. My grandmother on my mother's side was also born there. She was named after the springs, they called her Boomba. Her white name was Diana Johnny, a Punjima woman. This is the mother of two of my uncles, Mirru George and Listen Listen (prominent elders).

Dido moved to Ashburton Station. She worked there for years and years as a laundry girl, until she was a pensioner. I met her at Ashburton. She was a little woman with a big heart. She taught me matters of culture and land at the station when I came home from holidays. I used to take my swag and sleep next to her so she could tell me stories. When we went walking she'd tell me not to touch the bird nests, you know like kids do, because she said, 'That's a home belonging to somebody.'

She talked to me in Kurrama language and I talked back to her in language. But sitting here today I can't talk Kurrama. I can understand it but not speak it. The owner of Ashburton built a special house for her and told her that she could live there for as long as she liked. She did that. Dido passed away in the 1970s.

Living in the Carnarvon Mission run by the Church of Christ was a part of my life that I wouldn't like to go through again. The missionary was a very hard bloke. He used to lock me up in a little room that was used as a storeroom and flog me with the cane every time I got into a bit of strife — from neck down to my ankle and the marks stayed on for a good while.

I remember one incident. We used to wear those moccasins to school and some other style of shoe came in. But I didn't like the new style, I still wanted the moccasins to wear to school. So I put on the moccasins to go in the school bus. He said I shouldn't wear them and that I had to wear what the other kids were wearing. I didn't like that so he flogged me. That dark room used to scare me.

I was there for about five years, until I was eleven. Then thankfully, he kicked me out. I think the reason for my bad treatment was that I didn't like his methods.

So I had no school and my parents were working in Kooline Station. But there was an old white bloke working as a mechanic in Kooline. His name was Henry McLeod, old Don McLeod's brother. He said, 'Tell your mum and stepfather that you should really go back to school.' He came into Onslow and looked around for somewhere for me to board while I went to school. Onslow was a predominantly white town then. All of the Aboriginal people were out working and living on the stations. Only a few people lived in tents on the old Onslow reserve.

There was no hostel then. But he found an English school teacher, Mrs Rooney was her name. We called her Mother Rooney. She took me in as a boarder. The school then was near where the old goods shed is today. It was a little one-room school. Then the school moved to a vacant block down near the Department of Community Development (DCD) and we went there, me and my cousins, Elizabeth and Margaret Dowton, now living at Bindi Bindi.

When Mother Rooney moved down near the Onslow police station, I went with her. My cousins, Eva, Gladys and Marshall Smith also came. They had been living out in the bush. We all stayed with Mother Rooney and went to school in Onslow until the hostel was built in 1960 or 1961. Then the old girl went away. We all went to the hostel, me and my other two little brothers, Colin and Kevin. I went to live there because my two little brothers had come to Onslow. That is the same Gilliamia Hostel that is here today. I only stayed there for a little while because the manager was a very rough man. He was tall and skinny and used to flog me cruel. He had a big long cane which he flogged us with.

One night we girls pinched some potatoes and onions from the pantry. We took them back to the dormitory and were eating them raw. He sang out to be quiet, because we were giggling and making a noise. So we stopped for a while. The we started whispering and the next minute the whisper got louder and louder. Of course he heard this and sang out, 'Right,' but he didn't come down straight away. He sneaked down to see what we were doing, but we saw the flashlight, the beam. The girls all jumped back into bed and threw the potatoes and onions onto my bed. I grabbed the quilt and doubled it over to cover up all of these half-chewed vegies. The girls were chucking chewies around to kill off the onion smell on their breath and we all lay quiet, pretending to be asleep.

He came with the flashlight. He came to the first girl and put the torch to her face. If she blinked he would say, 'Out,' and the girl would have to get up for a hiding. He'd come to the next girl and she'd blink and he'd say, 'Out.' He kept going like this down the line of beds. Most girls were involved but there were a couple who weren't and were asleep. I was the last bed and he came to me now and he flashed that light in my face and I'm trying my hardest not to blink. And I did a good job for a while, so he said, 'Ah hah, there's something happened that you are not involved in.' I was a mischievous one. He reckoned,

155

'there must be something wrong.' He must have noticed the folded quilt or smelt onions on me because he grabbed the edge of the quilt and gave a quick pull and all of the potatoes and onions went everywhere on the floor, rolling everywhere. He yelled at me in triumph, 'get out. I knew you were in it.'

So he lined us up and went back to get his cane and bang, bang, bang. 'Put your hand out,' he'd say. We'd put out the hand, whack! And the other one, whack! He kept doing it until we cried. A lot of those girls cried straight away, others would tough it out. But with me it took about eight or nine, he won't give in on me and I won't give in on him, I wouldn't cry. He just kept bang, bang, left hand, right hand, left, right. Until I couldn't take it any more and cried. He was satisfied when I started crying. I don't think he liked me, you know.

One other night we kids took off somewhere, me, Tricia James and my other cousin, who was the aunty of the boy who's the Karijini coordinator. We came back to the hostel and as usual we jumped through the window. I was the last to come through. He was there and he let those other two girls jump through the window and told them, 'Sshh', not to say anything about his being there. I was comin' through the window last. I jumped through the window and he grabbed me by the hair and flung me to the floor, then got stuck into me with his fists. I had a black eye and a bunged up lip. I was about thirteen years old. He was a sexist too.

I told my stepfather and mother. They told the old McLeod. I dunno whether he went to see the welfare or the police about it, but there was a bit of talk, I know. They took me out of the hostel and I went back to Mother Rooney's and stayed. We did have some good times at the hostel. The boys and girls had mixed teams to play rounders, with a stick from the tree and a tennis ball. There was a good atmosphere between the kids. We went on picnics and places. Mrs Downs was a nice woman.

I finished primary school at Onslow and went to Derby for my high school, living at the United Aboriginal Mission (UAM). So I finished my school years. At Derby there were days when I was a bit homesick but I was one of those tough kids and didn't let anything ruffle me, didn't let it show. I only came home for Christmas holidays. I was the first Onslow kid to go to school at Derby. Later all the Onslow kids went there for high school. It was a school for all types of kids, but the Tech was only for Aboriginals. I was there for

Jarndunmunha, called Mount Nameless by the settlers at Tom Price. The irony is that this hill has had a name for thousands of years.

three years. Two years at high school and a year of some sort of Tech.

By this time I was growing up and I fell in love. I didn't return to Onslow to live but stayed up there and lived with this bloke, where I had my big son. I must have been about sixteen years old. I took my son to Halls Creek and was knocking around there. I found somebody else and I came back to Nanutarra Station pregnant. At Nanutarra I had my family. Lola was there by then, married to Wobby and with kids. The Parker mob was there too. It was a great time. We used to love horse riding and Margaret and I used to get up to all sorts of capers there.

I lived for a short time at Onslow while Vivian was born. She was my second one. I then went to Hedland and started drinking and going stupid. I had left Vivian with Lola and Wobby and my big son's father took the little boy, Frankie, back to Derby with him. I was in Port Hedland and on the loose, looking for an identity.

While I was in this state, Margaret's father, a powerful Aboriginal leader, said I had to marry Alec Tucker (who now lives at Roebourne).

He said to me, 'I think it's about time, instead of drifting around, that you get together with him.' Alec was my give away husband, my mother and father gave me away when I was born. Alec and his mother and father were at Coolawanyah Station and Margaret's father was going to a law meeting at the Shaw River. On his way back he took me to drop me off there. As it turned out I didn't get off because when we pulled up at Mount Florence Station Alec was there, sitting down with his girlfriend playing cards. Margaret's father sung out to him and he just come straight to the motor car. But that girl was saying, 'Oh don't go Alec, don't go.' She was crying for him and I was feeling shamed. I was hitting Margaret's father in the shoulder and saying, 'Don't make me stay here, I don't want to stay here.'

Coolawanyah is only about four miles from Mount Florence and we went there. Alec jumped on the truck and Margaret's father said, 'Well, I will stay the night here, I'll go along in the morning.' But he told me I had to stay there and oh, I didn't know what to do!

I stayed there, but not long, only a couple of months really. Then I started getting sick, I was getting pains, my gallstones started. I went in with the Flying Doctor to Port Hedland Hospital and when I was there thought, oh well, here's my chance, I won't go back. So Alec came to Hedland to find out if I'm ready to come back, but I was running away hiding from him. He got the picture and took off. Later he tried to make me go back, Margaret's father was there, they were both trying, but I wouldn't, I stood firm.

In the law Alec is the father to my kids. I was his wife by our law and he therefore was father of my children. So he and his mother claim them as their own until this day. He reared Vivian as his own to this day and Vivian knows him as her dad and calls him Dad and treats him as her dad. Alec also put my son through the law (initiation ceremony) as the boy's father, showing the strong obligations that exist today under our Aboriginal law in the Pilbara.

I had met Ronnie Councillor in Hedland and we got on well together. We decided to live together and went to Meekatharra where he came from. By this time my stepfather, mother and my brothers, were all living in Wittenoom. Ronnie and me went there to visit them and to get my daughter Vivian back. At that time Alec and his mother were rearing her up. Alec was her father at Aboriginal law. They were at Hooley Station, just out of Wittenoom. They wanted to keep her. They liked her. I got her back after a little bit of trouble because Alec and his mother didn't want to let her go. I wanted to settle down then with my kids. I had been split from them during my wild period. I tried to get my son back, they wouldn't let me. This was in the middle sixties.

But we took off for Carnarvon with Vivian and lived there for a while. That's where I was pregnant with my son, the one after Vivian. Then we came back to live in Roebourne and I had my next son there, the one that I lost. And from there we went to Wittenoom to live and there I broke up with Ronnie Councillor.

I met a white bloke and lived with him in Wittenoom for eleven years at Third and Sixth Avenues. There used to be a lot blue asbestos tailings in the driveways. It was also at the school. Neither me or my family ever had any tests done on our lungs after living at Wittenoom. I don't know anyone who did have such tests. Government health people certainly did not come around.

We left there when the town closed, about 1979. I was still living with this whitefella and we shifted to Karratha. He had a job lined up there. We lived there for six years. He was the one that reared my last two kids and that's when my little son was born. Finally that relationship broke up and I moved to Wickham for a while. That's where Margaret (Parker) lived, so that her daughter could go to high school. She had a house in Wickham and I stayed with her for a year, then moved to Roebourne until last year when I got this job working at the Onslow Safe House.

I've had a couple of jobs that I've liked: I worked at Wittenoom school as a teacher's aide (Aboriginal Education Worker, AEW) and I really loved the job. There was quite a few Aboriginal kids, the Guinesses, the Parkers — Lola had seven kids, Cooks, Stevens and some kids who would come from Roebourne to visit their grandparents, aunties and uncles. I worked in that job for two years before we moved to Karratha. I then worked there at Peg's Creek as an AEW. When there were no Aboriginal kids there I was transferred to Karratha Junior Primary. I worked there for a while until I developed kidney troubles and had an operation. We then moved to Roebourne.

My next job was field officer with the Roebourne Aboriginal Legal Service (ALS). This was a good job which lasted for two years. It was hard as I was the only person in the office. But it just suited me. Not so much because of the arguments in Court, but going out in the field and talking to the people and working with the people and for the people. Then I got involved in community committees. I became a committee member of the Mawarnkarra Aboriginal Medical Service at Roebourne. I finished up with ALS because I had a little bit of trouble with getting time off. I came to the Cane River and put my son through the law.

My next job was at the Weeriana Hostel of Roebourne, looking after the girls there. About this time I was elected as chairperson of the Mawarnkarra and held that position until I left Roebourne last year. I had become a diabetic in this period and lived on the pension, until I got the caretaker's job with the Women's Group in Onslow.

Land rights are really important to me and all Aboriginal people. Many of us have got together in traditional groups to go back to our land and to get a bit of our land back and it's hard. It's very hard. When you think everything is running smoothly we come up against a brick wall. We don't often get the land. We need the land to live, to take our children and old people back, there is nothing for those people to do in the town. They just get bored and the old ones turn to alcohol. The old people used to have a cultural life and be able to teach all those things in the bush. When they came to town to live they couldn't do all those. But in going back to the land the old people will have lots of things to do and maybe their alcohol intake will get less and less.

I have always carried out Aboriginal law. I am proud of our culture. But in town the kids are torn between two cultures. Taking them out bush will strengthen their culture. However it's difficult to maintain the law in all conditions. For example only one of my sons was initiated into the law. The other one didn't live with us at the time so I couldn't take him. I bring my kids up following Aboriginal law. I'd rather do that than bring my kids up in a white way. I still keep my language going and teach my kids to respect their elders, their family and how our kinship goes, who to marry and such things in our law. My kids are basically following the law.

The kids are bored, sport and things in town that Aboriginal kids like getting into don't last long. They need more meaningful things to keep them occupied, like learning the basic skills of their culture. What I see of these kids' town life really makes me want to cry, it doesn't have the richness and fullness that is possible in learning and practising their culture. By taking them out bush the old people can teach them the old ways, like hunting, tracking, making artefacts, bush medicine, corroboree for the kids to dance. They love all that, but not enough of that is happening in town.

My traditional land is Rocklea Station. This is the land with which my family identifies and has done for years and years. It runs from Tom Price right through back to Paraburdoo and right around. My grandfather and my grandmother's land, my mother and father's land and my land and my kids' land. And it doesn't matter that there have been miners, pastoralists and others on that land, I still regard it as my land.

We went out to that area on the Easter weekend. There was over thirty of us, nine cars, one bus and two big trucks and four-wheel drives. A lot of old people came that had never come for years. Our uncles and aunties who were working out in Burrangarra Aboriginal community. This used to be called Mount James Station. They are working there on this Aboriginal-owned station, waiting for us to get the land that we all belong to, so they can come back home to live. My old people at that meeting won't allow any one person to speak for that country. Only the elders, as a whole, are entitled to speak for

Cooling off at Millstream.

our country. In this way we hope to stop bad deals being made.

Since that Mabo case we've had discussions with the Rocklea pastoralist. He pledged to support our claim to some of his lease. He took us out there and showed us land he proposes to give to us. We agreed that the land is suitable, being in our traditional area and in the area of my grandfather's hill, Wakuthuni. We also have been to that land to talk with the surveyors appointed by the Aboriginal Affairs Planning Authority (AAPA) after we applied for this grant of land. We have great expectations of getting back to some of our country. This change in our fortunes has unleashed a new enthusiasm among our people. Some of the older ones have gone out to that block and are now camping there, waiting for the lease to be confirmed. They have caravans and bough shelters there. We look to being eventually confirmed as the owners of this land in either native or freehold title.

I think it's important because this face-to-face negotiation with pastoralists is a very important way for Aboriginal people to become self-acting about the struggle for their own land.

We went there with our two uncles and our father, my uncle, my father's brother. We still call him dad. Then there was me, my sister, brother and our nephew. We went and had a talk to the owner and his son. The owner sang out to his son to come a bit closer and join in the discussion because as he said, 'You have to be dealing with these people, when your turn comes.' We took it as a good sign that he would honour his agreement with us and wanted his son to also honour it. Di McCullam, the Heritage Officer with Karijini Aboriginal Corporation helped us on this trip.

The Wakuthuni hill is the main hill that has been mined at Tom Price. It's now been cut down to half its size. That's my grandfather's spiritual place. He was my mother's father, old Wakin. He was a very important Kurrama man, a mabarn, or Aboriginal doctor. He got all of his powers from that hill. That hill was recognised by Aboriginal people of the area as his spiritual place.

Before Tom Price was mined and before I was born, this old fella had died. But he had made up a song about that place and its future destruction. In the song it mentions that he could see his land being destroyed, hear loud noises and there were blinking lights on that hill. The old people knew of this song, long ago. But it wasn't Wakin that knew, but the spirits of that hill telling him what would happen to his land. One of our old elders has sung this song and we have recorded it.

It is part of our history. Our Wakuthuni group (incorporated association) is named after that hill.

This was one reason to form the Karijini Aboriginal Corporation. Three of our tribal groups got together in an umbrella organisation. Its aim was to deal with the matters of the land, the Karijini National Park, mining and to uphold and preserve our culture and heritage. Our Wakuthuni group was one of these. I really feel for Karijini because it's concerned about these things.

There is a question that I hear every day of my life from white people asking: 'Why don't the Aboriginal people get up off their arse and do something for themselves, instead of whingeing and moaning.'

Well Karijini was formed and the people are starting to get up and do things for themselves. So we are trying, but you get a lot of white people still putting us down for trying to do what's good for ourselves. But what can we do if white people and mining companies continue to throw shit on us for trying to help ourselves?

They don't want us to get up and do things for ourselves, it seems to me. They prefer to work with individuals not the Karijini organisation. We want to help them and at the same time help ourselves, but they must come through the right channels to Karijini so that Karijini can find the right people to help the miners. They should come through the front door and not go through the back door, that way hurts our feeling. They always deny not wanting to help us and that they want to work with us, but it doesn't look like that to me.

We think there has been some change in Aboriginal society today. I see that women are coming forward more and that men are taking the back seat. There is always women doing things, organising things and speaking out in meetings, joining in on committees. Menfolk just sort of sit back. I can't blame them. The white ways that wrecked their lives, they took away the thing the men used to feel when they had that power, you know, self-esteem.

Women are now setting up our own organisations and running community organisations like Safe Houses. Women are moving into the bad things in Aboriginal life and organising to stop them. There was a recent bush meeting of women in the Pilbara, women came from all over to attend. This means we can organise on a whole area basis. We need to do this with Karijini for it has an important role and it is recognised. It needs to be kept strong and it needs the women to keep it strong. Karijini has gone a bit flat.

It took two women to form the Wakuthuni Association. We needed land. Our people needed to live in their own country. Wakuthuni is the name of a hill at Tom Price which was my grandfather's. We need to be there where we can see that hill. So Lola and me talked it over with the old people to set up an organisation to get some land. They said to go ahead and we did. Now Lola and I are today sitting out on our block of land, our caravans are here. We are waiting for the Rocklea Station owner to put in writing the agreement to excise some of that land for our living lease. It took two women to carry the whole idea through and our two daughters are here with us. I think this is important.

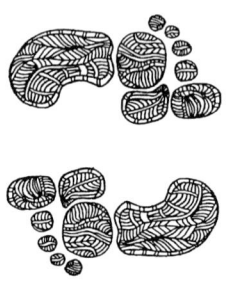

DONALD ARD

Birth Date: Not recorded
Birth Place: Onslow
Tribal Group: Dhalanyji
Skin Group: Milangka

*Where there has been a death in the family
I have to take time off work. This could mean
that I would be off work for about one week.*

I was born in the old Onslow Hospital and did my schooling at
Onslow. My father passed away. He was a member of the Kariyarra
tribe from around Port Hedland. My mother is Lorna Hicks a
Dhalanyji who lives in Onslow. I have a brother John who lives at
Carnarvon. A sister passed away as a baby at Yanrey Station. I am a
member of the Dhalanyji tribe which is from this area from the Cane
River to Nanutarra, Nyang, to Yanrey River. We are related to the
Hayes, Ashburtons and Irelands, large Dhalanyji families in Onslow.

The Aboriginal population of Onslow is mixed, there are people
from the Dhalanyji, Punjima, Yindjibarndi, Yinhawangka, Binnika and
Kurrama tribes here, all living together. Most of them are traditional,
believing in Aboriginal law. There are a few Dhalanyji boys out at the
initiation ceremonies being held right now, at the Cane River. They
have been through in previous years but have attend other meetings to
complete their learning, such as the one this year. They are following
the law. The Dhalanyji law is strict in not allowing brother and sister to
talk when they are growing up. They have to get someone else to talk
for them if they want to say something to the other person. In this way
we are stricter than other tribes.

Funerals are important in Aboriginal culture. Where there has
been a death in the family I have to take time off work. I would take
the time off in accordance with the Shire's award, but I might also
have to take another few days off on top of that. This could mean

165

that I would be off work for about one week. With me as the oldest in the family, apart from Mum, I would have to organise the funeral. These days this is made easy with the mobile telephone out in the bush. But I still have to meet other people who come to pay their respects and I will be there in case people come from far away. It depends on who has passed away as to the time needed to be taken off. I have attended funerals about 750 kilometres away.

The Dhalanyji people usually smoke their houses when there has been a death there.

The Dhalanyjis are involved in the practice of the law but this usually occurs around Christmas time when most people have their holidays. It is most unlikely that law leave would be needed outside this period. But even now there is a bloke working on the Council who should be out at the Cane River, so it doesn't always work out.

I worked on watering down the airstrip at Fitzroy Crossing for a long time. This was water binding of the surface. I was an acting airport foreman. I have had experience in the Main Roads Department. I've been a dozer driver, backhoe operator and other machine jobs. I have been employed by the Ashburton Shire Council since the beginning of last year. I am a truck driver. Out here we just look for a job, number one and then try to improve our skills, but most times this needs help from the employer.

DAVID SIMMONS

Birth Date: 19 June 1945
Birth Place: Perth
Tribal Group: Nyoongah
Skin Group: Burungu

Mum wouldn't give up her Aboriginality.

I was born in Subiaco, Perth. My mother is an Aboriginal woman from Kukerin in the Lake Grace area of Western Australia. My father came from the Margaret River area. He is an Aboriginal man. My stepfather is part of the Isaacs family from the Perth and Clarrie Isaacs is my young brother. My parents are Nyoongahs, from the south-west.

My schooling as a young fella was undertaken at different places. Our family used to travel around a lot then.

In 1951 the Native Welfare Officers were still active. My younger school days were occasionally spent hiding from the Native Welfare. My mother insisted that I go to school, but there was always that dread that I would never come home from school because of Native Welfare. We knew that if Native Welfare found out there were any Aboriginal kids like myself at those schools, they would take them away. Native Welfare didn't necessarily go and tell the parents that they had taken their child. We were all vulnerable to Native Welfare, who were always grabbing Aboriginal kids. I started school in 1950. I would turn six in June so I had to start when I was five and a half years old. It was at a very small place called Parkerville. I've been back since, taken my kids, it's just a one-room building.

Parkerville is up in the Darling Ranges, not far from Mundaring. We shifted there as the old man, my stepfather, was a returned soldier working at Hollywood Repatriation Hospital in Perth. Some of the old returned soldiers had country properties. He used to negotiate with them. The family had to keep out of the way of Native Welfare because Mum wouldn't give up her Aboriginality.

Not long after I started school we shifted to Mount Helena. It is another very small place back in the hills around Perth. I used to catch the bus to school myself. The school building there was the town hall. It was the only school they ever had. The reason seems to be that there was a bigger school further up the hills in Mount Helena, but it was too full. And all of us primary kids went to the town hall.

Quite a few kids went to the town hall. There was more than two bus loads, all mixed up, but I was probably the only Aboriginal kid at school. I can remember my mother taking me to school and asking the teacher, if the Native Welfare were to come, would they hide me?

I remember on several occasions that a Scottish teacher called Miss Lang raced into the class and grabbed me saying, 'Quick, quick, come in here.' And she got another boy, who is my friend to this day, to go with me and hide under the wooden stage. That boy's name is Peter White. We are about the same age. So we ran and hid under the stage. She said, 'Don't you kids come out until I tell you.' The Native Welfare man came in and asked if there were any Aboriginal children at school and the teacher said, 'No'. It was probably an hour or so before we could come out.

On another occasion we were out in the yard playing when the Native Welfare officer came. She told one of the kids to get me and go up under the hall. We had to climb right under the school. A few of the kids came with us and they thought it exciting hiding under the school until the Native Welfare bloke went. But it wasn't a prank for me. I think these visits were a response to somebody dobbing me in, but I'm not sure.

When we were in Parkerville there was a family called Green. I'm sure this lady was Dot Green. I'm almost sure they were related to the Greens from Geraldton way. Native Welfare knew that she was living in our area, but they never took her kids because they were big kids. Loma, her daughter was about as fair as me and about the same age. If they had made an effort to try and grab their kids I think old Mrs Green, who was a big lady, would have kept them at bay with just the thunder of her voice.

But we were dobbed in on a couple of occasions when we were at Parkerville because the bloke came to our house. But we had a system. Mum set it up. There was a tree two hundred metres away from the house and others about five hundred metres away. She would leave bottles of water under the trees. The system was that if the Native Welfare came we were to rush to the first tree and stay there. The dog was to come with us and he wouldn't let anybody come near without barking a warning. If the dog barked a warning and it wasn't Mum yelling out then we would go to the next tree, which was further out and hide there. We had about half a dozen bottles of water we'd take with us and mum would give us some bread or damper, whatever she had and we were off. You know, there was the four of us, four kids. There was three of us boys and our young sister. I was the eldest. We all had fair skin. Clarrie has got the darkest skin of all of us.

Native Welfare would have just grabbed us. The reason being that because Mum already had three kids to her first marriage, actually it was four of us. There was two boys and two girls and my elder brother and sister were in Sister Kate's children's home. Mum put them in Sister Kate's so she knew where they were. In this way she could stop Native Welfare efforts to grab kids. You see at the time when her husband passed away she had four kids. The grandparents kept the eldest daughter and they let her take the three of us. She put Alice and Bill, who are older than me, into Sister Kate's. Sister Kate's at the time had a lot of the half caste kids. Sister Kate's was in Queens Park and out near Thornlie at the time. It was ironic that later I bought a house about a hundred metres from where she originally started.

Unfortunately Native Welfare took the kids from the south and sent them north. They took kids from the north and brought them south. They crossed the people up all the time. So my schooling days were pretty traumatic right up to about 1953 when the last of the Native Welfare Act was repealed.

Mum's sister, Auntie Alice, and her husband, the old man's brother, uncle Les Isaacs, (my stepfather's brother), lived in town and they rented from an old fella who had a duplex flat in Gladstone Street, East Perth. They said to him, 'look my brother and sister-in-law want to come down to live in Perth for the sake of their kids.' The old fella said, 'yes, my son is staying there at the moment going to university and caretaking, I'll shift him out'. We were able to move in and live next door to our uncle and auntie which was very good for us kids.

In the meantime we had to get out of Mount Helena, it was getting too hot. We moved to a place called Belmay or as it's now called Newburn. There is a big railway yard there now. We lived on a small farm. We got this through another old ex-army mate of the old man's. He rented it to us. I went to Belmay school, we had to walk about two miles to the highway to catch the school bus.

My old man was one of the 'Rats of Tobruk'. He fought in Alamein. So when he came back he got a job in Hollywood Repatriation Hospital. Most of these places we rented were from ex-servicemen, because they all had this thing of looking after each other.

We went from Mount Helena across to Belmay which was a bit closer to the city. But it was still in the bush so we couldn't be detected. I think it was while we were living there that this section of the Native Welfare Act was repealed, instructing them to take the kids.

One of the Native Welfare Acts forbade Aboriginal people residing in the metropolitan area. Now you need to know that the only way you could reside in the metropolitan area was to give up your Aboriginality and take on a white citizenship. Then you were no longer considered Aboriginal. My mother would not give up her Aboriginality. When that Act was repealed, Aboriginal people were allowed to reside in the metropolitan area. We then moved to Perth. That was in 1953 and we moved to Gladstone Street, East Perth.

Mum always taught us about little things when we were kids in the bush. How to track rabbits, know the difference between the animals, how to catch the animals, where to look for them all and which animals we could eat those sorts of things, many's the time. The old man worked at Hollywood Repatriation Hospital. He only came home four days in a month. He didn't have a vehicle to drive home every weekend. We wouldn't see the old man for months at a time. What he would do is try to work for three months and then get twelve days off. In this way he had some sort of time off especially when we were on holidays.

So we spent a lot of time at home with Mum, it was really good. She always taught us to respect our elders, which I always follow. When we moved to East Perth we were among a lot of Aboriginal people who were like fringe dwellers. We never turned the people away and we were never afraid to mix with them. I certainly was never afraid of the people. Those were the things that my mother passed on.

Then there was the Coolabaroo League, it's a Nyoongah word, means black and white magpie. Back in '55, '56 it had a little meeting place in Murray Street. It was the Young Men's Christian Association (YMCA), I think. They had a lot of the old people come in there and sit down and tell us stories. In those days they still brought in the traditional spears and shields and boomerangs to those meetings. They used to have a lot of arts and crafts there to sell. Not so much art but craft. We heard all the stories about why the crow was black, how the red robin got red, how the emu and the goannas swapped feathers and all of those stories.

I was never part of a corroboree, never went to one in those days. But there was an elder, Bill Bodney. He was the old tribal top man back in the 1950s, responsible for Perth. I remember to this day when the Queen came, she had to be given the boomerang of peace by old Bill, to say that she could come to his country, because that was his place. He was on the airstrip when she came to Australia.

I don't think any Aboriginal boys of my age around Perth would have ever been initiated into the law, although a lot of them say they have. It's most unlikely unless they came up and went through the law in the Pilbara. That started in the 1950s and I know that people did come down and grab some out of the Nyoongah country and take them to the law at Cane River. I think this resulted from the inability of the local elders like old Bill Bodney, to get around. Unfortunately white dominance stuffed up a lot of our places, a lot of our sacred sites.

I joined the law at Cane River a couple of years back and I passed a lot of the things on to my kids. I've explained to them the skin group system, my skin group and their mother's skin group. Now they have their own skin group. I've explained to them all of the people that we are related to. It's information that you can pass on but my kids are at that stage where a lot of Aboriginal kids are, they grow up and chase the white side of life very early. But as they get older they'll see they have got to keep that Aboriginal culture alive. At the moment, they all stick together and look after one another. Yet, the need to get out and mix more in Aboriginal cultural life is there.

I always used to feel envious of people who came from areas where Aboriginal traditions were alive, regardless of whether they were unemployed or had a drinking problem.

I was married in 1966 in a registry office. We have four children, two boys and two girls. All the kids are here in Wickham, the youngest daughter stays with the wife and myself and the eldest daughter and the other two boys have got families of their own. They stay in Karratha.

My wife is Aboriginal, she comes from Moora, a Yamitji. They are a bit funny about being out of their country, but she mixes freely. But when we go places she is still a bit frightened, especially if they go to places of significance. They still believe that the bad things are going to jump on them because it's not their country.

I finished my primary school in East Perth and I went on to high school. It was for boys and I left halfway through the second year, as soon as I turned fourteen. In those days you were allowed to leave school at fourteen. I could have gone on to do wonderful things. I was told by the headmaster that I would have made an excellent accountant. But in those days, you had to know somebody who could get you into accountancy. We didn't have those sorts of contacts.

In those days there was plenty of work around for young blokes straight out of school. I started off working with my brother in a timber mill just up the road from us in Charles Street. The Tower Hotel was on the corner. The old fella next door had a little bit of a timber yard at the back and I worked there for about a year and a half. Then I left and went and worked for an old fella in a nursery.

At this time we'd moved to West Perth. I left school in 1959. We were there only for a short while and got our first State Housing house in Barney Street, Glendalough. Later, I was the last member of the family to live in that house. We lived there until 1986.

Once we were in that house in West Perth, Mum set it up as a halfway house for the kids coming out of Sister Kate's. There was a need which she saw. Kids coming out of Sister Kate's had nowhere to go when they turned fourteen or they finished high school, because then they had to get out.

Not far from us, on the corner of Fitzgerald and Carr Streets, was a place called McDonald house. McDonald house is part of the Aboriginal history. They taught the kids, in a TAFE type situation, to do things like bookkeeping, accounting, etc. It was the first sort of Aboriginal access in Perth. There were limited numbers of kids getting places there, so mum set up this halfway house. No government funding, just did it on her own bat. The kids who wanted to get into there came and stayed at our place. We had a big four-bedroom house. Mum put beds in, about four or five kids in each room like a little dormitory set up.

Bunurrunna (Mount Bruce), a place of significance for Aboriginal people, in the Karijini National Park.

They stayed with us. There was plenty of work around so they were able to support themselves and they had a place to come home to, three meals a day or prepared lunches. Then as places became available in McDonald house they went there and they were able to go on with schooling. That worked really well. Mum certainly made use of her time.

I worked for timber mills making things like fruit cases. I also worked in a brass founders and engineers. I've worked for a nursery, worked manufacturing spinning cast iron pipes and at Humes making concrete pipes and steel pipes. And while I was at Humes we made towers for the North West Cape.

I left Humes and went to the Water Authority where I worked for about two or three years. In about 1967 I came north for nine months contracting in earthworks building the coastal highway with Caratti Contractors.

When I went back home I got a job with Armstrong Nylex. They were the only people in WA at the time making crayfishing floats and styrene foam products. I worked for them for about two or three years until Nylex decided to sell the styrene foam. They did a lot of work using the styrene foam as insulation in walls for transportable housing on north-west projects.

Then I left there and went working part-time on the wheat bins. Every year they would start off about May. We'd bituminise wheat bins right throughout the wheat-belt area, the wheat silos. I did that for a few years, together with other part-time jobs, until October 1970 when I had a truck accident and broke my collarbone. I was driving and the truck rolled over. After I recovered I started with the Water Authority. I worked with the Water Authority right up to 1979 as a gang worker, then I graduated to service layer grade one, which is probably the highest level you can get on the trucks. The job was for two men who would put the water on for all the houses, repair burst mains and such things. I was in the water maintenance section.

In 1979 I started with another earthmoving bloke using scrapers, a bit of an old rogue, I worked with him for about a year or so. I used to come from Perth, all the way up to Shark Bay.

After this I went back to school, I went back to TAFE. This was 1982 and I was thirty-seven years old. I did the access course at Balga Tech College and I did really well. I also had a go at mature age matriculation but didn't do good.

The following year I went to Leederville Tech. I wanted to do accounting, something I'd always wanted. I went down there and had a go but it's something that you have got to be able to do every day. I surprised myself, I could do it, but I couldn't do it when they put me under an examination. I had a young bloke give me lessons after school. He'd give me all these little problems and I would sit down and do them. And he'd say, 'I can't understand why you can't do accounting, you've got it all right the first time.' There must have been something there that just didn't allow me to get it all together. I used to stumble through it at school.

I went back to education because I could see there were a lot of things happening in Aboriginal affairs. Our family had been involved in Aboriginal affairs for many years, doing all sorts of things. But we were never in a place, or able to get into a place, where you could really do something. I've always been involved with Aboriginal affairs from as far back as 1956. I thought what was needed was to change the situation where if you were a blackfella you were getting the job, to one where you were going to get the job because you had the education to back you up. I got a Year Twelve level of education. I'd done maths 1A, computers 1A, economics, all of those sorts of subjects that go towards accounting.

When I finished at college I worked for Stirling Council as a swimming pool manager. I'm probably still the only Aboriginal registered as a qualified pool manager. There has been a pool finally built at Roebourne. It should be run by the Aboriginal people of the town on behalf of the town's residents.

I managed the Balga pool. At that pool there were big problems; the non-Aboriginals just couldn't handle the black kids. It was a lack of understanding by the management. When I went there I got all the kids together and said, 'I'm a blackfella and I'm managing this pool. This is your pool as well as mine.' I told the kids that you got to accept the pool regulations. 'I won't throw you out unless you misbehave. I'll throw you out, Aboriginal or non-Aboriginal, just as quick. You've got to do the right thing.' Before this everybody that got thrown out was either black, or mid in-between colours and they went for things like running around, silly things, fighting in the pool, jumping in the water, dangerous things. The management didn't understand how to handle the kids. I think I finished the second season in this job. I would have lasted about a year.

When I left the pool I went and registered at the CES. They knew I had achieved Year Twelve and my other qualifications. At the time the Department of Employment, Education and Training (DEET) was trying to recruit Aboriginal people with education levels into the Public Service. I was offered a job as a health surveyor with the Swan Shire. I decided to accept. I was told that someone already had the job but they bombed out.

So I did all the interviews with the town clerk. Everything was going to be hunky dory. I went in and had an interview with the vocational officer who was responsible for the employment. About the job he said, 'Look, seventeen guys graduated last year, five are in the country, the other twelve are unemployed. At the end of the training there is no guarantee that you will have a job with the Swan Shire. They are offering the position as a training situation. But if you are interested in joining the Public Service you can start with us next week.' I said, 'That will bloody well do me.'

I signed all the papers there and then. That's how I got into the Public Service. But I didn't start as a health surveyor, I started as field officer, Aboriginal Employment Training branch. I started in Perth and I did my initial training at Innaloo CES. This was in July 1984. I was still working in the public service with DEET in 1992. In the meantime my employment had changed from Perth to Karratha in the Pilbara. I started at Karratha in December 1988.

The work in Karratha was different to that in Perth. There were opportunities for Aboriginal people but it was more. We were trying to get as many people as we could working for our own, so to speak, like the Ngurin Centre at Roebourne and places like that. Trying to get expertise and more training and developing positions. I learnt very, very quickly that the wider community wasn't accessible to Aboriginal people.

In the Pilbara they started a thing called REDSA, Roebourne Employment Development Scheme for Aboriginals. The committee that ran REDSA was comprised of all the bigwigs from Hamersley Iron, Woodside Petroleum, Robe River Iron, CES, the Rotarians and bloomin' business commercial mob. They all sat down and were going to do all these wonderful things for Aboriginal people.

After twelve months of attending these committees with the manager I could see it was just a 'mickey mouse' outfit. It was just a group of non-Aboriginals sitting down discussing what they were going do for Aboriginal people and nothing really happening. When you got right down to it, the amount of employment they offered was almost nothing. Out of six apprenticeships there were two positions available for Aboriginals if the Aboriginals were lucky enough to get any of the pre-apprenticeship positions offered the year before and successfully completed them. Many a time they bombed out. Not of their fault, but for cultural reasons.

Huge cultural differences existed. The cultural shock must have been massive for the guys to come straight out of Roebourne and into industrial enterprises like Woodside gas production and Hamersley iron ore mining.

The main target of DEET when it was up here was a special section called Training for Aboriginal Programs and the program was very,

very flexible. We could put Aboriginal people in anywhere they wanted to work as long as the employer was prepared to give them a fair go. They would be subsidised to the point where they became productive.

The employer was subsidised until the person was productive. Too many times in the past they spent a lot of money on short training schemes and the people got nothing out of them. But as we got more and more focussed on longer training periods and tapering off subsidies, we did better. For instance the guy walks through the door who will employ and train workers. In the first three months we subsidise him for 100%. He doesn't produce anything because he doesn't know what he is doing.

After three months we assume he was productive at least fifteen per cent, so we would reduce the subsidy by fifteen per cent. And that would carry on (if it was a trade) until the end of the trade course. At the end of the fourth year he'd only receive twenty-five per cent subsidy, because at the end of that time he would be a qualified tradesman and one hundred per cent productive.

Trades Assistants (TAs) would do much the same but on a twelve months period because only basic skills have to be learnt. At the end of a twelve month period that person would be productive enough to say this person is a TA.

We focussed on those types of areas to skill people. But the reality of it was that even with this assistance to employers there are many employers who jumped in for the money. At the end of the money, they had an extra hand at no expense, then they got rid of the Aboriginal person. Some of that is tied up with cultural problems. The Aboriginal people were getting little out of it. They got some skills but they got a bad taste of what some white people are on about.

I kept insisting that the department create a resource centre in the Pilbara. It could be the activity hub for community groups. The Ngarin Aboriginal Resource Centre at Roebourne started to operate in 1985. Unfortunately it didn't work effectively because of family favouritism and no management expertise in its leadership. It has failed to generate complete community support. It should have been very successful.

A lot of courses were run on a short-term basis. But a lot of the problems that the DEET programs had was due to the fact that they were designed in Perth for Perth and didn't work in the Pilbara. In the end we refused to send people to some programs. To give an example: a person on this particular program would receive unemployment benefit plus some school money 'on top' every fortnight. The program ran for thirteen weeks. It was six weeks before the students got their first pay. When they got the pay it was only ten dollars more than the unemployment benefit. By the time people received their first pay the scheme was down to about four or five people. The rest had withdrawn. The cost of living in the Pilbara is very high. I tried to shorten the thing up through my department but it just wasn't possible.

Yet, there are some good examples of Aboriginal training. Brendon Cooke did his boilermaker apprenticeship through DEET. There's young Kevin Guiness, he's a qualified motor mechanic. He did his apprenticeship at Dampier Salt. Aboriginal Employment and Training Branch (AETB) of DEET subsidised the employers in those training programs.

Company attitudes are often not always ideal. One miner set up a hostel there for the boys to stay during the week while they work in the area. But real jobs ... ! There is the one young Islander boy for instance, worked for Hamersley, finished his apprenticeship as a fitter and turner and turned out a very good tradesman. He was unemployed for about a year because at the end of the trade they kick the apprentices out. He applied for a job back with Hamersley. They interviewed him and offered him a job as a Trades Assistant, after he had become a fully qualified fitter and turner. And do you know the manager of the CES said, 'At least he's got a job.' I said, 'Yes but look, we subsidised that company for four years, so that he could become a tradesman, now they've got the cheek to offer him a Trades Assistant's job.' We've got more qualified Aboriginal apprentices unemployed than any other bloody race.

I'm now the coordinator for the Community Development Employment Program (CDEP) in Roebourne.

In the Roebourne community there are 103 Aboriginal people involved in the Community Development Employment Program (CDEP). It is a town-based program. There was one non-Aboriginal fella but he finished up on Friday. He was on the program because of his expertise. He had a B-class licence and he was able to teach people to drive and he was good support.

The people in the scheme undertake tasks which non-Aboriginal people wouldn't consider as work. But we work in the framework of Aboriginal culture and so we do things that are necessary for its survival. The work therefore involves things like we shoot kangaroos on Tuesday night and go around the village houses and give the residents a kangaroo. We collect wood and drop it off in the village so that people can cook on outside fires. We clean up the houses, yards, mow the lawns, prune the trees, keep the places looking neat and tidy. You could say it was a gardening service, but for us, it's a service that the people have never been able to afford. There was only those few with vehicles who were able to keep their yards neat and tidy. Now there is no reason why everybody can't have their yard neat and tidy.

Ngurin has got its own mob. They had about ten or twelve people to a proper camp out at Kurrabunya, a community cultural group. They are not able to live there simply because the infrastructure is not in place. I'm doing a budget for them now for the power supply. Then they will be able to live there. This will enable them to be more self-sufficient and develop the Aboriginal cultural enhancement programs, both in dance and in artefacts.

The main CDEP work force comes from the town itself and we have considerable capital equipment, backhoes, graders, tip trucks, front-end loaders, lawn-mowing gear and mobile welding outfits. This means that our people are learning new skills in the operation of this equipment while improving their own and the villagers' lives.

All the machinery requires operation by persons with B-class licences. There are only two guys, that I can rely upon, with the B-class licence. There is a bus that has to have a B-class licence driver and two trucks and a backhoe have to have a B-class. At the moment I've only got two guys who actually can use the machinery as well, about four or five women want to get B-class drivers licences. They should get licences next week. They are excited and I am pleased because we'll sort out some problems. My understanding of women's ability, from available information is that they make the best drivers because, first of all they are not 'lairs' and don't smash the machinery and also they appreciate danger enough to be careful.

Most of the training for the CDEP is done by Pundulmurra College. They train for plant machine operators which includes A- and B-class drivers licences.

179

Kalamina Gorge, Karijini National Park.

LORRAINE INJIE

Birth Date: 18 April 1962
Birth Place: Onslow
Tribal Group: Yinhawangka
Skin Group: Milangka

> *Different types of programs are suitable ... Aboriginal*
> *language maintenance, language awareness, language*
> *revival and retrieval and literacy.*

My mother is Joyce Injie and my father was Joe Injie. I was born in the old Onslow Hospital in 1962. We lived on the reserve where Bindi Bindi is now. Back then there were a total of eight houses on the reserve. The houses only had two bedrooms, which were separated by a kitchen with a wood stove. There was no running water in the houses, you had to get water from a tap outside. Some Thalanyji people, like auntie Rosey Campbell and Dora Hicks, lived on the reserve. And there was auntie Maudie Dowton's family, who are Binikura. There were also Yinhawangka, Punjima and Kurrama people who had moved on to the coast from the Hamersley Ranges.

Before I started going to school we lived wherever my father was working. He owned a truck and we lived on its back section, even when we went to town, because there weren't many houses. There was Mum, Dad, brother Ken, sister Tina, me and a younger brother who died of gastroenteritis in October 1968. He died when I was in Carnarvon hospital after being hit by a motor car. They flew me down there by Royal Flying Doctor Service and my whole family came down to see me. They came in the truck and he got sick. The roads were in poor condition and it took ages for them to get there and it was the beginning of summer. My brother was only a couple of months old.

We used the truck for everything. Every Christmas it was used to take people to and from the Cane River where we held ceremonies and it was used to travel to stations and my dad used it for droving.

My dad worked at Duck Creek (Kardajirrinha), Mount Stuart, Wyloo, Minderoo and Rocklea (Jarrungkajarrungka). When I was growing up and had to attend school, the family lived on the reserve, but my dad still worked on the stations.

I first went to pre-school in an old tin shelter. It was right on the edge of the Onslow Caravan Park and we would walk there and back every morning. Then I started school and lived in the hostel for two years. After the car accident Mum took me out of the hostel and I went to school from the reserve. One of the things I remember most about the hostel was that if we didn't eat the vegetables we would get hit on the leg with a wooden spoon and nearly all of us couldn't eat our vegetables. I used to throw up after eating cabbage. (Back then vegies from the shop were not a big part of our diet at home.) Instead, we must have eaten or tried to eat all of the seeds we came across.

In 1973 I started high school at South Hedland and lived in the Moorgunyah Hostel. In 1976 I went to Perth to finish my schooling and my first year of teaching at Mount Lawley Teacher's College. I deferred my studies when we had bad luck and graduated in 1988. My dad died while I was in Perth so I came back home to Mum and my family.

In the intervening years I married Reynold Martin. We have one child, a little boy, Aaron. I also commenced to work in Port Hedland, first with Wangka Maya, the Pilbara Aboriginal Language Centre, as an Aboriginal Language worker. There I worked on an oral history project and taught in the Language Awareness Program at the South Hedland Senior High School. I also did in-service courses on Aboriginal cultural issues for non-Aboriginal people, mainly teachers for their professional development and especially those at the Pundulmurra Aboriginal College at South Hedland. It is unfortunately true that government and other organisations who are interacting with Aboriginal people all of the time do not use the services of Wangka Maya to assist the delivery of their service to the Aboriginal community. The health, community development, welfare, police and legal systems would have some need of this service.

The work at Wangka Maya was rewarding and I received training there that would otherwise not have been available to me. It was the linguists with whom I worked, that provided me with that training in linguistic terminology and application and which gave me a good grounding for my current work with Pundulmurra.

My job with Pundulmurra is coordinator of Aboriginal language programs, training people to run their own language programs in their own communities and to develop resources and record their own languages. There are different types of programs which are suitable for different communities and language situations. These language programs are language maintenance, language awareness, language revival and retrieval and literacy.

Language maintenance programs are best suited to those situations where children use an Aboriginal language but mainly speak English. What happens today is that kids might learn their own language at home but when they get to school they lose it and as they spend more time at school and more time away from their communities, they lose more and more of the language they had first learnt at home. That happened to many of us, we grew up speaking English as a second language. Even though we don't speak our own language as fluently today as those people who did not go away from their communities, we have been able to maintain a lot of our first language.

Language awareness programs are used in those situations where kids don't speak or understand an Aboriginal language, but are able to relate or identify with a particular Aboriginal language. This is the type of program that Sue Smythe and I have been working with at the South Hedland High School. We talk to kids about the traditional locations of Pilbara languages, the language situation as it exists today, how the orthography has been developed and the sound systems of Aboriginal languages.

Language retrieval programs are for those situations where kids only speak part of an Aboriginal language, might understand some, but speak English a lot. At Pundulmurra we have many people who come in whose parents did not teach them to speak their language fluently. Some of them would have been beaten by non-Aboriginal people, missionaries, hostel supervisors, station managers etc if they were speaking the language. Such people now come because they now have an urgent personal interest, or there is a general community interest, for the language to be spoken again. We work with such people to develop their programs and strategies for teaching the language to the kids. They identify the gaps in their own language, ie, what they have lost and what they need to record immediately. Then we encourage them to use the language, so they develop resources in their own language.

Literacy programs are used in the situation where children speak the language fluently and they use it every day. It is in these situations that they are able to learn to read and write in their own language within a short space of time. Of the traditional languages in the Pilbara only some are strong, others are threatened or weak and dying, while a few are extinct. The strong languages are those which have up to a thousand people who can speak them, the others have less than five hundred people and some have only a handful of old people who can speak them.

Nyangumarta is one of the Pilbara's strong languages. It is one of the desert languages and it is the one spoken by people from the Strelley communities. Manyjiljarra or Martu Wangka, another desert language, would be the next widely spoken language, then Yindjibarndi and Punjima. There are no fluent speakers of Yinhawangka, most of the Yinhawangka people are speaking Punjima and/or Yindjibarndi. Other languages like Nyamal, Ngarla, Martuthunira and Dhalanyji are spoken fluently by older people, but the kids are not learning these languages, which is really the test of language use.

To revive Aboriginal language use we have to look at the school system. The school system has had the greatest detrimental effect upon our languages. The pressure is on kids to speak good English in school. If there were programs and strategies to counterbalance this then more people would speak their language. Where kids have had a solid first language education in the home before they went to school, the effect of Aboriginal language loss from schooling is minimised. But this is not happening. They are not being taught at home in those pre-school years. So because they do not have their own language before they come to school they find difficulty in picking it up when they are at school, because they are not hearing it.

Television has had a detrimental effect as well. The lack of TV is a factor in the northern languages being retained. Even Mum would say today that she has forgotten things because she's been watching TV. Television should have programs to assist language development and maintenance.

I prefer the terminology 'language group' as against 'tribal group' because it indicates that the person is a member of a group which spoke that language, whether or not the language exists today.

JULIE TOMMY

Birth Date: 1959
Birth Place: Roebourne
Tribal Group: Yinhawangka
Skin Group: Burungu

Society is compensating Aboriginal men by giving them the bloody dole cheque and grog and bullshitting about land rights ... And never giving work.

I am thirty-three years old. My mother is Mabel Tommy, a Yinhawangka elder. My father died when I was twelve. He was a Yinhawangka, born in the Tom Price area at that hill they call Nyimirli. That's my father now, that hill out near Tom Price.

I would like to talk a bit about my father because I honestly believe that I wouldn't have been able to accomplish the little things that I have, without what he told me, you know. Unfortunately, he died when we were young. But he would just listen to me with a lot of thoughts. I mean, even now, it is really painful for me to talk about him because he really was a spiritual person. He was a leader. And I get a lot of respect, not because what I have done, but because of what he was. I have been to Western Desert communities and if I mention his name, or his country, they always sort of give me a second look. You can sense that there was something about him. I suppose they often wonder if I got anything of what he had. I don't think I have but I like to think that he gave me good direction.

I feel that one of the things he left behind was his legacy and if he wasn't that particular type of person, I wouldn't be the way I am now. You will find the same thing if you talk to my mum, especially as he was an old man and she was only a young woman when she was given away to him. But, you listen to the way she talks about him, all she can do is admire the man and that's all I can do.

185

I have a twin brother, a younger sister and an older sister. There are four of us.

As a child I lived on Onslow reserve. There were quite a few people who lived there then. I lived with Mum for a while until I was about three or four and she left and went with my uncle dad. He died too, but she went out to Mulgul Station. So I lived with my brother and my father and my grandmother in a tent on the Onslow reserve. My younger sister was with my mum and the older sister was away in Derby. I lived there until I went to school and then went to the Gilliamia Hostel to live. But holiday time I would come back and stay with my grandmother and father. These were the days before there were houses on the reserve. But despite the fact that the reserve was only just up the road, you couldn't visit unless it was a Sunday or holidays.

I went right through primary school at Onslow. Then I went to high school in South Hedland because that was the thing at the time. We stayed in Moorgunyah Hostel. I did five years of high school at South Hedland. I was the only black kid in Year Twelve. One of the first, I think, to do Year Twelve and certainly the first one to go from Year Twelve to Curtin University, because that's where I finally ended up.

Looking back I think I was either naive, or unknowing, because I never felt I was any different to the other kids. Certainly that was the situation while I was in Hedland anyway. I never felt that I was any different.

I was an achiever in the class and this made working easier for me. I was certainly not looked down on. It wasn't an issue for me. Perhaps my involvement in studies and that I was advanced in those studies, was an accepted evidence of intellectual equality, to say the least. I think if I was doing badly at school it would have been more of an issue, you know what I mean?

I received a degree at Curtin University in social sciences. But I didn't start off in social science. I got into social work for two years, then changed to social science. This meant that I had to put in quite a bit of extra work. I not only swapped courses, but stopped mid-way and went to work in Aboriginal child care. I had started university in 1977 and it was in 1980 that I stopped my studies and went over to the Aboriginal Child Care Agency. I only had a few more units to do. But I stopped and went to work for a while, six years or something.

It was over ten years by the time I got around to finishing my degree. By then it was a case of have to, or they would have removed me from the course and I would have lost my course credits, I suppose. Of course this break in study was completely planned. You see, I had a baby son in 1978.

When I went down to Perth in 1977, I didn't want to be there, it was a really big cultural shock for me, right from the first moment. I don't know if it was the racism, but I really did feel different to everybody else, you know. It wasn't as if I was a Nor'wester and among Nyoongahs because there weren't too many Nyoongahs in the course. I just felt that I was really different to all the other students. Most of them were white students and I did really feel the difference.

It was when I went to Curtin Uni that I really felt my Aboriginality, when I first came across some of the paternalistic attitudes. Maybe it was academic kind of competition. I started to realise that I was an Aboriginal, studying. I felt the racism then, I think. Uni was a whole different way of life, I never had sat down and learnt with adults before. It was different to high school at Hedland, where there were other local kids, an Aboriginal peer group.

My starting a family began when I wanted to get out of studying in Perth. I didn't want to stay there. So I went to work with the Aboriginal Child Care Agency as a coordinator, a trainee coordinator initially and I stayed in that job for six years. It was a challenging job, it dealt with the issue of child removal from parents.

We dealt with two things. We would try to trace families who had children removed and trace children for parents who had lost their children. We were trying to relocate people. We were trying to push for changes to deal with this problem, the policy of child removal. I strongly believe that the Aboriginal Placement Principle in the Department of Community Services (DCS) came about because of the lobbying carried out. The principle was developed in the days of the Department of Aboriginal Affairs. The principle means that when an Aboriginal child comes into the care of DCS that attempts will be made to place the child within its known natural family. Failing that, they be placed with an Aboriginal caregiver, or if that is not possible then child be placed in an Aboriginal Hostel. The principle was a means of reducing the problem of identity crisis that had arisen in Aboriginal children.

My role at the time was to try and influence the Department's activity through discussing the shortcoming with key players in the system. Part of the problem was the egocentric attitude of some of its staff and also the lack of knowledge of Aboriginal culture by such people. These cases still keep coming because of the continued disintegration of culture and there is still the violence in communities. But it also has to do with the poverty of Aboriginal families and people.

Our existence as an agency, advocating changes in the way that Aboriginal people were treated by the welfare system, not just Aboriginal children but Aboriginal families, was very important to ensure that there was a process of change.

I had my son down in Perth. This bothered me because he was only a baby and I still had to go back to study. There was a lot of pressure on me to go back to study. To this day I consider that I must have been without any real direction, then. I always responded to what other people wanted me to do. I never really did anything for myself and I think to this day, if I had done something for myself I probably wouldn't have continued with the study and I probably would have stayed home with young Kirsten, because he was my baby.

As it turned out I put him into day care centres but that didn't work. I ended up putting him with Doreen Nelson, a friend and that was really good. I felt much happier because she was an Aboriginal woman with a licensed family care centre. Kirsten sort of fitted in because all her kids had grown up and were at school and he was the baby in the house. She had about six kids and he grew up within that Aboriginal type of child rearing system. When I would go and pick him up he would often be with one of the teenage daughters and they would take him into the shops and walk him. So they really looked after him. And he grew up in that household like that. To this day they still see him as family and they often ask about him.

My early history went like this: I went to university, then to work in the Aboriginal Child Care Agency. Then I came back to Onslow in 1986, married and proceeded to finish my studies externally. I graduated in 1989 by which time I had three kids.

In this period I started to work part-time at the Onslow Youth Centre. For a short while in 1987 I worked full-time, at the school, as an Aboriginal Education Officer while I was still studying for my degree.

When Adrian, my then husband, got that type of job in Karratha which is home territory, I applied for work with the Department for Community Services.

I see racism as a means of control. I just refer to work in the Department. There you are evaluating and trying to improve on your work performance and when you focus on that, that's when you see so many of the subtleties. It's almost like a conspiracy to control people. I read an article about internal pressure, internal racism and I think that's what it is, it's about controlling people.

The sort of practices that really bug me are those which exploit the Aboriginal people, their knowledge and customs. I have been subject to this practice myself, in my ignorance. Some people, particularly those responsible to develop Department policy, seek information about our culture and our way of life. This they store and use. And they are glorified for their use of this information in policy, or program. They don't ever state the source of their information. There is no credit to the Aboriginal people for this cultural material. We are victims of white paternalism. That happens constantly over and over again. I get frustrated and angry about it. But I can't communicate that message to the other people. I can't communicate with them because they don't see what is so wrong with it. They can't understand it and that is where it becomes really frustrating.

It's like when we did work with the Aboriginal People's Package. I did like the content of this package; the 1905 Native Welfare Act; the roots of some DCS practices; and the links to the past ration days by today's food voucher system. I did not like the way it was implemented. Nobody else but Aboriginal people can present that package. The package is not a training package that gives out information, but a structure that extracts information from you as an Aboriginal trainer. We become trainers of the non-Aboriginal staff and in that process must divulge intimate matters of our lives to make the necessary impact about our culture and of cultural differences. At the end of the day what has happened is that Aboriginal people have given personal information to other people about themselves. I find that quite exploitative. But the system doesn't. Its spokespersons say it is a training package. We who train are not seen as distinct from the package. There is something wrong with their approach and in the end it results in Aboriginalising the Department only to the extent of having more Aboriginal workers

189

and does not ensure that there is cultural equality in the workplace.

The policy and the practices haven't changed. At the end of the day you just get black people delivering a white middle-class service that is just as oppressive as it was when the white people were delivering it. That is why I have come from this phase completely disillusioned and have decided that I am not going to stay here. It might be another year because I'm involved in a program which I think will benefit Aboriginal people, if it ever eventuates. But I've decided that I would rather be on a pension and at home, being poor black, than working as an exploited black. It is demeaning. They take part of you, put their stamp on it and use it and you've lost control of your own bloody self!

Well, I won't give them any more information. It is not my information for a start. A lot of the knowledge I get is from my involvement with my own people, part of my own family and my own network. I don't have complete ownership over that information. I get it from other people.

I have told one other Aboriginal worker in the Department of my problem and she understands. I just said to her, well, I have to leave, because I feel if I don't leave I will lose control. It is not so much oppression, it's more like a threat. I feel like if I don't get out, they'll have me. They will be able to control me and I can't allow them to do that. I have always really been secure enough to be able to say, 'I don't need this job and I don't need to be treated like this and this job is not worth it.' You know, I could walk.

I always have that ability to be able to walk and go for other options. I've been unemployed and I've been on Social Security and that is not such an issue for me, because I believe I have more control of my situation. I'm not letting myself be exploited or used in a way that is not acceptable to me. That is what I want for my kids, to be able to feel secure enough.

One of my problems is that I have been prepared to battle, in my life, on the basis that the kids could later reap the rewards. But I can now see the kids having to take that same struggle on. I am aware that I have felt really disillusioned, primarily with work. I think that the disillusion may be like a bit of panic, you know. Like with my older son who is fifteen and going to be leaving school shortly and there is no hope for him. I mean you don't want them to get that message, but just tell them the only way they're going to get equality is to have to jump into the struggle. As a mother you prevent your kids from having to go through the pain and anger and the struggle you have had to go through. That is why you go through that. But all you are doing at the end of the day is just playing the game, so that they can come and play it and hopefully play a bit better.

A part of the problem is that social things have changed. Issues of racism, land and injustice, were blatant in my time. It was easy to have a purpose and with the Equal Opportunity Act you had a vision of getting legal equality to address issues. Now the rules haven't changed, there is still racism and justice issues, but it is all subtle stuff, what they call covert or hidden racism. That is harder to deal with. Like with my kids, that's what the struggle will be for them. I don't consider myself young if you look at the lifespan of Aboriginal people, fifty, sixty and I'm over the halfway mark now.

So you see the effects of the Equal Opportunity Act or Racial Discrimination Act 1975 have, in a way, pushed the open racism underground. And I think there is more discrimination now that

Cloud reflections in a rock pool, Karijini National Park.

racism is more subtle. I find this disillusioning because it just means that the kids will inherit the same struggle. It is not as if they are going to be equal. I mean you don't mind being part of the struggle if at the end of the day at least somebody is going to benefit, your kids or somebody. But I firmly believe my kids are going to have to continue with the struggle.

I went to Roebourne and applied for a job as a graduate welfare officer with Community Services. I suppose I worked there for over twelve months and then applied for a team leader's position. I did that for another twelve months in Roebourne.

I must say that I like Roebourne. I think the people in Roebourne are really worthy people. I won't say they are happy people, though some of them are. But they always appreciate other people, or they can see the worth in other people, I reckon.

I never really come across somebody that I didn't like in Roebourne, or somebody that didn't like me. Something about Roebourne gets to you. They criticise you, but not so much you, they criticise your behaviour if you haven't done something acceptable. But, in the long term, they always accept you as a person. I don't know what it is, but it is the only community that I got to know in that way.

Aboriginal families are the greatest resource Aboriginal people have. Our ability to care for our sick, aged, disabled, young, old, is one of the special qualities our family offers and Aboriginal people have that quality. I believe that we have to preserve the values our .Aboriginal families teach us. I have always been interested in that area because I feel that is the way to salvation. If you are going to survive then our families have to survive.

The work of the unit I am involved in is one of the divisions to empower Aboriginal families. To enable them to deal with those sorts of issues that are destructive and dysfunctional, but which regularly invade our family life. I think people have to understand that child abuse and domestic violence are elements of the violent confrontation we've had with the white invaders of our country. We've had that for years. This is just another form of that violence. I'm hoping if this program gets off the ground, we will be able to focus on where the violence is coming from and for people to understand that. At this stage people don't understand it. Some people have the feminist idea about men controlling women and that is how it is, they abuse their children and their wives in order to retain power. I find that hard to accept because in Aboriginal culture, Aboriginal women certainly had far more power than did their white counterparts, their white sisters. If you listen to old Aboriginal women, you know by the stories they tell, that they must have had considerably more economic and social power than white women at that age. I mean this is shown by a look at Aboriginal history and culture.

The situation of Aboriginal women's power in modern times may seem to have changed. I think it is as diverse as Aboriginal culture itself. I've certainly been in Aboriginal communities where you go in believing that it is the chairman you speak to. But what is revealed is that the chairperson is the person up front. The directions and information he passes on is coming from a group of women.

Certainly, there are men, particularly young Aboriginal men, who have adopted a more controlling presence. But even with them I think it's in part a symptom of their frustration and the lack of respect given to Aboriginal men generally in society. But there has been a change in the gender relationships in Aboriginal society. Aspects of this change relate to the numbers of our men who are in pubs and in jail. And on other hand, that more Aboriginal women are employed. This situation empowers the women.

I would have thought that the social welfare state efforts to break down culture by giving 'sit down money' and the easy access to grog, instead of giving jobs, has led men right off the 'straight and narrow'. But in a sense it has empowered women.

And it's not so much the giving, it's what is taken away in return that is the problem. If you gave Aboriginal men alcohol and didn't strip away their pride and dignity, then they wouldn't be as abusive, the alcohol abuse wouldn't be as dominant as it is. I think that is what has happened. They have stripped people of their pride and dignity and their culture. They have taken their land off them and instead they have been given money, social security and alcohol. This society is compensating Aboriginal men in particular, by giving them the bloody dole cheque and grog and bullshitting about land rights and never ever giving them. And never giving work. I mean that's it, they are destroying them and they are also destroying the young white generation by not giving them jobs either.

193

Sometimes I think that it is a conspiracy to finally rid the land of Aboriginal people. They can't go on with the traditional massacres and murder of people. But giving will eventually kill them and that is a medical fact, it will kill them.

So the trend of Aboriginal deaths goes on without abatement and without the widespread social anger that forces a change. That is what I mean about the subtlety. It is not as blatant as in the past. We can run off to the Human Rights Commission if there was a massacre. But we can't do that because the alcohol and the violence is seen as being self-inflicted. Not something introduced into the Aboriginal community and not part of a process of denying people's rights.

I was involved in an equal opportunity case in 1986. I walked in to the Onslow pub, to the so-called 'white bar', with Adrian another member of the local Aboriginal community. The bar was segregated by tacit understanding. No sign said 'This is a black bar' or 'This is a white bar'. But everybody knows it is there, like a convention.

On that night I walked in with Adrian and I sat up at the 'white bar'. I wanted to order some drinks. I waited for about thirty minutes to be served. Finally I said to the barmaid, 'Excuse me, can I have some drinks?' She turned and said, 'Oh sorry, if you want drinks you have to go on the other side.' I said to her, 'Well you can't do this to us, what is that supposed to mean?' She explained that because I mixed and socialised with the other people from Bindi Bindi (Aboriginal village), I had to go into the other bar because somehow I didn't have membership to the white bar, because I mix and mingle with the undesirables, in the establishment's eyes. That is their words.

Well, I said, no, I wasn't going to go back to the other side, this was a discriminatory practice. That wasn't the end of the matter, I would take this to the Equal Opportunity Commission and I made some comment about she ought to go and live in South Africa where they actually shoot blacks (this was during the apartheid era). I was angry and indignant. The bar attendant said that she was only following rules.

I refused to leave the 'white bar' but Katie Drummond, an Onslow friend, came to my defence. As a result the attendant decided to serve Adrian as he was a pub regular, but not me. So Adrian bought my drink. Adrian could be served in the 'white bar' because he mixed and mingled with these whites there. I didn't, I mixed with the 'derelicts and delinquents' and the 'no-hopers'. Therefore I couldn't be served.

This is the pub club mentality which justifies the discrimination against Aboriginal people. Only those who mingled with the 'desirables' could always get served. It was a type of class system which gives 'privileges' to certain blacks and breeds the racist practice which divides our people, trying to turn them against each other.

I put my complaint in to the Equal Opportunity Commission. It wasn't until 1989 that the case came on. I had filed the complaint in 1986. The fact that it took three years was disappointing. And it took a lot of persistence from me. At times I was at loggerheads with the Equal Opportunity Commission and its officers because it was so frustrating, it really was. I felt that I had done all of the work in bringing the case on. Then the Equal Opportunity Commission believed that the proper process was through conciliation and because of this approach they sought information on other complaints. So additional emotional and personal involvement, tension and frustration ensued.

My girlfriend, May Hubert, put in a complaint. It didn't happen to her personally but she could reinforce what had happened in my case about the black and white bars. She went through a conciliation process with them twice. We were told that the publican agreed to making changes, more equitable services to both bars and not restricting access.

Those things were breached time and time again and I had to ring up the Commission and tell them, hey look, they're not doing this or they haven't done that or these things weren't happening. I really did push it, but nothing eventuated. So in the end I said, 'Well, let's just go for the Industrial Tribunal, let's take it to the Tribunal instead of pussyfooting around the countryside.'

I was reasonably confident that I had a case and on top of that I had my girlfriend's complaint. Also that same night Marianne Tucker (another local) was told the same thing. She was told that if she wanted to get service she had to go in the other bar. Wobby Parker was told the same thing and so was his wife Lena. I had these witnesses. The Equal Opportunity advised me that these other people should lodge claims of discrimination and that their claims could also be heard. If the publican was found guilty he would have to settle all claims.

At the last possible minute I got a phone call saying that the publican was prepared to settle out of Court and there was no need for us to go before the Tribunal. I think he settled because he would have been convicted of discrimination, which would have been a bad mark on his record forever. The complaint was for unlawful discrimination on the basis of race, but it seemed very difficult for me to win. I think the Act is lacking in real power.

I felt the Equal Opportunity was really pushing the conciliation of the parties even though I was a victim. I felt that as I'm the one that had been treated badly, why should I reconcile with discrimination? To this day, I think one of the unfortunate things about the Equal Opportunity Commission is that conciliation focus.

If I hadn't a social conscience then it may have been beyond me to persevere with this case. People today say I'm aggressive. But when I was younger I was a lot more aggressive. So a typical Aboriginal person on the streets probably wouldn't take on this sort of case, even though they were discriminated against. They would have given up before the three years wait, let alone the hassle involved.

This is not a criticism of the legal officers. It is a criticism of the system which is needing an overhaul if it is really going to deal with racism. I was fortunate that at the end of the day I did get some benefit. But if people went through that process and got no reward, it would be very bad. It does not encourage socially responsible action.

I don't think Onslow has changed much since 1986. In fact I think it has deteriorated in terms of its service to people, not just with the 'Aboriginal black bar' but even with the other side of the bar in the sense of the service it provides.

I know a lot of Aboriginal people became chronic alcoholics. But it was the pub socialising that was attractive. You could go and socialise and mix, that's certainly what I used it for. I've never been a person to want to go and get drunk, but I certainly like mixing and mingling with people, especially my family and friends, they are important.

SUZANNE PARKER

Birth Date : 6 January 1953
Birth Place: Port Hedland
Tribal Group: Punjima
Skin Group: Milangka

Nobody has ever talked to me about the sort of work I would like, or what I might be suited for.

Queenie Yuline is my mother and Wobby Parker is my father. I was born in Port Hedland Hospital in the period when my mum and dad were working at Marillana Station. Mum flew to Hedland to have me. We lived on Marillana Station throughout my early childhood. Then Dad had two wives, mum Queenie and mum Lola and they all lived together for a time. Mum Queenie wanted her freedom and she moved out. She wanted to take me with her but Wobby wouldn't let go of me. So I was brought up by mum Lola and Wobby. All of this happened when I was just a very little child. It was not until I had completed my high school days that I found out that my blood mother was Queenie. It was Lola who told me. It was a real surprise to me and I didn't really want to accept it. I wondered what mum Lola was telling me. From then on I'd go on holidays with mum Queenie's family to get to know her more. Today she lives with me in Karratha. I care for her here. I really love my dad. He was there for me all that time.

I went to early schooling at Nullagine, finished my primary at Onslow and my secondary at Derby Junior High. I stayed two years at Derby then got homesick, it was about a thousand kilometres from home. There were other kids from Onslow and Roebourne at Derby so I had friends at school. I think Derby is too far away from home. I stayed at the hostel when I did my primary at Onslow.

After I left school I lived with Dad and mum Lola at the Nanutarra Station. I stayed there and then got a job at the house cleaning. When I was at school I had no idea what might happen to me later. Lola and Wobby were very strict in my upbringing. No going out with boys until I was at least seventeen. My father Wobby and my mothers were all very strong for the culture. On school holidays we would go to tribal ceremonies.

I learned about the most important cultural things from my grandmother, like skin groups, who we can marry and who we can't have any relations with. These things are rules of conduct for us and they still guide my life. Women of the same skin group we call sister, even if they may be an auntie.

Daisy Yuline was the one from Queenie's later husband's side of the family, from the Nyiyabarli tribe. She taught me a lot about Aboriginal dancing and who was my family on the mother's side. On the Punjima's side I got all of that information from mum Lola's mother, old nanna Dora Gilba. These things are still important to me as a woman now, because I've got to pass these things on to the young people. We try to teach the young ones even if they resist and go the non-Aboriginal way.

At Nanutarra Station there were three of us at the house. Margaret Parker, myself and the old girl, Ann Hayes' grandmother (Ann is married to Guy Parker) who passed on and Jim Roberts the yardman (he has passed on, too). I stayed there about two years, then I went to Hedland. I worked at the South Hedland kindergarten as an aide for a year. After that I found a fella and got married and lived at Wyndham for seven years. I had a daughter, Deborah. Since then I've worked at Mulga Downs, cooking, riding horses, station hand work. I liked that. I haven't worked since then, except for one week at the Pilbara conference last year. I've been living here in Karratha for the last six years. Deborah has two little kids, a boy and a girl, my grannies (grandchildren).

I've been to the college in Roebourne but I didn't really like it there. Then I tried at Karratha College at the start of last year. I didn't like that either; we were studying the same things I learnt at school. There was nothing new. We started on the Aboriginal Culture course but I didn't stick it out. I was sick. This year I started again and by the end of next year should have completed this preparatory course. What it will do for me is something I don't know anything about. I'll just have to wait until I'm finished before I know. I think that I would like to work in the community, but I don't think I'll get a job. There are fifteen of us in this class. One of the problems for me has been that nobody has ever sat down and talked to me about what sort of work I would like to do, or what I might be suited for. I have no idea about what I can do. I have no idea if there are jobs. People who know what jobs there are should come and talk to us and help us decide these matters.

I recently went on a trip to a women's meeting in the Western Desert. We were out there for a week, way out the back of Punmu. Aboriginal women came from everywhere. It was a great experience and I felt uplifted after it, but it's always the same when us sisters get together.

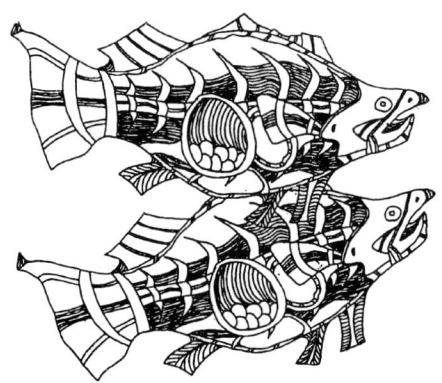

DARREN INJIE

Birth Date: 9 April 1968
Birth Place: Fremantle
Tribal Group: Yinhawangka
Skin Group: Karimarra

> *It's taboo to call someone's name once they have died.*
> *They couldn't refer to the house as Injie's. But we've got a*
> *lemon tree ... they called it 'the lemon tree'.*

I have spent most of my life with grandparents at Onslow in the North West. My mother is an Aboriginal woman, my father a whitefella. I don't know his name or anything about him. My mother now lives in Derby with my stepfather, brother and sisters.

The Onslow Hospital had been blown down by a cyclone in about 1967. As a result my mother had my birth at Fremantle, being one of the first local mothers to have a child born away. Today Onslow mothers go to Karratha, Hedland, Carnarvon or Perth. Onslow has a hospital but not a resident doctor.

I lived with my grandparents in Onslow until I was six years old and then I spent one year with my mum down in a small country town called Cadoux, near Wongan Hills. But I didn't like it there, I didn't like the cold and I didn't feel comfortable with my mother's other family. So when we came to Onslow for a holiday I refused to return with them. I convinced my grandfather to let me stay. I've considered this home ever since.

I did my primary schooling in Onslow and left to attend high school. I spent eight years in Perth living at a place called Kuta Kutu Hostel, in Mount Lawley. When I first arrived there was a group of five or six boys from this area and there was a group of girls in Cooinda Hostel around the corner. I spent five years at John Forrest Senior High School. I didn't like the first three years. Then I started to realise that I had to get serious about study. After high school I didn't go to university because I didn't have enough points and had to do a bridging course at WAIT (Western Australian Institute of Technology, now Curtin University). I passed at the end of the year and transferred to Edith Cowan Uni. I started doing a degree in Social Science and Behaviour Studies, with a double major.

For a while it was okay, but like all other country students, I ran out of time, energy, patience and had no money. To make matters worse I had a bust up with a girlfriend and was quite upset.

Finally I just said to myself, 'Well bugger it, I've been here too long, it's too cold.' Suddenly I realised I didn't even know the person next door. I was twenty years old when I stopped studying. I had completed two years and had eight units to go to finish. Getting back to my people in the Pilbara became more attractive than study.

I came back to my home district. I went up to South Hedland for a while. I had my twenty-first there and found a job with the Department of Community Development, now the Department of Social Development (DSD), as a District Officer. It didn't work out. I think the main reason seems to have been that I'd just finished eight years of studying where I had been constantly broke. This was the first time I'd ever got a job and had a wage coming in every fortnight and a car, it was too much. I think I just abused the whole thing. I couldn't handle it. It was a luxury out of the desert, so to speak. I lasted six months.

In all of my life I had grown up with having to walk down to the shop on a hot day to book up some food and then watch my grandmother go and work, work, work, to pay it back. At each pay day you are stuck in a cycle, you know — broke again. I recognised the problem years and years ago when I was a kid. I was never satisfied with that, living in poverty.

After the Hedland job I worked as a deckhand at sea, for two years. That's a totally different environment. I started working on a prawn trawler in 1989 and spent about eighteen months in Darwin.

Essentially I have lived in a town situation all of my life. I've never lived in the bush. Yet, despite this background I support a culture which is very much based on living a way of life in the bush. This is my old people's influence on me. I have had close relationships with the family elders all of my life.

I grew up in a little house called 'lemon tree'. Everybody knows it and that there is a lemon tree there. That's the Injie house in Onslow. That's where my grandmother Joyce lives and her extended family. She's lived there since 1971 when she moved from the old reserve and has been the backbone of our family. That's where I was brought up. The reason why they call it that is very much a matter of our Aboriginal culture. You see, my grandfather's name was Injie, that was his full name. The white people would call him 'Joe' Injie. They added the 'Joe' because that's white custom, but his name was Injie. The thing about Aboriginal law around here is that the Aboriginal people have only got one name. So the family then took his name, my aunties, uncles, nephews, nieces and of course myself.

It is also in our culture that we don't refer to the dead by their name. It's taboo to call someone's name once they have died. So when my grandfather died they couldn't refer to the house as Injie's because of the taboo. But because we've got a lemon tree in the backyard, it was referred to as the house with the lemon tree in the backyard for many years. Everybody knew where to come and get a lemon. Finally they just called it 'the lemon tree'. Some people still have a lot of respect for my grandfather. They even call to me, 'Lemon, come here.'

In this area when an Aboriginal person has died we do not say their name. We say kurnda to show respect for that person. If I talk about a person who I want to mention by name and he's got the same name as the deceased person, you say Jukari. If I don't want to mention any name, but want to say a fella who was dead, the word we use is marlkarri. It means a dead person. Like, 'the marlkarri they just lost'. If there's kids that survive they're called kamburda which means no mother or father.

Our family's tribal group is Yinhawangka, that's through my mother's tribal line. The relationship between my grandfather on my mother's side and me we call mabuji. He was one of four brothers and two sisters. Though they had the same father they had a different last name. The eldest was Jambu Giggles and the next my grandfather Joe Injie. The white people called them by this first name only. They were ignorant of the fact that we had our own system of names and in many cases gave our people 'Christian' names.

About sixty-five per cent of the population of Onslow is Aboriginal. This isn't traditional Yinhawangka homeland country. The people I grew up with believed that Onslow belonged to the Nhuwala people who did not survive the colonial invasion. But the Dhalanyji people also have a traditional claim to the area. Yinhawangka country is along the Hamersley Ranges, traditionally from Turee Creek, Thurriri in Aboriginal language.

I grew up in Onslow because my mum had to come to school here. My mum was one of the first kids to go to school in Onslow. My grandfather and grandmother brought their family here in search of work. There were two Aboriginal families living on the reserve at the time, the Injie family and the Dowton family. They were the first two Aboriginal families to come to Onslow from the Hamersley Ranges and for a while the only two families in Onslow. Our family finished up here as the result of government policy, all of the kids were made to go to school. Aboriginal families had to send their kids to the hostel here, because the main work in those days was for station hands, windmill mechanics, or droving stock.

My grandfather and grandmother grew up in the bush. My mother was born in the bush at Duck Creek Station. Toby Andrews, my great-grandfather, had died there at Waluruk Springs. He had been born on Mount Florence Station. The old people lived and worked at many stations in the Ashburton area until they came into town. There they lived in tents, near the old hospital, later to be the Aboriginal reserve. Today there are forty-five houses there and it's called Bindi Bindi village.

State Ships would come to this area to service the pastoral industry. They used lighters to unload the ships. Grandfather used to work unloading the State Ships and loading the camel trains. My grandmother was always the breadwinner. She had a stable job as a domestic and doing the laundry in the Gilliamia Hostel. Nanna had eight children.

I am a strong believer in Aboriginal culture. What a lot of people don't realise is that Aboriginal culture is moving fast and adapting. So the culture I grew up with is not going to be available to my kids and the Aboriginal culture of my mum's generation will never be seen again. It's changing and evolving that quickly. So you can't really generalise and say Aboriginal culture is a particular thing. What can be said is that the people around here are very, very sympathetic. Aboriginal culture stirs a deep emotion in a lot of people here.

People like my grandmother are staunch defenders of traditional Aboriginal culture, because that's the culture they understand, that's what they were brought up in. This culture is not going to last forever, there will be a culture which is an adaptation of the traditional Aboriginal culture. It will adapt to the standard Australian culture. But that will include our respect for our traditional lands.

I have always been a rather fierce supporter of land rights ever since I knew what land rights was about. When I was about fourteen the big land rights push was on in Western Australia. There were two books that really caught my attention, they were *A Bastard Like Me* by Charlie Perkins and *The Chant of Jimmie Blacksmith* by Thomas Keneally. They stirred my emotions. I was always for land rights. Not just having access to land, but what royalties we are entitled to. We can use the money for our economic development.

But the Aboriginal culture is based on land and if you are talking about retention of culture then you are talking about the need for land. I mean our traditional land. I'm a realist and am not talking about people going back to the land to live off the boomerang and spear. Nobody's going to do that. Yet there are a lot of our people who think about participating in the homeland movement.

We are largely limited by the amount of our resources. If you want to put a couple of houses out somewhere then you have to have money for infrastructure, water, power. The Shire has to service you, maintaining the roads and collecting the rubbish, or whatever else, all that sort of thing has got to come into consideration.

What is clear is that all people would like to go back, to participate in ceremonials on their traditional land.

The hope of the young people is for them to achieve status, to have equality of opportunity in Australia. For this it must be a multi-cultural society. What chance have the Aboriginal kids in Onslow coming through and being able to compete with non-Aboriginal kids in this society? Well, at the moment they don't have much of a chance. But I look at it as a long-term thing, maybe over a couple of generations of people.

When you get people who are teaching their kids about values, it all goes back to the basics, you have to go right back to the family structure. Why don't kids go to school? Why don't kids apply themselves at school? Because the parents don't really understand. Many kids go to school because their mother and father don't want to face a fine, or want a baby sitter for the day. These are really cross-cultural issues not dealt with by society. What is needed is that the process of adaptation only takes place to the extent that we do not have to compromise our cultural values. As an example, living in a three-bedroom house does not accommodate an extended family.

It would be a good idea to have Aboriginal language taught as a first language at school, that could improve self-esteem and performance. However, out here there are many Aboriginal languages, although only a few are constantly spoken. So teaching one language would discriminate against some other groups. The Punjima language is the dominant language in Onslow. It could be argued that Punjima language should be taught. But there are many Yinhawangkas living here, too, though neither group is on its own traditional country.

The Aboriginal kids are a majority here in Onslow school. They are taught English as a first language when clearly for them it is not. Teaching an Aboriginal language would be an advance. It could be an incentive for the kids to go to school and for the parents and grandparents to become involved. I think the sociologists call the Aboriginal society a gerontocratic society, run by old people. They basically decide the way things should go and what things should happen according to a set rule or kind of conduct.

Aboriginal people can participate in developing a valuable tourist industry. We can show off the Aboriginal culture with the aim of preservation and protection. The more people are made aware, in the promotion of culture, the more chance there is of protecting it. We can find the ways and means to preserve our culture and to pass it on by teaching kids what is important.

Tourism is an industry that we have been excluded from in previous times, as we were in other industries. We are now, however, realising that there is a great interest in nature-based tourism. We have the knowledge of Aboriginal culture and a cultural base. People worldwide want to get back to the land and traditional values. We hope to bring these things together.

This situation enables us to plan ahead and Karijini Aboriginal Corporation has been doing that. We are conducting Karijini Walkabouts in the Karijini National Park, teaching Aboriginal place names and revealing the natural beauty of the bush. We take groups of ten walkers with two Aboriginal guides. Karijini is now looking to put together a training program for eight Aboriginal tour guides to develop the indigenous people's input into the tourism industry in the Pilbara, increasing our employment and the quality of tourism.

DONALD HICKS

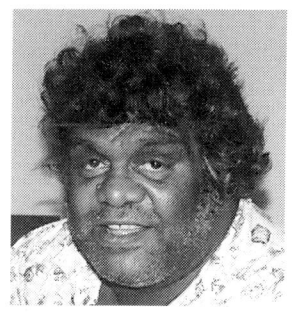

Birth Date: 17 September 1953
Birth Place: Mulga Downs Station
Tribal Group: Yindjibarndi/Punjima
Skin Group: Milangka

> *They usually talk to me. I've never been called*
> *around to the Safe House to deal with any violent*
> *or drunk males, they respect that place.*

I live on the hill in Onslow. My mother's mother was a Yindjibarndi from the Harding River. Ngurin is the Aboriginal word for this river. Grandmother died when giving birth to my mother. My mum's people were Punjima and Yindjibarndi. Her skin group was Burungu. My father is Dempsey Hicks of Roebourne, whose parents' tribal groups were Punjima and Kurrama. So I have these tribal connections in my family, but especially Punjima, from two of my four grandparents. Yet, in strict Aboriginal law I am Yindjibarndi.

I have four brothers, Cedric, Trevor, Rodney, Lawrence and two sisters, Leonie and Julie and three step-brothers, Angus, Michael and Davis, they are all Hicks. Rodney lives at La Grange, Cedric and me live here at Onslow, the rest live in Roebourne.

The family moved from Mulga Downs when I was very young, just a baby. We moved to the Ashburton Downs area, then to Nanutarra and Yanrey Stations. This was about the time when Aboriginal people could get a piece of paper giving them the right to go into a pub, around 1955.

I went to Onslow Primary School and stayed at the Gilliamia Hostel. The manager used to flog the kids with the timber from the vegie boxes. We didn't have to do anything to get belted. He had everyone frightened. It was a hard time. My mother at the time lived on the old reserve at Onslow where Bindi Bindi village is now. My father stayed at the station, they split up and he went off to Port

Hedland. I went to stay with my grandfather and the Parker family, at Nanutarra Station. He reared me up. I was going to school at the time this happened. Finally I finished my schooling in the Agricultural High School at Mullewa. It was the Tardun Mission. I was there from 1967 to 1969.

In 1970 I started working for the Shire at Port Hedland doing road maintenance work. I was there for about a year and a half. Then a job came up with CMM Contractors, the builders of the Dampier–Tom Price railway line. It lasted for about three years. It was good money and we used to get paid every week, not like now, where you get paid every fortnight. I went right to Tom Price with the work. I started in the first camp near where the Robe River rail line now crosses Hamersley Iron's line. Dawson Well it's called, near the old Tomalee Copper Mine. There was my uncle and my cousin brothers working with me, I was the youngest. There were about six of us Aboriginal blokes working and a big mob of wajalas (whitefellas) and Torres Strait Islanders (TSIs).

There were about eight in my gang and we were machine operators. We welded cracked rails and ground the weld. We packed the ballast between the sleepers with an electromagnetic machine. Sometimes I worked scraping the ballast up to make a bed for the sleepers and rails to be laid on. The machine would come along and tamp the ballast down level. There was no problems between the workers and I had a good time there. We'd work five days a week and I would go home to Wittenoom every weekend.

I came back to Onslow and worked for the Ashburton Shire. I've worked for the Port Hedland Shire and the Roebourne Shire at Karratha. I was mainly involved in patching the roads, cleaning out potholes and putting in the tar. I would drive trucks and loaders although I only had a ticket for driving. The Port Hedland Shire was best for me as I knew the bosses and blokes better. These were five-day-a-week jobs.

I was initiated in our culture and attend all the ceremonies at the Cane River. We are pretty strong with our law here, even with our young fellas, they all pretty well know everything, culture things, bush side. When I was younger we used to have our corroborees out in the scrub not far from the town of Wittenoom. My initiation was at the cattle camp down here and I went through the law with Jukari Solomon, he was yarlbu to me. He was my uncle and his father is my grandfather.

Land is important to us because we were all born in the bush and we just want to get back where we was born. I was born just the other side of Mulga Downs Station under a tree. When I was a baby, there were big mob of Aboriginal people living there, maybe thirty or something like that. I went back to work once since but there's none of our people living there now. Maybe one old fella could be working there off and on. Old Horace Parker is living in the area.

I've been painting landscapes for years. I learned when we had art classes down at the old Noualla building in the main street of Onslow. It's gone now. For the last three years I have started to do dot paintings. I paint in oils, also house paint with varnish. It comes out better. I draw in charcoal and lead pencil. I have changed to dot paintings because that's our culture. It is a Pilbara Aboriginal-style painting. You can see the dot style in some of our carving out in the bush in Yindjibarndi country. I did a lot of painting when I was in prison. I sell my paintings by street displays. People are interested. Once I do them, I get rid of them right away. There's one of my paintings in the Onslow Police Station.

I'm working in Onslow now as an outreach worker for the Women's Group. I organise things with the women, like sewing classes and art work. I look after domestic violence situations. I talk to the women and the men if they get violent. I handle it pretty good. In the main they are violent only when drunk. I leave them alone usually, go back in the morning and talk it over with them. Find out why it is that the man is flogging his missus, talk it over and try and help. They usually talk to me. I've never been called around to the Safe House to deal with any violent or drunk males, so basically they respect that place. I work daily on a part-time basis. This is up for review at the end of the month.

I have been married three times. One wife came from Port Hedland and had my son. He passed away. Another wife came from Carnarvon and had a little girl. The other came from Onslow and had a girl now fourteen. She lives at Wickham with relatives. Her mother passed away. I am not married now.

I've had problems with the police and the law in Hedland,

Roebourne and Onslow. I used to get on the grog and get violent with my wife. I was sent to Geraldton Regional Prison for two and a half years for assault because I had a bad record for this type of thing. I only came out last year. I still drink but I'm getting older and don't carry on as I used to. Maybe I'm changing also because I'm not married.

I used to live in Wittenoom when I worked on the railway line. And I also stayed there as a kid, with my grandmother on my father's side, Pidgy Hicks. She lived straight across from the power station. As kids we used to go swimming in the waterholes in Wittenoom Gorge. Other members of my family to stay with Grandmother at Wittenoom were my brothers, my aunt Shirley Walker from Roebourne. My uncle fathers, Nelson Hughes and Johnson Hicks, worked on Hamersley Station and came to Grandmother's with their kids. We would go to school in Wittenoom. I don't think our family has any problems from the asbestos, but I do have asthma.

SALLY CONDON

Birth Date: 1953
Birth Place: Boolaloo Station
Tribal Group: Yinhawangka
Skin Group: Milangka

*The ceremony starts next Saturday ... As his mother
I will go to the Cane River meeting place ... and he
will have passed the first steps of manhood.*

I was born on Boolaloo Station. Mick Condon is my dad, a
Yindjibarndi, who has lived down here in Onslow for years. Most
Yindjibarndi now live in the Roebourne area. Dulcie Condon, my
mum, is Yinhawangka. They are both living away from their
traditional country. Mum is very much involved with the
Yinhawangka group that have been trying to a get a little piece of their
land back out at Bellary Creek. My mother is very strong in Aboriginal
culture.

Not so my father, he was always away from his family ever since he
was a teenager. He had worked at different stations in the area:
Hamersley, Mount Brockman, Rocklea, Kooline, Wyloo, Mount Stuart
and Peedamulla, to name some. We spent many years at Kooline and
Wyloo. Dad used to break in horses. One of my earliest memories is of
running away from Mum and down to the stockyards to watch him.

I think even in those days it was the start of Aboriginal people going
away from their culture. It was still there but there was examples of it
breaking down. We went to ceremonies and corroborees as a kid. And
there was still the law things we followed, you know.

There are nine kids in our family. I'm the oldest. There were
actually twelve but Mum lost three.

I did my high schooling in Perth. But like most Aboriginal kids in
our area, I lived at Gilliamia Hostel and attended Onslow Primary
School. This situation was all right but the hostel was not always a

happy place. When holiday time came around we could go back out bush. The teachers thought I was smart and they skipped me a grade. At the end of grade seven I won a scholarship. But I repeated Year Eleven and when it came to Year Twelve, I couldn't be bothered doing it and went to business college instead.

At Perth I went to an ordinary State school. There were maybe half a dozen Aboriginal kids there. They all dropped off in about second year. I didn't feel any racial pressure at school. Maybe there was some culture shock. Basically I was a bush kid being taken out of my environment and plonked down in the city to live with white people. There was no support available for Aboriginal kids then, like there is today. I stayed until about third year, by that time I was the only one left. I was probably one of those kids that walk around with their head in the clouds.

My first job ever was as a receptionist typist with the old Native Welfare Department in Perth. Then I met my future hubby, got pregnant and we came back up here. I started living with him when I was seventeen going on eighteen. For the next twenty odd years I've been a mum. In that time I've had six kids. My only daughter is the oldest, she is twenty this year. The next one is eighteen, then a sixteen year old and there is a gap of five years. Then I started my second family. The oldest of them is ten, then eight and seven years old.

When I came home to Onslow for school holidays at the end of each term, I used to get jobs locally. I actually started casual work from grade seven when I was about twelve and did this until I was about sixteen. Most of the jobs were at the pub as a kitchen hand, laundry maid, housemaid. But I worked at a cafe in the main street, opposite where the supermarket is now, as a kitchen hand and served behind the counter. And of course I baby-sat for people. My cousin Nancy would sometimes work with me.

Between having children in my first marriage I worked as a relief cleaner at the single men's quarters at Dampier. And during my second marriage I worked as a Community Health Worker at Roebourne for two years, working mainly with the Aboriginal community. After that I worked as an administrator for the Ieramugadu Group at Roebourne. Later I worked for the Broome Shire as a labourer for three months. These jobs gave me financial independence and got me out of the house where you can go stark raving mad.

When I arrived back in Roebourne in 1988, I did a refresher course at the Roebourne Education Centre to update my office skills. I then sat the Public Service tests and got a job with the Department of Employment, Education and Training (DEET) in Karratha. I was there for four years, trying to get employment for Aboriginal and Torres Strait Islander youth. We had limited success. A few kids got apprenticeships with Robe River Iron Associates but as soon as they finish their time they get put off, the companies won't keep them working. And that is the period when they are qualified!

This is the usual practice among the big mining companies here, even Hamersley Iron, although they kept them on for six months after they'd finished their time. There were lots of young people coming in to register after they had finished their time. Woodside Petroleum employed about three lots of pre-apprentices for about six or twelve months. But out of those one got employed as an apprentice. So they were competing against each other for the job.

There are two Aboriginal apprentices at Woodside now. To get apprenticeships and that sort of thing they need to have a certain level of education and Aboriginal kids just didn't have that. Some managed to get into training programs with different employers. But often they never lasted, it's frustrating when you go to all that trouble, put in a lot of time and effort to get these kids employment.

My experience in DEET was conditioned by the fact that there just weren't the jobs for a start in the DEET programs. We couldn't find employment for the kids, because there just wasn't anything around. I don't know if it's peer pressure or racism in the workplace, but Aboriginal kids just weren't competitive, even with training programs.

Now I work for Karijini Aboriginal Corporation as a secretary. I've been there for four months. I enjoy the job and being in my home town. And the pay is better than I was getting at DEET, but that is the least of the considerations. I'm home and working for my own people, that's more important to me.

I'd like to see more support for Karijini amongst the local people. I think it is great what Karijini is trying to achieve and I would like us to keep it up and to expand a bit more, get more employment and that sort of thing. It was one of the issues discussed at our bush meeting, since then the three individual groups have had their own meetings. I think the Aboriginal people now realise that Karijini is here to help them. It is an umbrella organisation. Initially the umbrella had to be the spearhead to take up the fight for land. Karijini is strong for the Aboriginal culture and supports our customs and practices.

My older son went through the law two years ago and the younger one is going through now in December 1993. The decision on whether he is to go through the law is mine but I discussed this with the family members and we are all happy for the boys to go through the law. It should also be remembered that their father is a non-Aboriginal and so the pressure to go through the law is not as great. However the boys came to the conclusion themselves that they should follow Aboriginal law. The younger one has gone with others to various communities in the Pilbara so that they know that the ceremony starts next Saturday out at the Cane River. His brother has gone with him for support. As his mother, I have taken a month off work and will go to the Cane River meeting place for that period of time. Other family members will come out there and stay from time to time to support him. And the end of the time he will have passed the first steps of manhood. There are five young boys going through the law at this time from this area so there will be a big family celebration when they have finished. Other people from different places will come and put their boys through the law at this law ground next year. It is good to see the regeneration of our culture.

My daughter Lisa is my only girl out of the six children. She did a bridging course at the University of Western Australia at the age of eighteen. She completed it and did very well. Once she got into it, she thought it was really great because she met a lot of people she normally wouldn't have met, other Aboriginal people, kids from other areas. She's still friends with a lot of them.

She passed and she's going to do science. Since she was a kid she wanted to be a marine biologist. Well, she got into science but then decided to defer her studies for a couple of years. She got a job and found a boyfriend and now she is going to make me a grandmother. But she lasted a lot longer than Aboriginal kids normally do. Most kids tend to drop out as soon as they turn fifteen, some even younger. It is a real problem with Aboriginal kids. I know when I was working with DEET, it wasn't just Aboriginal kids, white kids would come in who could barely read and write and expect to get a job.

My son is eighteen years old and was doing a bridging course at Curtin University. He wanted to do the Arts Degree there but he had problems and dropped out. It's not so much homesickness with him because he's got his mates down there and he's into football. I think it is just he is not used to being so poor. Study doesn't pay much. That gets a bit frustrating because he's in a flat and he's got to pay rent etc. I would like him to stick it out because he is a real good artist.

My sixteen year old is in Year Eleven. He's a typical teenager. He's in training to be a heavy metal guitarist, so he says. He has long hair he wears in dreadlocks. Out of all my kids he is the brightest, it would be a shame to see him just letting it all go. The younger ones are at primary school and are doing very, very well. My three youngest kids live with me. The others live in Karratha. I would have liked to see them all go on to do great things but, it's their life, once they reach a certain age you can't make them do what you simply want. My kids are just typical of most kids.

RUBEN MILLS

Birth Date: 7 October 1967
Birth Place: Narembeen
Tribal Group: Nyoongah/Punjima
Skin Group: Burungu

> *When I first came to this area I knew very little about Aboriginal law and its importance, I was a young male looking for a good time.*

I started kindergarten and primary school in Salmon Gums, in the wheat-belt area of Western Australia. But because my father was working for Westrail we were required to constantly move and so was my schooling. I continued primary school at Esperance, then Merredin, Bencubbin, Mukinbudin, Kalannie and Perth.

I did three years high school in Perth at Midland, Governor Stirling Senior High School. If I had the opportunity I would have gone to university. I wanted to get a Bachelor of Science degree. At this stage my employment ambition was to be a policeman.

I believed then that to go further with my education I had to go to a TAFE college and be financially supported. It was not as today where students are required to go to Year Twelve, then make a choice as to whether to go to university. Then you had to prove your academic merit through qualifying exams to study Years Eleven and Twelve. There was little encouragement to take this path. I was not a poor student, except economically, but I didn't invite such hassles. Besides at Year Ten I was presented with the opportunity of going to work, if I could get a job.

My first job after leaving school was lumping bags of potatoes from West Perth to outlets in the metropolitan area. This lasted three years. After this I worked as a salt stacker, again for three years. The salt came from Esperance and we bagged it and stacked it and sometimes carted it around the town.

Around this time the Mills family moved to Wickham in the Pilbara. I had to question whether I was going to move with the family. I was a solidly built young bloke, playing a lot of football at the time and with a strong peer group. The idea of tearing up my roots to go to an isolated place did not appeal. Nevertheless I did go and I suppose it's the result of the strength of family in my life and the old man's force of character. So when they said, 'Are you coming?' I felt it was a big ask, but I went.

We settled down in Wickham. I started to play football with the Wickham Wolves and put down new roots. There wasn't much work around. I was pretty lucky because the footy club got me a job in the first year with Robe River Iron at Cape Lambert. They needed more land for stockpiles for their iron ore and were reclaiming ocean land. I worked on the heavy earth-moving equipment for twelve months.

At the end of this period there were about six of us with little to do except shovelling up spillage from the conveyor. It was a day-to-day proposition. Each day we returned to shovel up more spillage. This type of boring repetitious work did not suit, I had wider visions of life, so I left.

Then I got a job supervising the building of a fence around the Roebourne village, for Boral Cyclone on contract to Homeswest. There was seven of us local guys: Dougie Cooke, Rodney Parker, Terry Mills, Wayne Boona, Sid Walker, Mego Woodley and myself. It was to last three months, but on condition that if we finished earlier we would be paid the three months wages. We finished in six weeks and the fence is still standing.

I was on and off the dole and got a job with Austrack at Wickham. They were contractors for Robe River Iron making these new cement sleepers to replace the old wooden ones. We were stacking cement sleepers on twelve hour shifts. It lasted six months, then it was the dole again.

My next employment was the Support Accommodation Assistance Program (SAAP), Commonwealth funded with a job relationship to the Women's Task Force in the campaign against domestic violence, in Roebourne. It involves taking a holistic approach to containing and reducing domestic violence. It's a support scheme that works on everything that is associated with

What a mob! Aboriginal kids at Wickham.

domestic violence, like household abuse, child abuse, physical abuse, mental abuse, poverty, etc. This was my first job as a government employee. I was in the 'deep end' but found my feet after a couple of months. The job opened up my eyes to new possibilities to help my people, especially the youth.

We were invited to go to Perth at Easter 1993 to take thirty-two boys aged thirteen to sixteen and seven girls to play basketball. There were seven senior players as well. I was responsible for their organisation for the duration. It was funded by Aboriginal Affairs Planning Authority (AAPA) who made the initial approach. This was a great experience for these young people and for me. The kids went to Perth and played against their own age and adults. They played twenty-two games of competition in four days. And while it really opened their eyes, they also impressed people in Perth.

Six months later it was suggested that a group of Roebourne boys would go to Canberra for a national competition. I was asked to supervise this trip. I was involved in feasibility discussions in Perth. AAPA agreed to put up $20,000 of an estimated $40,000 budget based on plane travel. We had to find the other $20,000. We had two weeks to do it. The task was impossible as there was only two weeks to find the money. I was convinced of the importance of our kids going. So I approached it on the basis of cutting travel costs and went by bus. My wife, Mary, and I took forty boys away for nine days.

They played four teams from Canberra, two from Western Australia, one each from South Australia, Tasmania, Darwin, Queensland, Alice Springs, New South Wales and Victoria. Our young learnt something from this experience, that they were better people. They had more respect for themselves. It opened up a lot of things. Their ability to do things for themselves grew. They knew that they didn't need other things in life to be happy.

As a result of this trip, ten of them went back to the local TAFE College and about eight of them got employment, something that had never happened to them before. I think this indicates that there was a change in their attitude to themselves and that they'd had a good experience with people from different cultures. They are more motivated and less willing to just sit around any more.

I continued to work with this group but the SAAP program was put on hold while the Department of Community Development (DCD) is restructured. I was put off work. However, I got a job with the Department of Social Security. I'm working in Roebourne on an agency basis. It's just a short-time job assessing youth and adults applications for the dole programs.

I see my future work very much tied up with the youth of the area. I still play football and basketball. I'm always involved with the young fellows. I assess each individual young person so I know where he is going and how he's going in life. I can't treat any one the same as the next. They've all got different qualities. This morning I received a phone call offering to take another group of youth to Perth at Christmas time. Of course we are seriously considering the offer.

Roebourne Aboriginal community has been abused by non-Aboriginal society especially by the workers from the mining camps in the 1970s and 1980s. The whole fabric of the culture was at risk from men demanding women. But the Aboriginal culture survived and the law remains a strong and positive force today, guiding the conduct of the people.

When I first came to this area I knew very little about Aboriginal law and its importance in everyday existence. I was a young male looking for a good time if I could find it. It wasn't long before I came under the notice of the Aboriginal elders. In the old people's eyes I was a bit of a troublemaker. I formed relations with young Aboriginal females and this was the cause of concern.

I became involved emotionally with one of the young women of the area. My father was a Punjima who had been taken from the Pilbara as a child. But the old people keep a very strict reckoning on who one's relatives are, they use it as a guide to the daily interaction of people. Through my father's family there was some relation between myself and this young woman. Discussions with my father took place.

As far as the elders were concerned it was an unacceptable relationship and should be terminated. In any event, it was clear that if I was to be accepted by the local Aboriginal community, I would have to be initiated or would not be accepted as a man. This was in 1988.

At first I could not accept that I had to give up the relationship and it took me a while to accept that I would be initiated. Gradually the idea took hold however, as people would drop hints that my turn was nearly due. I knew it would happen if I stayed.

One morning at my friend's place a knock came at the door. It was 5.30 am. My mother was standing there very upset. She told me that some men had come for me. Despite my fears, I assured her that this was no cause for worry, that I was ready to go. We went to a house where a group of nine blokes were waiting. They would not look me in the eye, no matter how I tried for eye contact. A couple of the group were talking to my old man. They were ones I knew and respected, but they would not eyeball me either. So I went and talked to my brother. I thought, well, there's nothing wrong with me, but underneath I was starting to feel there was something going wrong. Suddenly they came over and asked, 'Are you ready?' I said, 'Yes,' and they said, 'Then let's go.'

I was out bush for the next seven months. This was about three months before Christmas and I had had other plans about how I was going to use that Christmas, but they were blown sky high.

I was waiting and learning out in the bush and waiting for my yarlbu mob, the other boys who were going through the law at the same time as me. It was January 1989 that we were initiated and released. My whole family were there to support me, even some relations from Perth. They stuck with me from day one. It was a long time in the bush before I was released into the wide society.

When I came out, I had a very different view on life. I was not the same person. I think I was more relaxed and open. I learned to respect other people, not to be jealous of others, to listen to other people and to respect elders. And I learned about the culture and language. Now I am one of the local Aboriginal people and am accepted as one of them. I am more respected in the community and I respect the community. I can better assist to solve people problems now and my life has changed completely, for the better.

Mary Smith and I are now married and live at Wickham. We have four children: Stacey ten years, Dwayne eight, Kalen three and Brodie who's nine months. Mary was my girlfriend at the time of initiation and was really my number one supporter in that time. We look forward to giving our kids the best education we can and our ongoing support.

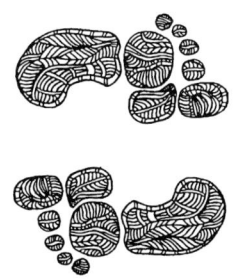

VIVIAN COOKE

Birth Date: 1969
Birth Place: Onslow
Tribal Group: Kurrama/Yinhawangka
Skin Group: Banaka

> *They had to choose either alcohol or their*
> *culture, they chose their culture. This is the type*
> *of decision that has to be made in Australia.*

The Environmental Health Worker is a job I really liked. It was practical and necessary for the Aboriginal community. But it also had a theory side. We were trained by Pundulmurra College. To be a qualified environmental health worker you've got to pass about five modules of study. Every so often we'd go back to Pundulmurra for a session.

I prefer outdoor jobs and don't like sitting down in the office. So on the practical side of the job we would clean out ponds in the communities. We'd go to Ngurawaarna, Cheeditha, Kurrabunya, Cheerida on septic systems, cleaning the tanks out if they got blocked. We'd work with the shire to do this. If it was really bad we'd get the environmental supervisor from Hedland. Most of the problems are associated with the habits of the kids chucking stones and pieces of bikes and things like that down into the system. We'd have to jump in and get all the things out. It was a dirty job, but it had to be done. It was good wages, but they are better now. We also carted water out to the communities like the Three Mile, where they had none.

We spend time educating people on environmental health. We have workshops with people. Sit down and talk about the problem. Educating the mob not to have too many dogs and cats. They can be a health risk. There can be an outbreak of scabies because Aboriginal people like their dogs on their beds. We'd also dip and cull dogs and cats, every month if it was needed.

222

Learning the culture. A Corroboree performed by Aboriginal youth at Karratha. Photo by M Young.

At the time when I stopped working there we were starting a health program in school. We had a positive effect: Today there are still environmental health workers. The problems continue. But I think they will work it through the Community Development Employment Program to place responsibility to monitor problems and to solve them back in the smaller community groups. In other words the programs are decentralising and emphasising community control.

My next job was with the domestic violence unit. The Commonwealth Employment Service approached me to see if I would apply for a project officer's job for the Roebourne Housing Project, dealing with domestic violence. I applied, was interviewed and got the job. I have been working there for two years now.

When dealing with domestic violence you have to do basic counselling of the women and assist them in any way, like getting a Homeswest house and showing them resources. We also help the kids. Involving them in programs so the mother and kids can spend more time together. Like every day you find many mothers just playing cards and they don't spend much time with their kids. In the Roebourne Housing Project we take care of the men, too. We had a male worker there who could work with the men and help them because they needed help.

We had a good response with the men. We try to get the men and the women together after we have talked to them separately and try and solve the problem. We've had a couple of successes. The problems come down to alcohol, unemployment, boredom, lack of self-esteem by men, because the women are most often bringing home the money.

I personally have never experienced domestic violence but I have seen members of my family going through it. This has helped my understanding. I like working in this domestic violence area because I've never approved of a man hitting a woman. And I've always wanted to work helping my people. This is what I'm good at. I feel comfortable doing this work.

I also reckon it is one of the most important jobs in our community. Domestic violence is really bad. A lot of people who are bad offenders don't front up, or don't want any help. We can't tell them, we have to wait 'till they come. We go into the streets and talk to the people. They seem to be open with us when we talk about it. And they admit they have a problem: they talk about jealousy and such things as factors. You get virtually the same people, although lately we've been getting different people, men and women and all ages. The most are the young, those around about their twenties to early thirties. These days I notice young people getting married really young, at fifteen, sixteen, or whatever. Then it's kids having kids. Then you get young people fighting each other. So we've started a program to tackle this situation. It will go into schools, teaching the kids so they know what's happening.

I don't think the situation in places like Roebourne is getting better. It's on hold. In one respect it seems to be worse because I see the young kids starting to drink alcohol, take drugs and such stuff. And they've got no Aboriginal culture, no respect for their family.

I recently attended a worldwide Healing Our Spirits Conference in Canada. It was hosted by the Canadian Native Americans, who invited indigenous people from around the world. We went for two weeks. What the Canadian indigenous people had to show us was that they had beaten alcohol. They had been able to give it away. So I see the drinking here in Australia, but I know that they can give it away, it can be done. It's just a matter of the community getting together and wanting to help each other. I learnt about freeing oneself spiritually, how to be open about yourself, never keep things to yourself.

The Canadian indigenous people have based these main personal steps on their culture. They recognised that their culture was being lost if the process continued. There would be no one left to carry it on, as the old people were passing away rapidly. So they had to choose either alcohol or their culture and they chose their culture. This is the type of decision that has to be made in Australia.

I firmly believe in Aboriginal culture. My mother's mother Dora Gilba taught me a lot. She was living at Wittenoom at the time. Mum and her de facto were following work. To go to school I had to live with my grandmother. She insisted that we show respect for elders and that we should sit with them and hear their stories. She always talked language and she'd go out hunting. She was a Kurrama, their country is around Hamersley Station. I'd pick up everyday language from her. The same as I would learn from Doris, my mother. But it's when we'd go bush with grandfathers and others that I would listen and learn a lot more. It's only lately that I've started to talk. We would always talk our everyday language. We also learned respect for our elders and other aspects of our culture.

The skin group is a key aspect of Aboriginal culture. My own skin relationship to others was something taught by my mum and my grandmother, but it's the kind of thing that comes naturally. I'm of the Banaka group. I learned this when I was about ten or eleven. I was a promised wife in our culture. This shows that our culture is very much alive today, even if the arrangement doesn't take place.

When you're growing up you kinda learn about such things as respect, especially at funerals. Our family always had this attitude. So we saw how the grown-ups greeted each other on these occasions and when they cry and grieve. When you get to fifteen or sixteen that's when your mother or grandmother says you're old enough to be part of that process. My old grandmother's auntie passed away at 102 years of age in the 1970s. They called her Dido. I was in grade four or five when she went, but not before she had taught me how to make her burlku (tobacco mixture). In our culture if you have a long life it means that you are a kind person.

I believe that a person isn't Aboriginal if they don't have their culture. You are lost without your culture. Examples of people breaking our customs and cultural rules show that those people haven't been brought up right. If you are brought up with the culture you're right. In some of those communities where young people have no respect for the elders, where they get drunk and make noise all the time, the best thing for the elders is to go and live in the bush. There is no hassle there.

I am a member of the Wakuthuni Aboriginal Association, which is part of the Karijini Aboriginal Corporation. We are in the process of setting up our own community on our traditional land out near Tom Price. In setting up this community we aim for it to be alcohol-free. We've been living in Roebourne, Wickham, Karratha, Onslow and other places scattered away from our lands. We've been living in other Aboriginal people's country. It's a good feeling to be back here. I don't like living in the town, it's just too much stress on me, seeing people always drinking and no respect and out of control. And I lost my young brother twelve months ago and this is the pressure of society. Town tends to breed sick people.

ADRIAN CONDON

Birth Date: 28 September 1965
Birth Place: Onslow
Tribal Group: Yinhawangka
Skin Group: Milangka

The basic culture in schools is non-Aboriginal,
but often the majority of children are Aboriginal
and so there are constant problems.

My parents were members of local Aboriginal tribes. Dulcie, my mother, was from the Cox family, Yinhawangkas living at Onslow. She married Mick Condon, my father, a Yindjibarndi. Both of the old people still live in the area, though time and tide has seen them go their own ways in life. My mother originally came from the Rocklea Station area, down near the Karijini National Park. There used to be a big mob camped down there on the station.

Mick Condon was born in the Roebourne area, traditionally one of our Aboriginal living areas. This family background makes me a Yindjibarndi and Yinhawangka mixture. But in Aboriginal law here I follow my mother, I'm a Yinhawangka. We always follow the mother's line.

Sometimes you'll see that this line of descent has been broken. That's an effect of colonisation and tribal break up. Today many Aboriginal people take their descent from the father's side as is the custom in the rest of Australian society.

I am an Onslow man. My people were moved from their traditional living areas before I was born. All of my primary schooling was done at Onslow. I did all of my high school in Perth, that's fourteen hundred kilometres from here and my family. I went by choice, I wanted to go to Perth. I went right up to Year Twelve, passed all my subjects. After I finished high school I did a little bit of college, then I went to university. The Murdoch Uni had an annex up in South Hedland and I applied to study there. I went there for first year Psychology, Time Management and Welfare Practice. It really was a Child Welfare course and at the end of two years I had received a diploma in Welfare Practice and Child Psychology. This enabled me to get employment as an Aboriginal Liaison Officer with the Education Department.

I worked at the Karratha District Education Office. I was there for three years. After that I moved to Hedland. At the moment I'm working for the Pilbara Aboriginal Language Centre in Hedland, I'm doing administration work for them.

Aboriginal Liaison Officers (ALOs) are a feature of government schools in the Pilbara. ALOs do important work in trying to introduce Aboriginal families to the Western-style education. They spend most of their time talking with students and parents about the need to attend school and the problems for both parents and pupils when they go to school. I provide support to all Aboriginal children in schools and some counselling for the Aboriginal parents at home. Parents need counselling because a lot of times there are conflicts at home with the parents and the kids and you go in there, sit down and talk with them and the kids.

There are always conflicts between the Aboriginal kids and the teachers at the schools, so you sit down and talk with them and liaise between the teachers and kids. The basic culture in schools is non-Aboriginal, but often the majority of children are Aboriginal and so there are constant problems. A lot of it is because the teachers don't understand the background of the Aboriginal children and their Aboriginal culture. They don't realise that these kids are really coming from a different culture. A lot of the teachers that come up here are first-year teachers out of college. It is the first time they have worked with Aboriginal people and they don't know anything about them.

At home a lot of parents don't insist on their kids going to school. I think that's because of the way the parents have been, they've been with a lot of government departments. They just let the children do whatever they want, because that's the way they've been brought up and so the kids are going to be the same way.

In our Aboriginal communities kids are kind of special people, they can get away with a lot of things that they wouldn't get away with in non-Aboriginal culture. This is because the Aboriginal child grows up by himself, watched by his parents, but can go and explore anything, walk wherever. But if the European child walks off, his parents get out and chase him, say, 'Come back here.' If he gets hurt they cuddle him, whereas when the Aboriginal child gets hurt, he mends.

These differences happen in the same way when they go to school. The non-Aboriginal parents say to their children 'You must go to school,' whereas the Aboriginal parents allow the child to make the choice. That's the main thing about being a Liaison Officer, you try to bring out the importance of going to school. It's a big job here, I looked after not only Karratha but seven other towns. In all there were Karratha, Dampier, Roebourne, Wickham, Onslow, Exmouth, Tom Price, Paraburdoo and Pannawonica. Many of these are iron ore mining towns. There were none or very few Aboriginal families in such towns. But I would go and talk to the kids there to bring the Aboriginal culture to them, face to face in the classroom. This was part of my work, I would take them out bush, do bushwalks and show them the importance of the bush, what it meant to us, how we lived in it. They loved it.

The kids find it difficult to keep studying until Year Twelve. A lot of them just find growing up as an end. They believe that for them there's nothing positive in being grown up. They see that once they get to the age of eighteen, there's nothing for them. And that's the main problem Aboriginal people find everywhere. That's why it's hard being a Liaison Officer trying to convince them there's more, to keep going on and on, keep up being at school, or be in the work force. The problem is there are no jobs. Another difficulty is just to find role models — and the welfare system is there. There's no jobs on the one hand and on the other the system and we're stuck in the middle.

I believe in our Aboriginal law, every bit of it. I was initiated in the law. And I attend the law ceremonies each year like most people around this area. Our traditional lands are up there in the Karijini National Park area. I and other Yinhawangkas look at those lands believing we have ownership rights. If we were able to get some of that land back it could improve things for us. People might get their family unit back together and make us as one people, one group, not as little individual groups here and there. Because once you get the land back you find unity again. Many things are needed to improve life for our people here. That's why Karijini was formed. The main thing is for us to be recognised as the people that belong to this country here and the Pilbara itself. Look at the Northern Territory Aboriginal people, they have been treated as owners with royalties. We are not treated as the people who own this place. I think that's the most important thing, people should start to recognise that we are important people here.

RODNEY BUTLER

Birth Date: 1965
Birth Place: Carnarvon
Tribal Group: Punjima
Skin Group: Banaka

> *It's very difficult for Aboriginal workers to get
> jobs out on the islands; they pay better and
> the jobs are taken by non-Aboriginal labour.*

I went to school in Carnarvon until the beginning of third year of
high school in 1979. I then left the Carnarvon area and moved up to
Yarraloola Station to work.

I had two brothers and one sister living up here in the Pilbara. My
sister is in Port Hedland, one brother is in Wickham and the other
was at Peedamulla Station but is now working with me out in the
Karijini National Park. I've got my grandmother's name. I am a
member of the Punjima tribal group on my father's side.

When I left school I only wanted to work on stations. I wanted to
get out into the bush. I used to do this during my holidays with my
uncle Ernie and auntie Bella Randell. She's Mum's younger sister. At
Middalya Station near Carnarvon I used to go to the bush all the
time before I ever came up to Onslow and met my other family and
before I left school.

I was taught about the law when I came up to the Pilbara. I've
been initiated on Peedamulla Station. And I believe in doing things
in the traditional Aboriginal way, just like at the funeral today. That's
the way I'd like my kids to be brought up, too.

I worked at Yarraloola for three years as a general station hand,
mustering cattle or whatever. Then I went and did a twelve months
course at Pundulmurra Aboriginal College as a plant operator. This
enabled me to get a job driving the loader, backhoe and truck with

the Shire of Ashburton for two years. I got the job with Ashburton Shire on the recommendation of Pundulmurra. I had the papers then because I was awarded the plant operator of the year at Peedamulla Station. I then moved to Carnarvon with the family for two years and worked for the Carnarvon Shire doing the same thing.

After working for the Carnarvon Shire I came back to Onslow and got a job on Thevenard Island, off the coast there, as a trades assistant with a welding mob. I was on the island for about twelve months and worked for five different companies: Chicago Bridge Iron Company (CBI), Electrical Power Transmission (EPT), RM Lee Electrical, Leightons Contracting and McDermitts, packing explosives.

It's usually very difficult for Aboriginal workers to get jobs out on the islands, they pay better money than most places and the jobs are nearly always taken by non-Aboriginal labour. I got the job by persistence, I reckon. At first I just went and asked for work but they weren't looking for anybody. But I kept going up and down to their office every day. I told them, 'I need a job, I need a job.' I kept going and they said there are no jobs, until I walked in one day and some bloke had got the sack that morning. I had seen this bloke being sacked so the fella couldn't say he didn't have any vacancies. He said, 'I'll sign you up and see how you go.' That was with CBI but I moved on to other companies like Leightons and EPT.

After the island I went back to Carnarvon and worked with Dampier Salt. That was on contract, operating scrapers. They are like bulldozers. Then I spent a couple of months in Meekatharra in the goldmines on a scraper as well. I went up to Derby working for the Main Roads Department. The contractor was the same guy I was working for at Dampier Salt at Carnarvon. It was just a fill-in job for four weeks. I next worked out of Dampier and Karratha with Skilled Engineering. We were on front-end loaders doing night shifts over Christmas, working from 6.00 am to 6.00 pm daily.

Between jobs I go back to the bush at Peedamulla Station. I do a bit of cattle mustering until another contract comes up. I did a lot of work off and on for Northern Transport of Onslow, driving trucks and a grader. I was employed for a week, with other young fellas, helping to prepare an Aboriginal Employment — Mining, Tourism and Culture conference here in 1992. Our people were hoping to talk to miners and the tourism people about land use and jobs. It was a good experience for me, but I didn't see too many miners there.

I also worked for Karijini Contractors in the National Park. Karijini's first contract in the park was maintenance work building new paths, walkways, low fences, new toilets and that sort of thing. Now I'm supervising Karijini's work there. We've got a few young blokes working out there, fulfilling the Karijini's contract. The park is home country to the Aboriginal tribal groups who are members of the Karijini Aboriginal Corporation. The Corporation set up its contracting company to help maintain the park. It's employing young Aboriginal workers there. At the moment there are four of us, all in our twenties. It's good to get young people work there. They're doing a good job too. We like being there because not only do we get paid but we are working in our traditional country.

The work is casual at the moment. It goes from contract to contract. But we are hoping to be able to engage in full-time work. This could certainly happen as more tourists come through and when the construction workers from the Marandoo mine start living in the area. I reckon CALM will need to get some people in there with Ranger training. Preferably Aboriginal Rangers who come from that country. They should start training some now for the future.

We've developed good working relations with the Department of Conservation and Land Management (CALM) operators. I think they are satisfied with our work. The toughest thing about the work, for me, is not being out on our own for two weeks at a time, but making decisions about the work. The boys count on me see, to make decisions, especially when machines break down. And the blokes back in the office leave everything up to me. And I've got to make decisions when you are going to do that, or this and which way will it make the job easier for the boys, without over-spending our finances.

It's difficult to see a future in the Pilbara for young Aboriginals. We hope there is one in tourism and in mining, but we'll wait and see. There is so much unemployment here among our people that it's hard to say. This has been a mining area for iron ore for the last twenty-five years. But we've had no jobs. To get into the mines our people need training. But most of them are not getting this.

There is a training program that just started in 1992 with Hamersley Iron, but there is only a handful of boys involved. There's a couple from Onslow and some from Karratha and Roebourne.

About six or seven are involved. They are learning to operate machines, like bulldozers. And the work they are doing is cleaning up on the train lines. I have already had this experience.

I think our people might feel a bit more confident if they saw another Aboriginal like myself in such training programs who, because we know the ropes, could assist with the training.

At present I'm working out at Urala on the LPG gas construction project. It's a big operation for this area, but there are very few other Aboriginal workers there. Yet you don't need many skills to do some of the work being performed. The failure to take account of Aboriginal needs in industry is continuing.

RODNEY PARKER

Birth Date: 29 September 1965
Birth Place: Onslow
Tribal Group: Punjima
Skin Group: Banaka

> *Aboriginal people do not have good health today ... the lack of traditional land and loss of their culture affects their health.*

My mother was Lola Parker (now Young) and my father is Wobby Parker. My eldest brother is Ronnie Mills, then there is Susan, Dawn, Johnny, Mervyn, Cecil, Rhonda Parker and myself. Only Susan and Ronnie had different mothers. I also had a young brother, Keith, who passed away as a teenager.

I'm from the Punjima tribe. My father's land is on the top end of the Karijini National Park. And down to Rocklea and Paraburdoo is my mother's area.

I believe in Aboriginal culture and was taught by the old people. I was initiated in the Wamulu law system, but my brother was put through the hard way. I went through the law at Woodbrook, but it was Wamulu law as I was the oldest of the group of boys being initiated. My brother Cecil, who came after me, went through the hard way. At the time I thought this was all right, but now I think he was the one who did this for me. My skin group is Banaka and I'm married to Josie Samson by agreement of the parents, Aboriginal way. I have two kids and they will grow up to respect our culture.

I was born at Onslow Hospital and I went to Onslow school. In the early days the government would get the kids to go to the closest school and as Dad was working at Nanutarra, Ashburton Downs and other stations we went to Onslow school. I went to Gilliamia Hostel until Mum came and got us, they had split up then. Mum got a house at Wittenoom and we went there to live. I was at Onslow Primary

School until grade four then I started at Wittenoom. I went to high school at Hedland. Wittenoom started to close at this time because of the asbestos hazard. I was in high school when the family moved.

Later I transferred to Karratha High to be near the family. But I didn't finish the third year at high school and left about two weeks before the end. I just wanted to go back to Ashburton Downs and Rocklea Stations where my father was working and which was the area that I believed was home. Dad and brother John were working there so I started working on the station. I saw no need to finish high school.

At school I noticed discrimination but thought that the best way was to try and teach others about Aboriginal culture. One example was when we were doing Social Studies about how Captain Cook came here. There were some things in Social Studies which were different to what my old people had taught me, so I didn't agree with the lesson. I stood up and said, 'That's not right, that's not the real history. I can tell you the real history.' And I did not get any appreciation from the teacher. She disagreed with me.

At Hedland there was a special class for Aboriginal kids if they didn't have good marks, this was the project class. My marks were good but I tried to get in because that was where all the Aboriginal kids were. I did attend for a while but soon they told me I had to go to one of the ordinary classes with hardly any Aboriginal students and all the white kids. I had to make it on my own, though I didn't like it at the time, I am glad about it now. In the project class the kids learnt at their own pace, whereas in the other classes we were pushed.

The teachers then didn't understand Aboriginal kids and their culture. They didn't understand that we came from a country place where we were all together as Aboriginal kids. All the Aboriginal kids at Moorgunyah Hostel didn't have bags, pencils and pens ready when we got there at the start of the school year. The first couple of days at school we didn't have anything. And to get these things we had to fill in a form and take that to the store and receive the necessary school equipment. I couldn't get any of my gear because I didn't have any forms. I had to wait a couple of days. The teacher called all of the kids' names out and she asked that everyone put their name on a piece of card and place this on the desk so that she would know who each kid was. And what I felt so low about was that everyone else had their pens and bags and things and I had nothing. I was sitting there with nothing and I was the only Aboriginal boy in the class. So I was sitting there and the teacher said, 'You're supposed to come to class prepared, you're supposed to have a pen.' What she didn't understand was that I had to wait for a form. She didn't understand the system. But there I was with all of these white kids looking at me. Finally one of them got sorry for me and offered me the use of his pen.

I had trouble from a couple of white boys in school, but there was also one white kid who was big and chubby and they used to pick on him, too. So I thought, well I can make a mate out of him. And we got along okay together. But one day I did get into a fight in class with two boys and I flogged them. The teacher sent me down to the headmaster's office. I got the third degree from him but at the time I didn't explain what was happening in the class. I had been taking their name-calling but got sick of it and retaliated. There was two Aboriginal girls in the class and at first one of them stood up for me. But I thought I can't let the girls fight my battles for me, so I stood up for myself.

My first job was at Rocklea as station hand. My brother John was the head stockman there and he got me and Aaron Hubert a job. During the holiday time I got a job at Karratha and stayed there for a year. After this I had a job with the Ieramugadu Gardening Service at Roebourne, they had a contract with Hamersley Iron, looking after their gardens at Dampier. I worked there for three or four years by which time I was a leading hand, but I knew we were being underpaid. I started on $200 a fortnight and when I left was getting $260 a fortnight. I had got married in the meanwhile so the money didn't go far enough and I didn't like some aspects of the work system.

I did some work with the Department of Conservation and Land Management out in the Karijini National Park, working alongside the rangers. I did fencing with brother Ronnie and other jobs, like making pathways. After this I applied for a job as health worker with Mawarnkarra, the Aboriginal Medical Service in Roebourne. I got the job and have been with them for the last three years.

When I started I knew nothing about health work, but I enjoyed the job. In those days it was mainly going out and picking up the people that the registered nurse wanted to see or to attend to, there was no health function for me, I was just the odd-jobs man. Since then there has been career paths opened up for health workers and we are getting involved in this side of the work which is needed. There are training programs where health workers specialise in different aspects of the community work. Now I have just finished training as a qualified health worker and have a piece of paper to say this. In this way I can see that I can have a future in this organisation and can increase my skills level and ability. In the earlier days I didn't know if I would stay at the job, but now I've found my feet there.

I've also realised that health work is important for the Aboriginal people. The training means that health workers attend block training sessions at an Aboriginal college in Perth. Now I am a health worker, not an Aboriginal health worker. In the past white nurses would refer to us, or introduce us, as their Aboriginal health worker. We wanted this to change so that we are introduced as a health worker. If the boot was on the other foot they would think it ridiculous if we were out in the Aboriginal community and introduced them as our 'white nurse'.

We have two male health workers and two female health workers, a registered nurse and a doctor. We see the clients and assess them to see if they need to see the doctor. There is a male and a female health worker working in the clinic at all times with the doctor and nurse. Other health workers will be out in the field seeing people, or carrying out their programs. All health workers meet daily to discuss their work and so the daily schedule of work is known. And we rotate the work which is good for all of us.

Mawarnkarra is an Aboriginal organisation, run through a committee by Aboriginal people for Aboriginal people. It has to make things go right for Aboriginal people. The health system has been set up by people who are non-Aboriginal and who do not know about Aboriginal custom and culture. This is why it is so important that the health workers are Aboriginal. They can relate to the people in the community and bring the information back into Mawarnkarra so that we can do what is required. We deal with a lot of traditional Aboriginal people and we respect their needs. If they want to see a mabarn man, a traditional healer, then we'll take the person to one.

Aboriginal people do not have good health today. One of the things that affects their health is their lack of traditional land. The land and culture go together. There are a lot of things in their lands that are holy to them. And without their land they lose their culture. This affects their health. The world we live in, TV and such things, distracts us from our culture and without culture we are not Aboriginals.

Take Roebourne as an example. Here there are different Aboriginal tribes from everywhere living in the one place, practising their own culture, so there's got to be ill feeling. There's only one tribe who are the traditional owners of that land, yet you have others doing things without permission of those owners. So they are stepping on each other's toes all of the time.

At the moment we are trying to be strong as peoples in other people's land, we want to be strong in our own land. That's why we want to go to our homelands. Karijini was set up to help the homelands movement. Wakuthuni, one organisation in Karijini, has recently negotiated to get some of their land back near Paraburdoo and our people are starting to live there. Now Karijini has to push this process forward. We need strong organisations and strong people.

When I was a kid at Wittenoom we used to climb up above a pool in the gorge and roll down over and amongst the asbestos and into the water. We played in it. All my school friends played there. I don't know what's going to happen to us. There was no check up on us when we left Wittenoom. But there should be a mass screening of the people of Roebourne. In the past the death certificates didn't always mention the effects of asbestos contamination, so our people had difficulty in processing the legal side.

Appendix 1
Aboriginal Peoples Mentioned

There are different orthographies used to spell tribal or language group names. The text of *Karijini Mirlimirli* uses the spelling shown in bold below. Alternate spellings are included to provide certainty of meaning for the reader who may have encountered these.

Baijunka
Bailyku — Balyku — Pailgu
Binikura — Pinigura
Dhalanyji — Thalandji — Talandji
Kartujarra —
Kurrama — Gurrama — Kurama
Manyjiljarra — Manyjilyjarra
Martuthunira
Ngarla
Ngarluma — Ngaluma — Ngalooma — Gnalluma
Nhuwala — Noala
Nyamal — Njamal
Nyankumarta — Nyangumarta
Nyiyabarli — Niabali — Nyiyaparli
Nyoongah — Nyoongar — Nyangar — Noongah — Noongar
Punjima — Panyjima — Pandjima — Bunjima — Banyjima
Wariangka
Wongi — Wangkai
Yamitji — Yamadgee
Yindjibarndi — Indjibandi — Jindjibandji — Injibarndi
Yinhawangka — Innawonga

Appendix 2
Glossary of Aboriginal Words

The words used in the stories are based on the Punjima language, being the most common Aboriginal language used by the Karijini. Yet words from other local Aboriginal languages are used in the text as the authors of personal stories come from a variety of language groups. Further, Punjima, as a main language, tends to incorporate words of the other languages with the passing of time.

The orthography used prefers b to p, k to g and d to t. The reader will note some inconsistency as words such as Punjima start with a P but should start with a B. This is a case that breaks the rule simply because most Punjima people appear to prefer the P letter use. Yet the spelling of words is essentially consistent. The reader may find it helpful when reading to consider that p and b sound the same as in buh.

Aji	Lucy Toby's name
Baddawa	A medicine tree
Badjeri	Kangaroo
Bahbinah	Henry Long's father
Bailyku	A Pilbara Aboriginal tribe
Bajarri	Big kangaroo, Euro
Bajiwana, Bajiwanarra	Plains kangaroo, has long arms
Balinkunha	Palm Springs (Paraburdoo)
Bambajinha	Mount Whaleback
Banaka	A skin group
Bangkabara	Shaw River
Bankarnu	A goanna (black)
Barlkabi	A traditional dance using two boomerangs to make music
Barlkanu	Rain coming
Barlkanu buldaku	Rain falling
Barlkanyjinha	Law ground near Mirrurdanha

Barnbarnmunha	Bee Gorge
Bathara	Bush fruit like mulberry, or a wild plum
Bayunku	A Pilbara Aboriginal tribe
Biddi Biddi	Dignam's Well
Bilyabilyanku	Ashburton River
Bilyankarra	Brothers
Bimbanha	A spring where Mabel's mother was born near Marandoo
Binbirrnha	Jimmy Daji's wife
Bindima	Alice Smith's grandfather
Binikura	A Pilbara Aboriginal tribe
Biniyanku	One of Mabel's grandmothers, also Listen Listen's
Birdarra Burndurr	Yindjibarndi Law Dance
Birluba	The woman given away in marriage
Bithankara	A medicine tree
Bithinybanku	Roy Tommy's name (Mabel's twin son)
Bulina	Big lizard
Bullenkarnu	Turee Creek
Bumbanha Springs	Once people's main camp on Hamersley Station, now dry
Bundaliny	Mabel's grandfather, a great hunter, buried in a tree
Bundinha	Bundaliny's birth place, a waterhole
Bundiyanha	A waterhole between Hamersley and Mount Brockman Stations
Bunhthalku	Rain is falling
Buniyanku	Listen Listen's grandmother, married to Bundaliny
Bunku, Bunkurra	A goanna
Bunurrunna	Mount Bruce, a place of special significance
Burdangka	A tree burial site
Burdardu	Bush fruit like mulberry
Burlinkarnu	The creek at Carbery's camp
Burlku	Chewing tobacco and ash mixture
Burndurr	A Yindjibarndi law dance
Burradu	Sandalwood
Burungu	A skin group

Buuminyjinha	Ceremony ground at Tambrey near old ration camp
Darraru	Sunset
Dhaji	'Jimmy', Limerick's uncle
Dhalanyji	A Pilbara Aboriginal tribe
Dharlibiri	The creek at Coppin Pool
Dharraki	A scrub turkey
Dhurandaji	Mabel's great-grandfather, the greatest song maker in Hamersley Ranges
Dhurdu	A big sister
Dhurlja	Lola and Doris mother's father; Chubby Jones' father
Dhurriri	Turee Creek
Inyji, Injie	Mabel's brother Joe Injie
Jabikal	Site on the Ashburton River
Jajiwirri	Birth place of Mabel's father
Jajiwurra	Robe River
Jambu-nha	Mabel's brother Jambu
Jandaru	Wild honey
Jankurna	Emu
Jarndu	Small plain's Kangaroo
Jarndunmunha	Mount Nameless at Tom Price
Jarrdu	Joyce Injie's great-grandmother
Jarrungkajarrungka	Rocklea
Jibulyu	Bush fruit like gooseberry
Jidarka	Fruit bird
Jiddha	Yam
Jijinbunha	Joffre Gorge
Jilarn	Green bush used, after boiling, fro treating sores, by washing the skin.
Jilbukarri	Bush fruit, like passionfruit
Jilkuwanna, Jilywanna	Peter Steven's birth place at Hamersley Station
Jilunnhu	Waterhole near Marandoo, Peter's father's birthplace
Jinkajibuka	Echidna, porcupine
Jirrirdinku	Mabel's Tommy's birth place on Mount Brockman Station
Jirrirdinkurri	Mabel Tommy

244

Jirtijirti, Jitijiti	A willy wagtail
Jiwarlank	'William Jeealong', a great singer of Aboriginal songs
Jubula	Fortescue Falls
Jukari	The replacement name spoken to a person, who has the same name as a deceased
Jumbunha	Stone hut near the Mount Bruce Road
Junakerra	A featherfoot
Jurna	Waddy, or hitting stick
Jyntarndah	Racehorse lizard
Kaarbun, Kalidah	A dove
Kabarli	The term used for one's father's mother
Kabawarra	Part of the Ashburton River
Kajardi	Little lizard
Kajawari	Bush fruit, a wild orange
Kajiwinha	The Fortescue River where Mabel's father was born
Kaki	A bird (generic)
Kakurla	Bush fruit, wild pears
Kalbari	Seeds for grinding
Kalharramunha	Rio Tinto Gorge
Kamayi	Mother's younger sisters
Kamburda	The name given to the children of a deceased
Kanaji	Lightning
Kanaji binbaku?	Is lightning flashing?
Kannabugka	Doris Parker's father's father
Kantharri	The name for one's mother's mother
Kanyjiyanyji	A law ground near Millstream National Park
Kardajirri	Duck Creek
Kardakarli	A place at Rocklea, 30kms south-west of Paraburdoo
Karijini	The name for an area of the Hamersley Ranges
Karimarra	A skin group
Karlaya	Emu
Karlikarra	Fast running lizard

Karlkatharra	A meeting place on the Turee Creek
Karnku	Looking after a son and daughter when grandson is going through the law
Karrpu	The sun
Kartujarra	A Pilbara Aboriginal tribe
Kijiyamba	Bonny's mother's mother, also Jonah
Kininkra	Dress stick to wear in the hair
Kinnapougah	Doris Parker's Father's father
Kiya	Grandmother's sister
Kudjibunghu	Alice Smith's grandmother, mother's side
Kughali	Lizard
Kulandinha	Old road to Rocklea and Murimamba
Kulyu	Wild potatoes
Kumbali	Brother-in-law
Kumbalnha	A waterhole
Kumbu	To urinate
Kunangkawanjarrinha	Horace Parker's birth place (old Mulga Downs Station)
Kunangkawinghadetha	Herbert Parker's birth place (new Mulga Downs Station)
Kunankwarri	Yanrey Station area
Kunduwanha	The big hill Jack Barry drove over
Kungkanhawarra	A hill near Newman that belongs to Lena Long's father
Kungkuna	Wobby Parker's uncle
Kunkinna	Mabel's brother Limerick
Kunkurrnardi	Mabel's husband, old Tommy
Kunyika	'Spider', Mabel's brother-in-law
Kupawarra	Turee Creek
Kurdakurda	Mabel's grandmother, married to Bundaliny
Kurlarndinyjarn	Name of a spring
Kurnda	A mark of respect for a deceased, shame
Kurrabunya	A Ngarluma meeting camp
Kurrama	A Pilbara Aboriginal tribe
Kurri	A marriageable girl
Kurri Kurri	The seven sisters

Kurrubunya	Lola's father, his given non-Aboriginal name was Cookie Cutacross
Kurrumanthu	A sand goanna, yellow
Kwarnura	Flock of crows
Mabarn	An Aboriginal healer
Mabuji	The relationship between one's mother's father and his grandson
Madawandi	Marshall Smith
Makarli	Old Jidi, Mabel's grandmother
Makurndu, Makuntu	A punishment spear
Mangkalyi	An initiator in that law
Mangkarnba	Spirit, featherfoot
Manyka	A son
Mardamarda	An Aboriginal person who is not 'full blood'
Marla	A white carrot
Marlakan	Place at Minthi Spring, horse shoe
Marlbanunku	The sweet residue of lerp
Marlkarri	A person who has passed away
Marlumalank	Peter Steven's father
Marlumarlunha	Place of Joyce Injie's birth
Marlumarlunurri	Joyce Injie
Marlurlu	Young boys taken as initiates
Marna	Beans, Seed
Marndamalu	Big plain's turkey
Marndiwindi	Burial place of Marlumalank's brother, Doug
Marrian	Marrina Springs
Marrkamarrka	Difficult
Marruwa	Snakewood tree
Martuthuni	Fortescue River
Marundu	A goanna
Mayali	One's father's father
Milangka	A skin group
Milykan	Snappy gum tree
Minbanha	Bonny's aunt
Minderu	Name of Sport's Creek
Minhthukundi	Hamersley Gorge
Minjiyanha	Mount Meharry

Minthacoogina	A spring in the Karijini National Park
Mirlimirli	Paper with writing on it
Mirru	Spear throwers
Mirrudanku	Water pannikins
Mirrurdanha	A spring near where Mirru George was born
Mirwida	A well on Rocklea Station named after Mirru George
Mubuji	One's mother's father
Mulkunnaddi	Peter Steven's grandmother
Mullalu	Young boys
Mullamallunha	A spring near Rocklea Station
Mullu	Old law grounds at Mulga Downs
Mullwadu	Turner River
Muminna	Koolkanari's first wife
Munkinah	Echidna, porcupine
Muntha	Fast slender lizard that waves its foreleg
Murruwa	Snake wood tree
Muyirdnha	Mabel's sister Amy
Ngalirinku	Mabel's sister-in-law, Ivy
Ngamarribala	The name for Nanutarra
Nganuwirra	Small pinnacle of Mount Bruce
Ngarlku	Bush vegies, white onions
Ngarluma	A Pilbara Aboriginal tribe
Ngurin	Harding River
Nhaandawanha	A windmill at Minderoo Station
Nhaddiwah	Dance
Nhadi	Wirndawari's brother born at Minthi Spring
Nhiidi	A substance to treat sores
Nhuthabah	Henry Long's mother
Nhuwala	A Pilbara Aboriginal tribe
Nirdi	A type of hawk
Nurabunna	Mud Springs
Nuwala	A plant with berries and leaves used to treat sores
Nyamal	A Pilbara Aboriginal tribe
Nyimiliny	Peter Stevens
Nyimirli	Hill that belonged to Mabel's husband

Nyirrilyi	Bush fruit like a cherry
Nyirrimba	A place on the Turee Creek
Nyirti	Mother-in-law
Nyiyabarli	A Pilbara Aboriginal tribe
Nymbiliyundah	Henry Long's father's country
Nyoongah	An Aboriginal person of the south-west region of Western Australia
Nyuba	Sweetheart or partner
Punjima	A Pilbara Aboriginal tribe
Wadirra	Eagle hawk man (story)
Wadjina	Kangaroo
Wajalas	White people (Nyoongah Word)
Wakin	Lola and Doris father's father; Nellie's father
Wakinbanku	An alternate name Wagin
Wakulanha	A Rocky spring at Murimamba, 'Donkey Pool'
Wakurra, Wangkirna	A crow
Wakuthuni, Warrkuthuni	Hill next to Mount Tom Price owned by Wakin
Walakurru, Waluku	A feather
Walhibindamunha	Circular Pool
Walkayinya	Julie Tommy's name (Mabel's twin daughter)
Waluruk	Camping place near Duck Creek Station
Walybala	A whitefella
Wamulu	Form of law, called 'free law'
Wanaki	Three men in the sky (story)
Wandika	Former ceremonial ground
Wangkawili	Stop the noise, talk
Wankja	Chubby Jones' mother
Wanmala	Further north
Wanu	Digging stick
Wardirra	A form of Aboriginal law
Wardirrba	When boys come back from the bush at initiation
Wariangka	A Pilbara Aboriginal tribe
Warlibi	A young man, the three brothers

Warlkangka	Julie Mabel's song
Kawurrbarndi	
Walkayinya	
Warrirda	An eagle hawk
Wartalba	North
Wathinkinha	A place, location
Waya	Joyce's grandmother's sister
Wayangka	Telegraph
Waylku	A little kangaroo
Wilarra	The moon
Wilga	A gap between hills, a pathway
Wilgi	Peter Stevens' mother, Jessie
Wilyinha	Old Winnie, grandmother
Winda	An emu spear
Winya	A fruit tree
Winyjinha	Mabel's brother Limerick
Winyjukundi	Peter Stevens' grandfather born in Hamersley Gorge
Wirlbiwirlbi	Mount Meharry
Wirlimarra	Pelican Creek
Wirlumarra	A Law Ground at Hamersley Gorge, Mabel's brother went through the law here
Wirndawari	The father of Bundaliny who died at Rottnest Island
Wirra	A boomerang
Wongi	A central desert Aboriginal
Wungina	Peter Stevens' uncle, Doug
Yaba	Ivy's name
Yallakarah	A goanna
Yallumarra	Alice Smith's mother's name; Windmill area on Hamersley Station
Yamitji	An Aboriginal tribal group from Carnarvon
Yandi	Dish for seed collecting
Yandiwogka	Turee Creek at Rocklea Station
Yangkalinha	Old name for Mulga Downs Station
Yankuna	A lizard

Yarlbu	A person who goes through initiation with you
Yarnbanku	Grandmother of Mabel
Yilykarri	The sky
Yindjibarndi	A Pilbara Aboriginal tribe
Yinhawangka	A Pilbara Aboriginal tribe or language group
Yunbu	Tip of a hunting spear
Yunibah	Henry Long's grandmother on his mother's side

Appendix 3
Contributors and Their Family Relationships

Despite the random nature of the individual contributors to this book, their strong extended family relationship is evident. The following list of contributors, their relationships and place of residence is informative. Asterisks denote the Elders.

Donald Ard	Cousin to Margie Hughes	Onslow
Rodney Butler	Son of Doris Parker	Onslow
Adrian Condon	Son of Dulcie	South Hedland
Dulcie Condon	Mother of Adrian, Sally	Onslow
Sally Condon	Daughter of Dulcie	Onslow
Doris Cooke	Sister of Lola	Tom Price
Vivian Cooke	Daughter of Doris	Tom Price
Mirru George*	Lola's mother's brother	Tom Price
Donald Hicks	Cousin to Lorraine Injie	Onslow
Darren Injie	Grandson of Mabel	Onslow
Doreen James	Niece to Joyce Injie	Onslow
Listen Listen James*	Brother to Mirru	Tom Price
Chubby Jones*	Doris' father's brother	Tom Price
Nellie Jones	Wife to Chubby Jones	Tom Price
Judy July*	Joyce's younger sister	Onslow
Tadje Limerick	Mabel's sister-in-law	
Henry Long*	Brother-in-law to Jukari's brother-in-law	Tom Price
Ruben Mills	Son of Beryl and Ron	Wickham
Jukari Parker*	Mother of Slim, Maitland, Guy, Margaret, Marjorie and Trevor	Onslow

Maitland Parker	Son of Jukari	Karijini National Park
Margaret Parker	Daughter of Jukari	Onslow
Marjorie Parker	Daughter of Jukari	Onslow
Slim Parker	Son of Jukari	Onslow
Suzanne Parker	Daughter of Wobby	Karratha
Wobby Parker*	Brother-in-law of Jukari	Tom Price
Guy Parker	Son of Jukari	Karratha
Trevor Parker	Elder son of Jukari	Peedamulla Station
David Simmons	Friend (accepted as family)	Wickham
Mabel Tommy*	Sister-in-law of Joyce	Onslow
Julie Tommy	Daughter of Mabel	South Hedland
Bonny Tucker	Auntie to Lorraine	Onslow
Greg Tucker	Stepson of Bonny	Roebourne
Lola Young	Sister of Doris	Tom Price
Queenie Yuline*	First wife of Wobby	Karratha
Lorraine Injie	Daughter of Joyce	South Hedland
Joyce Injie*	Grandmother of Darren	Onslow
Peter Stevens*	Uncle of Doris and Lola	Karratha
Rodney Parker	Son of Lola	Roebourne
Alice Smith*	Aunt to Peter Stevens	Roebourne

Appendix 4
Water Places Mentioned by the Contributors

Where the Aboriginal name is known it is given in the glossary, Appendix 2.

Ashburton River
Bellary Creek
Bimbanha Springs
Boomanna Springs
Cane River
Coongan River
Coppin Pool
Dale's Gorge
Dignam's Well
Duck Creek
Fortescue River
Fortescue Falls
Hamersley Windmill
Hancock's Gorge
Harding River
Joffre Gorge
July Springs

Kuralanha Springs
Marrina Spring
Milli Springs
Millstream
Minthacoogina Spring
Mirwida Well
Mud Springs
Palm Springs (Paraburdoo)
Red Gorge
Robe River
Shaw River
Turee Creek
Turner River
Waluruk Springs
Weano's Gorge
Weeli Wolli Creek
Yule River